Librarian's Guide
to Games and Gamers

Librarian's Guide to Games and Gamers

From Collection Development to Advisory Services

MICHELLE GOODRIDGE AND
MATTHEW J. ROHWEDER

LIBRARIES
UNLIMITED®

An Imprint of ABC-CLIO, LLC

Santa Barbara, California • Denver, Colorado

Library of Congress Cataloging-in-Publication Data

Names: Goodridge, Michelle, author. | Rohweder, Matthew J., author.
Title: Librarian's guide to games and gamers : from collection development to advisory services / Michelle Goodridge and Matthew J. Rohweder.
Description: Santa Barbara, California : Libraries Unlimited, [2022] | Includes bibliographical references and index.
Identifiers: LCCN 2021026454 | ISBN 9781440867316 (paperback) | ISBN 9781440867323 (ebook)
Subjects: LCSH: Libraries—Special collections—Games. | Readers' advisory services—United States. | BISAC: LANGUAGE ARTS & DISCIPLINES / Library & Information Science / Collection Development | GAMES & ACTIVITIES / Reference
Classification: LCC Z692.G36 G66 2022 | DDC 025.2/896—dc23
LC record available at https://lccn.loc.gov/2021026454

ISBN: 978-1-4408-6731-6 (paperback)
        978-1-4408-6732-3 (ebook)

26 25 24 23 22   1 2 3 4 5

This book is also available as an eBook.

Libraries Unlimited
An Imprint of ABC-CLIO, LLC

ABC-CLIO, LLC
147 Castilian Drive
Santa Barbara, California 93117
www.abc-clio.com

This book is printed on acid-free paper ∞

Manufactured in the United States of America

Matt would like to dedicate this book to his Mom—I wish you could have read this. You always rolled your eyes at my love for video games, but your unwavering support got me to where I am. Thank you.

Michelle would like to thank her Dad who spent countless hours playing Diddy Kong Racing *with her and didn't mind always losing and to her Mom who taught her how to play* Canasta.

Contents

Acknowledgments

Writing a book is never a single player experience and can sometimes take a whole cast of non-playable characters (NPCs) to make this a reality. The authors would like to acknowledge the following people for helping this book evolve into its final form. To those people who spent time talking to us about gaming, games, and gaming in libraries. To those who patiently listened to our ideas, read sections of this book, and offered sage advice—we thank you. The list is many: Nick Walker, Joe Fahey, Darryl Andrews, Michael Rogowski, Blair Beveridge, Lauren Bourages, Meredith Fischer, Darryl Blake, and Lee Puddephatt.

A big thank you to Emma Cross, who started on this journey with us and got us thinking about VR in the library.

Matt would especially like to thank his husband, Ian, for always being an encouraging ear and being willing to watch him play countless hours of video games over the last couple of years.

Introduction: "Roll for Initiative"

In keeping with traditional readers' advisory techniques and tools, this book will help librarians and library staff develop an ongoing relationship between themselves, their patrons, their gaming collection, and the larger gaming (gamer) community. This volume will make gaming, and its numerous genres, accessible to library staff and create a larger understanding of gaming in libraries. It is intended for librarians, future librarians, and any member of library staff who might find themselves working in a library with a gaming collection or patrons interested in gaming. This volume can also be used in any library environment: public, academic, or special. In particular, this guide will look at how libraries can adapt readers' advisory for the gaming community. Because the community of patrons that will be served through this volume have their own unique needs and characteristics, we are stepping away from "readers' advisory" as a terminology and instead establishing "gamers' advisory" in its place. Whereas the majority of literature on gaming in libraries looks at developing a gaming collection or assisting gamers in finding similarly themed reading material, this volume moves beyond that and looks at how to serve library users interested in gaming and gameplay.

Although games have been present in library collections for several years, this is one of the first comprehensive resources for library staff in assisting patrons in discovering game materials in the library. There has been little done in the area of readers' advisory in relation to gaming collections at libraries. Jin Ha Lee et al. recently surveyed the literature on game readers' advisory with little luck.[1] This was one of the first empirical studies done to analyze patrons and game appeal. There are some nonlibrary resources that can help in guiding users to new material, including such online sites as BoardGame Geek, GamesRadar, IGN, or previous episodes of Geek & Sundry's *TableTop* hosted by Wil Wheaton, but these do not include important context that library staff need to make informed suggestions for their users. Furthermore, there have been several academic articles published on establishing game collections (in both public and academic libraries) and some articles written on helping game enthusiasts find game-related reading material that is either based on the game or follows a similar genre or story arch. But again, this does not broach the topic of helping patrons find or engage with a gaming collection. This volume will begin addressing this gap by providing library staff with some of the necessary tools and ideas to help bring concepts of readers' advisory to the world of gaming and games. The collection will cover a wide range of gaming genres, including digital games (video games and virtual reality), board games, and other tabletop games such as role-playing games, miniature tabletop role-play, and card games. We hope that through this volume, libraries will find greater engagement between their gaming collections and their patrons using the principles of gamers' advisory.

Before moving into a discussion of readers' advisory and gaming, it is important to consider how to best build up and maintain a gaming collection in your library. Furthermore, to best serve your patron base, it helps to understand some of the fundamental issues behind gamer behavior—exactly as you might when thinking about how to best serve readers. Therefore, this volume will briefly address fundamental concerns as collection development, cataloging, programming, and user behavior. We hope that you find this volume informative, useful, and enjoyable as you begin the process of opening up your library to gaming and gamers.

This volume will cover a number of essential issues and concepts that can make building and maintaining a gaming collection in your library a worthwhile endeavor. In Chapter 1, we provide an overview of existing literature about gaming collections in libraries to help you see why it can be important and some of the trials and tribulations other librarians have faced. In Chapter 2, we start delving into the day-to-day operations of collection development, followed by Chapter 3 where we discuss maintaining that collection. Chapter 4 shifts focus and looks at offering programming using your gamissng collection, with key examples that can help you get started. We then look at user behavior and gaming to help you select the right game for the right patron. In Chapter 6, we introduce the concept of gamers' advisory, with some key reference interview examples. Chapter 7 provides a list of controlled vocabulary as well as an exemplary list of games both tabletop and digital that you can use in developing a collection and offering gamers' advisory services to patrons. Chapters 8–11 cover additional gaming formats in a similar way and include collectable card games, miniature figures (mini figs), virtual reality and augmented reality games, and role-play games.

Now . . . play on.

Note

1. Jin Ha Lee, Rachel Ivy Clarke, Hyerim Cho, and Travis Windleharth, "Understanding Appeals of Video Games for Readers' Advisory and Recommendation," *Reference & User Services Quarterly* 57, no. 2 (Winter 2017): 122–139.

Part I
GAMING COLLECTIONS AND GAMERS

1
Gaming Collections in Libraries: A Primer

There has been quite a bit of discussion and research regarding games in libraries, so this chapter is dedicated to highlighting the literature. Some libraries struggle with justifying a gaming collection; this is especially the case in academic contexts. So by providing a brief summary, we hope to help with creating a case for a gaming collection and to provide the groundwork needed to create a proposal for funding from your library board or administration for the appropriate resources to ensure the collection is successful.

Public libraries have long been leaders in bringing games into libraries; however, academic libraries can offer unique insights into how we might want to go about collecting and later suggesting games for patrons. While "[there] have been relatively few studies that specifically address academic gaming collections,"[1] Diane Robson and Patrick Durkee have noted that the literature on video games in academic libraries focuses on five issues:

1. "the role of video games in research and curricula on university campuses,

2. the support services university libraries provide to facilitate that use of video games in research and curricula,

3. the selection policies university libraries establish to build collections that serve campus needs,

4. the particular challenges of acquisition, preservation, and continued access amid video games' rapid format evolution, and

5. the role of game collection librarians in shaping the character of video game studies in academic settings."[2]

Academic Gaming Collections: More Than Just Curriculum Support

Creating an impressive gaming collection that is accessible to all can build a bridge between libraries and patrons, helping to further engage them in their studies, hobbies, and communities. Eli Neiburger discusses how, in an increasingly visual society, the ability to interpret on-screen stimuli is a valuable new form of literacy.[3] Bill MacKenty found students are willing to expend considerable energy to understand and play games successfully; students learn how to work together to solve common challenges in games and are enthusiastic about the material. According to MacKenty, it's the act of problem-solving along with the risk of failure that makes games fun.[4] Gaming not only meets an educational need but also facilitates the building of a game-based community in an academic context.

Community Building

The key to any successful community is creating a sense of belonging through social interaction. A successful gaming collection would attract students from all faculties. The strengthening of community and the cross-pollination of knowledge and ideas by bringing together the university (both students and faculty) through gaming would be beneficial to students individually and as a whole. It is important to build not only a collection that supports curriculum requirements but also one that has mainstream, highly popular games to ensure the broadest of audiences can be served.[5] These are ideas that can easily be applied to any type of library—while academic libraries focus greatly on students and their learning, the ability of a gaming collection to strengthen ties between a public library and its community is also extremely essential to consider. It is also important for academic libraries to consider potential programs and community connections that the collection could support; for example, you may want to explore using board games for fostering relationships between domestic and international students, while supporting the development of second language learning.[6] As an example, while in public libraries, you may want to establish board game cafés specifically targeted toward immigrant and newcomer populations to help build relationships and encourage second language learning. The role of gaming in supporting second language learners will be further explored in our programming section.

Patron Groups

When building and managing gaming collections in an academic context, there are two additional populations of patrons (besides the general student body) to consider collaborating with: educators and game scholars. Educators may be interested in the potential of games to motivate and educate their students. There is a growing discussion over the use of games in regard to education, and this in turn will entice more educators to explore these resources. The second population of patrons are game scholars who are interested in exploring issues such as innovation, artistry, and the positive and negative effects of games.[7] In order to satisfy the needs of these two user groups, faculty consultation is encouraged—this also will help in the creation of a "core collection" of games that faculty expect students to have familiarity with.[8]

In public libraries, there are many different patron groups that may be interested in using and engaging with a gaming collection. If you have an academic institution nearby, students and faculty may be drawn to the collection for similar reasons discussed earlier. There are also support materials of a more traditional, monographic nature that may be of interest to them, for example, a book on the artwork of *Final Fantasy*. Teachers may be interested in incorporating gaming materials into the classroom or partnering with a local library to run a workshop or event (see our section on programming for ideas on how to do this). Community members may want to explore gaming programs for at risk youth to give them more options and events to attend. The opportunities really are endless, and these are all cases to be made to encourage the development of a gaming collection.

Using Your Gaming Collection in Unexpected Ways

When establishing gaming collections, there is more to consider than just how it will serve your general population (whether that be the public or study body). For instance, there are multiple benefits to having board game collections in libraries that go beyond supporting the game studies programs and students. These include supporting teaching and learning outside of the game studies program and the unexpected increase in teamwork and morale of library staff.[9] This added benefit can be applied to all types of libraries: namely, games can be used for team building workshops and as a way to bring staff closer together; after all, who doesn't enjoy playing a game every once in a while? There is a growing movement to bring popular or leisure book collections into the academic setting for similar reasons including providing students with more leisurely materials to use in between their studies.[10]

Academic Gaming Collection Development

When you are developing an academic game collection, you should keep in mind two major functions that the collection will serve—these will inform how you build and focus your collection. First, it will support the curriculum of a game design program, and second, it will provide scholarly and recreational resources to the rest of the institution. The NYU Game Center has game faculty select games that are directly tied to the curriculum; this includes the inclusion of several European games as they have had a different evolution than games in North America. This may be an area worth exploring depending on the interests of the faculty and students in the program. Aside from creating collections that support faculty research, there is a need to create an exemplary collection for students to use as examples when they are designing their own games and completing assignments. To do this effectively, you would work closely with your faculty members to get their opinions and see what games they are suggesting their students play. This is a service area that academic libraries can support; providing games on reserve that students need to play. This can be done using the traditional reserve model or setting up a console in the library and having sign-up times for students who need to play the game.

From an organizational and collection development perspective, Christopher Thomas and Jerremie Clyde suggest that rather than looking at video games solely based on platform you should try to evaluate them based on discipline-specific knowledge. Traditionally, video games have been located within media collections, but Thomas and Clyde suggest that this may limit their potential use within academia. They suggest cataloging the games based on subject using traditional library classification schema and shelving them accordingly.[11] While there is most certainly merit in this particular approach, it may be wise to colocate all the gaming materials into one section, but still use the Library of Congress classification system in case a change is required in the future. There is further discussion on collection maintenance that addresses this concern in Chapter 3.

When selecting digital games, it is important to cover all gaming genres to create a representative collection and provide students and researchers with the tools they need to appropriately study the medium of gaming. This includes first-person shooter, action-adventure, racing, role-playing games, party, and more. Kym Buchanan and Angela Vaden Elzen suggest seeking advice from experienced gamers and noted that *Library Journal* occasionally posts video game reviews and best video game lists. They also note that there should be a mixture of popular games and critically praised games from each gaming genre to provide a more diverse selection.[12] Many of these games require specific hardware or peripherals to play, and rather than assuming the users have access to these critical elements, the library should provide access to them for a variety of reasons, specifically to ensure that the game is experienced how it was intended. It is also important for the library to have on hand extra controllers, game pieces, rulebooks, and so on. Reasons to maintain an excess of material might include: to replace any missing elements or to meet a specific need, such as a patron who needs the rules in another language or if a patron is hosting a gaming event and requires more than the standard two controllers.

Academic libraries are excellent resources for other types of libraries to refer to in terms of planning and implementing unique collecting areas. Part of the reason why academic libraries are so useful as examples in this way is the increased output of publications regarding their work, as it is required by many academic librarians in their role; competing demands for library collections as a whole (e.g., supporting academic programs and providing recreational support); the ability to partner with outside organizations including potential donors; and the rigorous (and sometimes prohibitive) process of developing new programs and services at an academic institution. For instance, while public libraries tend to be nimbler and more inventive, academic libraries are often required to complete lengthy research and discovery phases before being able to act on a new opportunity. This means that by the time academic libraries are investigating a new area of librarianship there is a wealth of information available to discuss. Building on the work done by some academic libraries, other library systems can develop clear justification for unique collections when facing administration restrictions. Once you have jumped this hurdle of proving why a gaming collection is essential and how you intend to go about developing that collection, you need to start thinking about some of the logistics of what that collection will do. Therefore, the rest of this book is aimed at creating a sustainable collection, which includes collection development, maintenance, programming, and providing advisory services.

Notes

1. Diane Robson and Patrick Durkee, "New Directions for Academic Video Game Collections: Strategies for Acquiring, Supporting, and Managing Online Materials," *Journal of Academic Librarianship* 38, no. 2 (2012): 80.

2. Ibid.

3. Eli Neiburger, *Gamers . . . in the Library?! The Why, What and How of Videogame Tournaments for All Ages* (Chicago: American Library Association, 2007).

4. Bill MacKenty, "All Play and No Work," *School Library Journal* 52 (September 2006): 46–48.

5. Christine L. Ferguson, "Ready Librarian One," *Serials Review* 42, no. 1 (2016): 43.

6. Michelle Goodridge, "Conversational Gamers: Developing Language Skills and Connections through Games," in *Supporting Today's Students in the Library: Strategies for Retaining and Graduating International, Transfer, First-Generation, and Re-Entry Students*, ed. Ngoc-Yen Tran and Silke Higgins (Chicago: American Library Association, 2019).

7. Kym Buchanan and Angela M. Vaden Elzen, "Beyond a Fad: Why Video Games Should Be Part of 21st Century Libraries," *Education Libraries* 35, no. 1–2 (Summer–Winter 2012): 15–33.

8. Scott Nicholson, "Playing in the Past: A History of Games, Toys, and Puzzles in North American Libraries," *Library Quarterly* 83, no. 4 (2013): 341–361.

9. Emma Cross, David Mould, and Robert Smith, "The Protean Challenge of Game Collections at Academic Libraries," *Source Information* 21, no. 2 (May 2015): 129–145.

10. Pauline Dewan, "Why Your Academic Library Needs a Popular Reading Collection Now More Than Ever," *College and Undergraduate Libraries* 17, no. 1 (March 2010): 44–64.

11. Christopher M. Thomas and Jerremie Clyde, "Game as Book: Selecting Video Games for Academic Libraries Based on Discipline Specific Knowledge," *Journal of Academic Librarianship* 39 (2013): 522–527.

12. Buchanan and Vaden Elzen, "Beyond a Fad."

2
Collection Development

Considering collection development needs (acquisitions, processing, cataloguing, collection maintenance, etc.) is a crucial step in establishing a game collection in a library. Libraries have always been somewhat involved in games and gaming (puzzles count, too)! Video game collections have long been in the domain of public libraries, and it is only recently that academic libraries have begun to build their own gaming collections.[1] The following chapter will discuss collection development as it pertains to board games, console games, role-playing games, and online games in most library settings with the understanding that there are also localized challenges to consider.

Video Games

For all intents and purposes, video game collections can be viewed as specialized media collections. This viewpoint can help alleviate some of the apprehension when developing video game collections, as libraries are already familiar with developing and maintaining traditional media collections. Similar concerns with video game collections to media collections include:

- availability of necessary playback equipment,
- rapid technological obsolescence,
- classroom support for technology, and
- a lack of format knowledge.

Furthermore, from an academic library perspective, a general disconnect toward understanding a game's role as a primary source in research can make administrative buy-in challenging. There are multiple ways in which a library can secure funding for a gaming collection, and this chapter will discuss some of avenues and provide tips for librarians. It should be noted, however, that some of these suggestions can be dependent on where you are located, whether there is a strong presence of the gaming industry in your city, and other mitigating factors.

With regard to video game collections, however, there are a few special concerns that need to be taken into account when building a collection, including:

- the release of the same titles across different platforms (e.g., Xbox and PlayStation),

- games are rarely reprinted (unless they are later released as "classics"), and

- some games are not commercially available or are "indie" releases.[2]

One final concern worth noting is that there is a movement toward video games (or digital games) not being available in hardcopy anymore and shifting toward downloadable content only. This can pose some acquisition and circulation challenges (and archiving content), but this will be discussed further in this chapter.

Board Games

Analog game collections (e.g., board games, card games, role-play games—namely any non-digital game) have their own special considerations that make them different than their digital counterparts. Although sales of board games are continually on the rise, many libraries have been reluctant to include them in their collections. The thought of creating tabletop collections can be daunting and comes with a host of presumptions around cost, durability, complexity, and lack of subject knowledge. Discussions about tabletop collections in libraries have received very little academic research in comparison to the work that has been done on video game collections.[3] In a 2007 survey of 313 libraries, only 12% circulated board and card games,[4] and in a similar article from 2016, they found that out of 78 responding libraries 44% had circulating tabletop collections.[5] This demonstrates a noticeable reluctance of libraries to develop circulating tabletop collections that is slowly changing over time. Maintaining all the pieces of a game is big obstacle in the willingness of a library to circulate these types of materials. We have provided several suggestions throughout this chapter to overcome this obstacle.

Role-Playing Games

Role-playing materials are often found in libraries but not as a genre of games, rather they generally fall into the category of reference. For example, the *Monster Manual* is an encyclopedia of monsters that players may encounter during a Dungeons & Dragons (D&D) quest and is necessary during gameplay.[6] These books are essentially rule books and scenario builders that help the game progress. While also giving it structure, these manuals will need to be shifted out of a noncirculating reference collection and into their gaming collection to allow patron access. From a collection development standpoint, libraries need to recognize that it is important to build a complete collection of these materials because if you are missing volumes your patrons may not be able to carry through with their role-playing adventure. It is not enough to simply provide these resources on shelves, as many of your patrons may be using these resources for the first time; it is important to have a general understanding of what a patron will need to successfully play the game.

Should a group of patrons want to learn and play D&D for the first time, there are specific considerations and elements a library needs to accommodate such a request. These could include providing specific material, such as one-inch grid paper to draw out the scenarios, or assisting players with creating characters through extensive research—namely, providing D&D manuals. D&D requires a skilled dungeon master (DM); thus, a library may need to provide resources to help a patron train to become one. D&D gameplay also requires a number of specific physical resources, such as a cardboard screen to hide the DM's actions from the players in the campaign, the ability to consult with scenario builders, all of the required handbooks (which must be the same version), and plastic miniatures to help players visualize the campaign. In order to help facilitate a full D&D campaign, libraries may want to build special programming around the role-play collection to encourage non-familiar users to engage with the collection. See "Intro to Dungeons & Dragons Campaign" in Chapter 4 for how to set up a D&D program.

Sourcing Games

Video games and tabletop games are unfortunately not available through traditional library vendors, so there will be a need to do some exploration. Large online retailers such as Amazon carry a comprehensive stock and can be an easy starting point, as many libraries already occasionally order from them. You may also want to explore smaller, local retailers or game stores, which can offer volume discounts and may allow for invoicing rather than having to front the money upon ordering. Given the rapid rate at which games (board games and digital) become out of print or hardware becomes obsolete, there can be an increasing need to look for used games. There are several ways to go about this (e.g., yard sales and online classifieds), but one of the safest ways to do this is through a used game store. Although buying used games from sources other than registered businesses can be more economical, there is also a chance that the software or hardware may not be in excellent working order or you may be missing essential pieces; if this is the case, there is generally no recourse. Many used games stores will offer some sort of warranty on their product and may allow you to test it out in the store before you make a purchase. Forging such a business relationship with a local store can become quite fortuitous, as you can build a working relationship that may include donations, sponsorship, help with running events, and so on. The game stores can also advertise events that you are having in the library, which may attract a crowd of patrons who normally wouldn't have come in.

Tips on Buying Used Games

Buying used games can be a more economical way to build your library's collection. This section of the book will provide some guidance on what to look for when purchasing used games, but this can also be used as a guide for accepting game donations as well. As game collections are popular, this can be a good opportunity to run a fundraiser event in the community to build the collection, but you do need to be cautious to make sure that the games you acquire are in working order and that you are prepared to maintain them.

Used Video Games

- Look for noticeable wear and tear and the general condition of the hardware or software you're purchasing. Take note of any dust or scratches that are present on the surface of the game disk if it is in this format. Dust and minor scratches can be removed/repaired, but a spot inspection will not provide enough detail to know if the game will be playable.

- Ask to play the game before purchasing and if that is not an option ask what assurances and warranties there are if the game does not work.

- Buy from trusted sources such as registered businesses rather than through buy-and-sell websites or yard sales.

- Be aware of what it is you're buying and what the requirements are to be able to use the game (e.g., does it need special hardware like a Nintendo glove or a gun?). There are many online sites that you can take advantage of when doing research on a game prior to purchase to see what it requires.

- Use sources such as PriceCharting.com to look up the current selling price of a used game to ensure you are not overpaying.

- Foster a relationship with local game stores to further benefit you, they might have buy-back or trade-in programs where you can trade-in some of your older, lesser circulated material to help fund getting more current titles.

- Finally, be prepared to test out any used games that are donated to the library. It is very time-consuming to process donations (custodial history, cataloguing, barcoding, etc.), and it would be a shame to put out a game that ends up not working when a patron borrows it. Taking that step to test that the game is working is important—this can even be an issue with new games, as sometimes there is a scratch or they are damaged and do not work.

Used Board Games

- It is important to take note of the condition of the game—starting with: Is the box in decent condition? Are there any noticeable pieces missing? If it is a game that you are unfamiliar with, you will want to do a bit of research to make sure you are getting the right supplies and parts for the game.

- If you're looking to purchase a used copy of an in print tabletop game, have a look at BoardGameGeek.com, as they have suggested retail price and the price of the game at major U.S. retailers (e.g., Walmart, Amazon, Target, and eBay) to ensure you don't overpay.

- BoardGameGeek.com has a feature called "geek market," where members of the page can post their used games for sale. Again, look for trusted sources—Amazon and other online retailers have fantastic selection of board games across all genres, but source out local retailers and board game cafés.

- Some cafés might be looking to cycle out their older, well-played games and might be willing to sell at a discount.

- Think about partnering with local board game cafés, which might help you with donations or programming.

- Are there tabletop developers in your area? If so, they might be interested in partnering with a library to showcase their games or local designers may even donate copies of their published games.

- Local board game groups or local enthusiasts. Collectors will regularly cull their collections, so if you have a contact you may be able to get copies of games that are in good condition for less than retail price. There may also be local meetups or swaps of games that you can attend to build your library collection.

Naturally, like any collection development project, there are a few generalized things to keep in mind when selecting games, including:

- Does age appropriateness matter?

- Are you creating a loanable collection or one just for programming?

- Which game systems are you able to support?[7]

While these are essential elements to consider, the scope of this volume will not engage with these larger questions. However, by referring to our Resources section, where we have included a number of additional resources for further reading, you can address some of these issues when developing your collection.

Online Gaming

Online gaming has been separated from the rest, as it has its own unique set of challenges and considerations. Diane Robson and Patrick Durkee address some of the possible issues with supplying subscription access to online games. You will need to enter into licensing agreements with diverse commercial and noncommercial entities that are not the typical vendors that libraries deal with. This being said, many of these online gaming purveyors, such as Steam or Gametap, offer subscriptions for nominal annual costs and then the library would instantly have access to hundreds of titles. You can also purchase individual titles rather than entire subscriptions.[8] Steam is a software program and online game purveyor that allows one to create an account and obtain access to many online PC games (some free content and some paid content). For instance, NYU has one account per PC in their lab (4), and they were one of the only academic libraries that provided this service to their students in 2016.[9] (See Chapter 9 for more information on Steam, an online game platform.) Other institutions cited cost, digital rights management, and firewalls as reasons why they have yet to explore a similar model but increasingly more are willing to take the calculated risk and provide this service to their patrons.

Licensing

One of the key considerations with online gaming is that of licensing. Robson and Durkee note that

> licensing itself is a crucial issue for libraries entering into purchase agreements with online gaming . . . since purchasing subscriptions customarily entails acceding to a long and detailed licensing agreement. It is essential to work out a procedure for vetting and permitting agreements between the university library and subscription services, a process that potentially involves both the library's legal staff and its information technology division.[10]

Libraries should carefully read any licensing agreements and take stock in whether they can adhere to the agreements or in some instances it may become a matter of calculated risk. Items often listed in a user agreement are limitations on the number of users on one account and how users must conduct themselves online. Libraries need to take into account their limitations and community base before committing to these subscription services. Namely, if you are serving a large community, you will need to purchase multiple subscriptions, whereas if you work within a very small community, you can get by with one or two, depending on the end-user license agreement (EULA).

Another aspect about online gaming, especially Massive Multiplayer Online (MMO), is that they demand a long-term commitment for the creation and evolution of a character. Providing access to these games raises the possibility for library staff to have to monitor online activities pursued with a library collection MMO account, which may make MMO play ultimately too difficult to manage.[11] For example, a participant's actions could break the user agreement or terms of use and get the library account banned from a particular game. Libraries must consider whether purchasing MMOs is a viable option for their collection—given the staff, resource, and time commitments. One way to try to combat this potential issue would be to create a detailed code of conduct that holds patrons accountable for their actions while playing online games using library accounts. For a simple example of how to write one of these codes of conduct, check out Wilfrid Laurier Library's "Game Collection—Code of Conduct and Acceptable Use Guidelines."[12] You will also note that part of this policy includes holding students accountable for their actions while using library gaming accounts, these policies include the Use of Information Technology Policy and the Non-Academic Student Code of Conduct. Libraries or institutions should consider developing similar policies to protect themselves and their users.

Technical Requirements

To run some of these online games requires the most up-to-date computer technology. The computers needed far exceed the average public computers the library supplies to its users. This becomes challenging for libraries as the hardware quickly becomes obsolete, and it is rather costly to replace. Most libraries who do provide this type of service to their patrons do so on desktop computers housed in the library that are typically located in a separate area from the regular public computers. Providing access to online gaming is challenging and not something all libraries are capable of doing. There are also potential issues in working with IT departments, as the programs needed to run games on computers are not part of the typical software suite that the IT department would be familiar with, and in some cases, they may not agree to support it. At Wilfrid Laurier University, the game lab run by the Game Design and Development program has its own network that is managed by the director of the program, not the IT department. The director is also responsible for maintenance of the desktop computers, as IT will not do any installations, troubleshooting, or repairs. This type of arrangement may be cost and/or resource prohibitive to some libraries, so it is important to weigh the pros and cons of offering online gaming to patrons.

Notes

1. Christine L. Ferguson, "Ready Librarian One," *Serials Review* 42, no. 1 (2016): 42–46.

2. Mary Laskowski and David Ward, "Perspectives on . . . Building Next Generation Video Game Collections in Academic Libraries," *Journal of Academic Librarianship* 35, no. 3 (2009): 267–273.

3. Teresa Slobuski et al., "Arranging the Pieces: A Survey of Library Practices Related to a Tabletop Game Collection," *Evidence Based Library and Information Practices* 12, no. 1 (2017): 2–17.

4. Scott Nicholson, "Go Back to Start: Gathering Baseline Data about Gaming in Libraries," *Library Review* 58, no. 3 (2009): 203–214.

5. Slobuski et al., "Arranging the Pieces," 2–17.

6. Edward Schneider and Brian Hutchinson, "Referencing the Imaginary: An Analysis of Library Collection of Role-Playing Game Materials," *The Reference Librarian* 56, no. 174–188 (2015): 174–188.

7. Kym Buchanan and Angela M. Vaden Elzen, "Beyond a Fad: Why Video Games Should Be Part of 21st Century Libraries," *Education Libraries* 35, no. 1–2 (Summer–Winter 2012): 15–33.

8. Diane Robson and Patrick Durkee, "New Directions for Academic Video Game Collections: Strategies for Acquiring, Supporting, and Managing Online Materials," *Journal of Academic Librarianship* 38, no. 2 (2012): 79–84.

9. Library staff at NYU, in-person visit with Michelle Goodridge, July 2016.

10. Robson and Durkee, "New Directions for Academic Video Game Collections," 17.

11. Ibid.

12. "Gaming Collection," Wilfrid Laurier University Library, accessed February 2020, http://library.wlu.ca/research-materials/gaming-collection.

3
Collection Maintenance

Once you have built your collection—taking into account the different users who might engage with your game collection, as well as the larger community—you will need to consider how you will treat that collection within the library. Some questions you might want to address include:

- How will you allow patrons to discover and engage with your gaming collection?

- How are you going to catalog the games?

- How will you shelve them?

- How do you intend to preserve them, if at all?

- What kind of programming will you develop around this collection?

One of the first questions any library needs to consider when developing a gaming collection is how their patrons will actually discover that collection—will it be through the library catalog, or will it simply be through a display shelf that is placed prominently in the library? Regardless of how you intend for users to interact with the collection, it is important to ensure that the gaming collection is properly cataloged.

The "if you build it, they will come" mentality will not lead to successful use of your gaming collection. Many libraries with gaming collections don't catalog them properly, and the collection is lost to the patrons. There are several models for how to store and make your game collection discoverable and depending on your particular library's situation you may decide to do one or a combination of several of the following ideas.

Table 3.1: Open versus Closed Shelving

	Pros	Cons
Open Shelving	• easily accessible by patrons • inviting and highly discoverable • can be stored anywhere in the library	• potential of theft, damage, lost pieces • harder to keep accurate usage statistics • requires additional security features (e.g., RFID and jewel cases)
Closed Shelving	• easier to gather accurate usage statistics • less chance for theft, damage, lost pieces, etc. • you don't need special security features	• requires more staff time you need to provide secure storage (e.g., a back room or lockable cabinets) • less discoverable • you may outgrow storage space

Open Shelving versus Closed Shelving

There are many different ways you can store gaming related materials and the path that your library chooses will depend on a variety of factors. You may want to consider looking at either open shelving, where the materials can be seen and selected by the user, or closed shelving, where materials are locked and can only be physically accessed by a library staff member. This section will look at both forms of shelving and help you consider the pros and cons of each. How a library shelves their gaming collection can depend on such things as space, security, financial resources, community engagement (i.e., programming), and patron or staff needs. It is important to consider exactly how your gaming collection will be used when you develop storage (see Table 3.1).

Cataloging

Cataloged Records versus Non-Cataloged Records

In a recent survey of libraries with gaming collections, it was found that cataloging practices are largely inconsistent. While there are records available in the Online Computer Library Center (OCLC), the completeness of these records varies. Further to this, the survey found that of the 94 libraries that responded over 51% never created catalog records for their games.[1] This can impede the ability of your patrons to discover what games are in your collection and therefore decrease use and engagement. Data from the PEW Research Center in 2016 indicated that 27% of Americans visited public library websites in the previous 12 months,[2] which demonstrates the need to include online records for your gaming collection. Patrons are increasingly going to the online catalog and website to learn more about library programs and collections. It is not uncommon to have encounters with patrons who are genuinely shocked that the library has a browsable gaming collection and that they are able to borrow these materials. This is important information to consider when deciding what is best for your users to enhance discoverability.

Despite wanting patrons to use library catalogs to discover gaming collections, we need to be cognizant that many patrons may be looking for other avenues to discover these collections. Therefore, many libraries look to other ways to build an online presence for gaming materials to ensure their games are discovered and used. Board games and digital games do not have their own classifications in Resource Description and Access (RDA), so some cataloging librarians have improvised to increase discoverability online. Some libraries create resource pages that include visual and written information about what is in the collection, how it can be browsed, and so on. You can do this within the existing Library Management System (LMS) by supplying "canned searches" that bring up all the catalog records with the click of a link rather than relying on patrons to perform the entire search. This usually involves the use of tagging rather than altering the MARC records. Other libraries also provide in-person, paper listings such as a binder with all of the games alphabetized. Every library will be different, and the solution for your library may be a combination of several of the proposed solutions.

Traditional Cataloging Practices

As noted by the librarians at Simon Fraser University, traditional cataloging practices mixed with library specific software can pose some challenges for discoverability. When they began cataloging the gaming materials for their collection, they were using copy-cataloging, grabbing records from OCLC, but then added specific field notes to indicate which gaming system the game belonged to reduce false hits and also included notes for PC games that had CD keys.[3] Many online public access catalogs (OPACs) and library discoverability tools do not contain a lot of options for displaying and organizing game content. This leads libraries to get creative with how their records are displayed in the systems. Some libraries will classify the games as media, while others have more specific options they can use. At Wilfrid Laurier University (WLU), there was some trial and error to try to make the records more accessible. WLU used Primo for their library catalog, and because they were part of a consortium, they ran into issues with digital game records deduping and not displaying what game console they belonged to. A quick solution to this was creating tags in the catalog to generate listings by gaming console.[4]

When it comes to cataloging materials and assigning call numbers, there are a few other considerations to make. Libraries have been flirting with the idea of abandoning Dewey or Library of Congress (LC) in favor of adopting bookstore models in an attempt to make items more discoverable and intuitive to users.[5] The call numbers assigned to the games are within several ranges rather than them all being within one range, which makes shelving them by call number challenging as most patrons will be searching for a digital game by title and by console. The Library of Congress has placed most board games in the GV (Recreation. Leisure) range:

GV1232–1299	Card games: Poker, patience, whist, and so on
GV1301–1311	Gambling. Chance and banking games
GV1312–1469	Board games. Move games Including chess, go, checkers, and so on
GV1469.14–1469.62	Computer games. Video games. Fantasy games
GV1470–1511	Parties. Party games and stunts
GV1491–1507	Puzzles

In game stores, board game cafés, and some larger bookstores, games are typically filed alphabetically (occasionally they are filed by game type or theme). This poses a potential issue with discoverability as the collections will not be fully alphabetical if they are shelved according to LC or Dewey call number. If you have a small collection, then this may not be an issue, but if you have several dozen titles, you may want to consider shelving them alphabetically, while maintaining the proper call numbers in the catalog. This will require some staff training as this is not the typical way to shelve material, but it may increase the likelihood that patrons will find a particular game by title. Digital game organization has the same considerations that board games do.

If you do choose for your library to use cataloged records for video games, a good resource to have on hand is the "Best Practice for Cataloging Video Games: Using RDA and MARC21," April 2018 report prepared by the Online Audiovisual Catalogers, Inc. It can be found online at https://www.olacinc.org/sites/default/files/Video%20Game%20Best%20Practices-April-2018%20Revision-a.pdf.

Collection Preservation

Board Games

Little work has been done on the preservation of circulating board game collections. One study, completed by librarians at the University of North Texas, does shed some light on best practice for maintaining this type of physical collection. The team decided to do various preservation techniques on different parts of the board games. This included more involved methods such as cloth box corners, binders for the instruction books, and waterproof sprays and dips. While this study concluded that extensive processing and preservation measures are not cost-effective or necessary for a circulating collection, a library can use simple, less invasive, and inexpensive measures that can extend the longevity of their collection.[6] Some of the more essential and cost-effective considerations around board game protection that libraries may want to consider as they grow their gaming collection include:

- **Board games should be stored on shelves horizontally rather than vertically.** The game boxes are designed to be stored this way, and if you store them vertically, they may warp should there be any gaps in the shelf. Also, you may have pieces fall to the bottom of the box so the box will not close properly. If you must store them horizontally, try to keep the games shelved closely together to prevent any warping from happening.

- **Use elastic bands or ties to prevent warping and keep the boxes closed.** There are some archival considerations to take into account (e.g., rubber bands become brittle over time and may stain the box), so using cotton ties or purpose-built silicon ties for board games may be worth exploring. This will also help keep the boxes together when they are returned in a book drop. If you do use some type of tie be prepared to educate your patrons on the importance of returning the games with the ties to minimize potential damage when the items are returned.

- **Reinforce the box corners to help prevent potential damage when games are returned in a book drop.** The University of North Texas did not see this as an effective strategy based on the resource cost to do this versus the damage to the boxes. You may also want to explore padding for book drops to minimize damage to the board games that are returned, but overall you need to account for game replacement similarly as you would for other types of collections in the library.

- **Invest in card sleeves.** Card sleeves are plastic protectors to prevent damage to cards in the game. They are relatively inexpensive and can be purchased online or at a game store. These are helpful for games that rely heavily on card components and will be handled a lot (e.g., Munchkin, Exploding Kittens, and deck building games). The sleeves are not waterproof as they remain open at one end, but they do help with bending and surface dirt.

- **Box inserts and plastic bags.** Although they are quite expensive, box inserts can be helpful in keeping board games organized and prevent pieces from falling out or getting mixed up. Box inserts are custom made for the specific game and can be found online, or you can 3D print them if you have access to a 3D printer. A cheaper alternative is to take pieces that are loose in the box and put them into tiny plastic bags.

- **Create piece count sheets for the games.** This will help keep the box organized and to determine if all the pieces are present and accounted for. Piece count sheets include a listing of all the pieces in the box and perhaps have visual representations of them. You can also include an image of how the box should be organized to encourage patrons to return the games in an organized manner.

- **Photocopy rule books and include the photocopied version in the box and keep the original copy in the library.** This is increasingly becoming unnecessary as most commercial games have copies of their rules available online, even in multiple languages, which can be helpful for programming. That being said, if the games are "indie" rather than mass-market produced, there is a chance that they do not have rule books available online. By providing a copied version you ensure that if that version is lost there is still a version of the rules available. It should be noted, however, that you should consult with your copyright laws to ensure you are not breaching copyright.

Ultimately, you need to prioritize your board game budget to see if these are the options you want to explore. In the case of the University of North Texas, they found that most of the more invasive preservation techniques were not effective uses of resources, and it was easier to just replace a damaged game. If you are building a collection with grant-based money, you may want to add some of these features to increase the longevity of the games, as some can be over $100 to replace. Some of the cheaper options, such as plastic bags, card sleeves, and purpose-built ties, are beneficial without being cost prohibitive and will extend the life of your board game collection. Regardless, it is up to the library and the financial resources available to determine which approaches will be best for you as you build the collection.

Video Games

Luckily, digital games (digital media) have been extensively studied in both the library and archival professions, so we have pretty clear guidelines on how to ensure the longevity of the collection. If the collection is a circulating collection, there are some easy things to implement, such as:

- doing regular inspections of the games to look for scratches,
- using disc cleaner to remove any dust or debris,
- regularly playing the games to ensure they still work,
- storing them in a temperature- and humidity-controlled environment when possible, and so on.[7]

If the plan is to keep the items even longer, then you may want to refer to literature written by archival professionals on the subject.

It is also important to maintain hardware used for playing digital games, as many are not backwards compatible, meaning a specific game can only be played using a specific piece of hardware. As we discuss in Chapter 7, a library may need to consider purchasing multiple systems if their budget allows. Hardware can be costly and requires regular maintenance, and most libraries that intend to have more current circulating collections will likely only have newer models. There is a growing market for "retro" games, and many companies, such as Sony and Nintendo, have been releasing new hardware systems with older games preloaded into them, for example, the Nintendo Classic has 30 Nintendo games preloaded onto the device. These retro alternatives make it easier for libraries to fulfill patron needs from a nostalgic perspective and are fairly inexpensive versus maintaining the older hardware and game cartridges. (Further discussion of retro gaming consoles can be found in Chapter 8.)

Moving to Digital Only Releases

One particular topic that is being discussed in the literature is the movement away from having physical releases of video games (e.g., on a disk or cartridge) in favor of having downloadable only content. This poses a number of risks for libraries as decisions need to be made around this new model. Do libraries only purchase physical format games, or do they create online accounts and download content for their users? Both have their pros and cons. If you only purchase physical format games, you end up excluding many indie titles, and if you only purchase online content, you then must agree to loan out expensive game consoles and monitor user behavior online, as they could be banned while using a library account. Online content also tends to be less expensive than the physical version and is more likely to go on sale or be part of a bundle. However, while the content can be cheaper, you may need to make adjustments to your consoles to store all of this content, and it becomes challenging to provide access to users if all your games are on one physical game system. Downloaded games take up memory on the system, and most systems come with very limited memory. You can go ahead and purchase additional memory cards in many instances, but you do run the risk of the card going missing or temporarily losing some of that content if a patron accidentally erased it (although it can usually be re-downloaded). Lastly, there is a chance you could lose your entire catalog. This recently happened when Nintendo announced they were closing the Wii Shop Channel in January 2019.[8] While the Wii is an older system (released in 2006) that had been around for 14 years, users still had content on there and found out they would no longer be able to re-download any content that they owned in the event they needed to (e.g., having to factory reset their Nintendo Wii). In many instances, it is easier to maintain a physical collection of video games than it is to maintain downloaded content. Having said that, more digital games are incorporating downloadable contents (DLCs) along with regular updates and patches. As the systems and games age, it is possible that these important updates will no longer be available, so this is something to think about from a long-term preservation perspective.

Notes

1. Teresa Slobuski, Diane Robson, and P. J. Bentley, "Arranging the Pieces: A Survey of Library Practices Related to a Tabletop Game Collection," *Evidence Based Library and Information Practices* 12, no. 1 (2017): 8.

2. John B. Horrigan, "Libraries 2016," Pew Research Center, September 9, 2016, https://www.pewinternet.org/2016/09/09/libraries-2016/.

3. Natalie Gick, "Making Book: Gaming in the Library: A Case Study," in *Gaming in Academic Libraries: Collections, Marketing, and Information Literacy*, ed. Amy Harris and Scott E. Rice (Chicago: ACRL, 2008).

4. Deduping occurs when catalog records have the same title, the cataloging program consolidates the records into one bibliographic (bib) record rather than having duplicate records in the system with similar titles. This process is called deduping and is problematic if items have the same title, but are available in different formats.

5. Jeannette Woodward, *Creating the Customer-Driven Library: Building on the Bookstore Model* (Chicago: ALA Editions, 2004).

6. Diane Robson, Jessica Phillips, and Steven Guerrero, "Don't Just Roll the Dice: Simple Solutions for Circulating Tabletop Game Collections Effectively in Your Library," *LRTS* 62, no. 2 (2018).

7. Fred R. Byers, "Care and Handlings of CDs and DVDs: A Guide for Librarians and Archivists," Council on Library and Information Resources, October 2003, https://www.clir.org/wp-content/uploads/sites/6/pub121.pdf.

8. Frank, Allegra, "R.I.P., Wii Shop Channel," Polygon, January 30, 2019, https://www.polygon.com/2019/1/30/18203844/nintendo-wii-shop-channel-closed.

4
Programming

You have built a gaming collection, now what? Having a gaming collection in a library is about more than just physical space, policy, or technical and financial requirements—you will need to consider how to best encourage your patron base to actually use the collection. Namely, there is a need to do more than build a collection of games and hope that library patrons will serendipitously begin using them. It not as simple as building a collection, you need to actively engage your patron base with it for it to be successful. This chapter will look at considerations around space, questions to consider prior to consider when creating and implementing game-related programming, and then it will outline several gaming programs we have run to get you started on your journey.

Need for Space and Programming

Gaming patrons have a host of needs that are not entirely dissimilar to other patrons, but they can be unique. On one hand, reading a book requires little in the way of hardware or space, and it is largely an individual activity; gaming, on the other hand, has a high hardware/object requirement along with space and ability to play with others (in most cases). It also requires some knowledge around technologies when it comes to digital games as well as access to the hardware and software needed to engage in the experience. Tabletop games, while analog in nature, require some know-how along with the physical space for group play; this can get boisterous and may upset patrons who are used to libraries being quiet spaces.

There are three main areas where libraries can provide service to game users: access, motivation, and guidance. Access is rather straightforward and pertains to the library supplying not only the games but also the hardware and technology needed to run and support them (e.g., an Xbox One). Motivation refers to librarians and staff encouraging users to visit the library and borrow material. Finally, guidance refers to connecting to user needs and interests and being able to help them find the right material.[1] Libraries should make an effort to create space and programs around these unique collections, which can include developing gamers' advisory policies and strategies.

Space requirements vary depending on the type of library and the intended users you are trying to attract. In a small, rural library you may not have much space to dedicate to a gaming collection so you will need to work with what you have and perhaps have some storage solutions that allow for easy access to gaming equipment when needed. In a larger institution, you may be able to dedicate an entire space just to gaming and include gaming computers, permanently hooked up gaming consoles, and more. In Chapter 5 of the ALA *Library Technology Reports* (April 2008) on gaming in libraries, a number of different case studies are presented showing the need and success of doing such work.[2]

Library Programming Considerations

It is important to not only have a robust collection of gaming materials in the library but also complementary programming to generate interest in the collection. These collections tend to be very popular and users tend to get excited about related programming. These programs also tend to be very well attended. We have started you off with a list of popular programs that we compiled from our own experience and from other libraries. A lot of the following examples require fairly limited resources and can be modified and adapted based on a particular library. As you build an appetite for gaming in your library, you can start to expand the programming and increase your budget—the sky is the limit!

Before running any program that incorporates games, it is important to ask yourself some key questions.

Who are you targeting to come? Is that the right group?

If you want families to come, then you need to cater the program to that demographic. You will see examples of programs that are intended for families but can also be geared toward an older audience if that is who you are targeting. The age and skill level of participants is also important. If you have well-versed gamers come to your event and you only have basic family games, they will likely leave disappointed. Likewise, if families come and all of the games are two to three hours in length and very complex, they too will be disappointed in the program. Just because the game fits the theme or genre doesn't mean it fits the intended audience. Also be prepared to learn that you targeted the wrong crowd or made an incorrect assumption. When we ran our Intro to *Dungeons & Dragons* program for tweens and teens, we ended up having adults call the library asking if they could attend or if we would create an adult version of the program.

How are you marketing this program to your patrons?

We found listing just a general board game café in our newsletter became problematic to adult patrons as the program was listed in the Teen section of the newsletter. Adults tended to not look there, and if they did, they didn't think the program was meant for them. Likewise, putting the program in the adult section meant that teens and families did not feel comfortable coming. While multigenerational gaming programs are possible, it may be necessary to create clear messaging about who you are targeting to come. It is also important to not just assume patrons will be able to understand if the program is meant for them just based on its theme or title. Some programs are easier to make intergenerational, whereas other programs may need to be slightly modified and offered to different groups to encourage their participation. We found if a program was successful that it was worthwhile modifying it and offering it to a different audience to see if they also would enjoy it.

Who will/could be assisting with this event?

Finding willing and enthusiastic staff members to play games with patrons can sometimes be a little harder than you would think. If you do not have staff members who already know a lot about games or who are unsure where to start, having them read this book can help prepare them for running game-related events. Reaching out to people who are into games or local businesses may be an untapped market of volunteers who are looking to get involved with their community library, whether as a participant, donor, or volunteer. For example, we sought out community members who were established "Dungeon Masters" (DMs) to come in and teach tweens how to play Dungeons & Dragons. This turned into a multiyear partnership that continues to this day. When we ran our Live-Action Clue event, we had a local gardener come in and pretend to be Mrs. Sprout, and the gardener also brought in seedlings for the participants to plant. We also had a local hobby store donate Warhammer figures and paint sets for children to learn how to paint models. Sometimes these community members can even help create the events themselves and assist staff with areas they are not as knowledgeable in.

What materials and resources do you have available?

Are you in a situation where you can buy specific games or materials for an event or do you need to work within your existing collection? The better you know your collection the more aware you will become of potential uses for it. Maybe you happen to have a lot of games that are educational—this may lead you to consider partnering with a local school board. Maybe you got a large donation of role-play books, so you may want to experiment with launching a role-play campaign in the library. Maybe one of your staff members is really good at graphic design and wants to teach a "create your own board game" workshop. There are so many genres, themes, and mechanics in games that the opportunities really are endless!

Will this be a themed event?

Sometimes, you can get very creative with your game programming. For example, if you are planning a storytelling month event, you can focus on a lot of games, as many have some sort of storytelling function versus picking games solely because they are listed within the storytelling genre. If you're planning an event around world building or exploration, again many different games whose main theme isn't necessarily an exact match may have elements within them that can fit the theme. This is why it is important to know your collection well and be willing to get a bit creative. You can also consult websites like Boardgamegeek.com and IGN (www.ign.com) to get ideas for what games may fit within your theme; keep in mind, you should pick games that will satisfy more than just your theme—being mindful of age, time commitment, player ability, and so on.

What are other libraries already doing?

Why reinvent the wheel? Libraries are always sharing and borrowing ideas from each other. We've included some sample programs that we have run at our library, but we have also shared these ideas with other library systems before this publication was even a thought. In our experience, we have collaborated in many different ways including academic libraries partnering with public libraries, local municipal government partnering with academic libraries, and we even had one of our more popular programs turn into a bit of a traveling roadshow where one of this book's authors travelled to four different regional library systems to teach staff how to do a specific program. Some libraries are more adventurous than others or some may even have a resident gamer on staff who puts on a lot of this type of programming. Reach out to them and cross-pollinate ideas surrounding using games in the library.

Game-Related Programs: Ideas and Suggestions

Here are some examples of game-related programs we have run in our libraries. We have tried to clearly layout the programs. Feel free to use these ideas or modify them so that they fit your library's situation.

Intro to Dungeons & Dragons Campaign

Supplies:

- copies of the Dungeons & Dragons Player's Handbook
- an experienced DM to lead the campaign
- mini figures
- blank character sheets
- five to seven sets of dice designed for Dungeons & Dragons
- one-inch grid paper

- table set up with chairs in an area where players could be loud but also concentrate

- a staff member experienced with Dungeons & Dragons or a volunteer

This program can be run with tweens, teens, or adults. Dungeons & Dragons is a thrilling role-playing game, but it can be hard to get into as most venues where one might engage with it outside of your friend group (e.g., game café) have already established campaigns and seasoned players. The library can find itself in a strong position by tapping into this local player market to recruit DMs to teach people how to play Dungeons & Dragons (or any other role-playing game). These campaigns will typically need to last a few months so that players can see their characters develop, and you also need a large block of time to ensure players can carefully think out their moves and have more than a few turns. Running a seven-week campaign in three-hour weekly sessions is an appropriate amount of time for new players to get into the game. They can then use this knowledge to start their own campaigns and borrow the library's resources to do that. In order to have a successful program, you need to limit the number of players for each campaign to five, as each player's turn is very time-consuming, and it becomes a challenge accomplishing anything within the three-hour window if you have too many players.

In the first week of the program, players will go through the process of selecting their characters. This involves choosing the race and class and also being assigned attributes that players will use while playing the game. The DM will also introduce themselves and explain the game and how the campaign will be played. In the following weeks, the DM will lead the players through an adventure, drawing out the scenes using the grid paper and populating it with the mini figures that will act as monsters and playable characters. As players move through the campaign, they will increase their knowledge and abilities and become more familiar with the game. We ran a program like this at a public library for youth ages 10–13, and it turned into a regular weekly event after the seven weeks had finished.

3D Game Avatar Printing Program

Supplies:

- character sheets and resources to match the game that participants are interested in playing (e.g., Dungeons & Dragons and Pathfinder)

- access to computers with Internet access

- access to free 3D design web-based programs like Tinkercad or SketchUp that allow existing files to be uploaded from Thingiverse

- access to a 3D printer

- model paints and paintbrushes

- staff member

This three-session program (normally run over a three-week period) can be run with tweens, teens, or adults. In order to play most role-playing games, participants need some sort of 3D object that represents their character, as they need to be able to move it according to the actions they take in the game. Since these characters are highly customizable, there is an interest in being able to model a specific character to play with—your avatar. By creating a 3D Game Avatar Printing program where participants create their 3D role-play game avatar, libraries can entice a group of users who may not have taken advantage of the 3D printing services available within the library. This also encourages them to play more role-play games and to tell their friends who also may be interested. A program like this would pair well with the Intro to Dungeons & Dragons program.

In the first week of the program, participants will take time to learn how to create a character for the role-play game they wish to play. They will look through the resources and plan out their design. After they have decided on their character, the program facilitator will teach them how to use a 3D design program. Tinkercad is very easy to learn but is not as precise as something like SketchUp, so depending on the abilities of the participants you may want to choose one or the other. Participants can also import files from Thingiverse, as it has many freely available designs including many mini figures from role-play games like Dungeons & Dragons. These imported files can be modified (e.g., you could add wings or a tail to a character) or printed "as is" depending on the skill level of participants. Once their designs are completed, you would queue them up to print. The last week of the workshop participants could come in and paint their characters so that they are ready to go for their first role-play campaign.

Painting mini figures is a real art, so we also ran a program where we had local experts come in and teach participants advanced painting techniques like antiquing, weathering, adding 3D material to the bases (e.g., adding sticks and moss to the base to make it look more real), painting patterns like flames or ombre colors, and so on. These paints can be very expensive so we partnered with a local game store who donated the materials. It's best to use the higher quality paints, so that they adhere to the 3D printed plastic with minimal preparation.

Visiting Virtual Reality (VR) with Seniors

Supplies:

- a laptop with preloaded games and experiences
- a VR headset and required hardware and software to run it
- a trained staff member on VR

This passive activity involves taking whatever VR hardware your library has out of the library and into a retirement home or long-term care facility. Typically, the best "games" to use are scenic views or tours through different vistas. Seniors can wear VR goggles and stay seated for safety while a library worker can navigate them through the experience.

The most labor-intensive part of this program is to transport the VR equipment from the library to the desired location and setting it up. Ideal locations to set this up are open areas that are level where all obstructions can be removed. Depending on the particular VR equipment you are using, you may need a larger space for sensors, or you may want to project what the participant is seeing onto a screen so that passersby can view what is happening, in order to spark their interest in participating. Some seniors are comfortable with being more active in participating, so they will walk around and use the controllers themselves. Others are a bit more limited, so you should have them sit comfortably in a chair and have the program facilitator use the controllers to move to where the participant wants to go in the VR experience. It is also important to make sure program facilitators work with the retirement home or long-term care facility staff to ensure safety of the participants.

Google Cardboard Maker Day

Supplies:

- Google Cardboard Kit (available at https://arvr.google.com/cardboard/) (you can also get free printable mounts online)

- experienced staff member

- smartphone (user provided) with software equipped, software may include:

  - Google Official Cardboard App (Android & iOS)

  - Cardboard Camera (Android & iOS)

  - Google Arts & Culture (Android & iOS)

  - Google Spotlight Stories (Android & iOS)

  - Google Street View (Android & iOS)

  - YouTube (Android & iOS)

This program is intended for a variety of patron groups—including children, teens, adults, and seniors—but many libraries focus this event toward a younger audience. For this event to be successful, you need to ensure that attendees will be able to bring a smartphone, usually equipped with the Google Cardboard App or a similar software to enable VR experience for the user. This is often best done in a large group, with one or two experienced library staff members participating in and facilitating the event. Libraries will need to acquire the Google Cardboard kit, or its equivalent, which are readily available online and can range in price from $9.00 to $25.00. Given the start-up costs, you may want to consider making this a pay-what-you-can type event. Alternatively, you can also have your patrons make their own mounts using free patterns online and minimal supplies to limit costs and allow them to continue their experiences at home. You may want to spend some time at the start of the event getting everyone to download a suitable software, see the supplies list. If you are focusing the event toward children, you can also encourage them to decorate the cardboard set. You might also want to encourage participants to work together in getting the set configured correctly or have them play different games in pairs—but make the event fun and exciting by generating and fostering a community atmosphere.

Running this program is fairly simple. You can use the Google Cardboard App to get started or a host of other apps available that are compatible with Google Cardboard (e.g., Expeditions). These apps can take patrons through both VR and augmented reality (AR) experiences and can be planned around a theme or event already happening in the library. For example, the Expeditions app allows patrons to "roam with dinosaurs," or the Paul McCartney App allows you to experience a Paul McCartney concert in 3D (this would likely appeal to a little bit older crowd). You can also take photos and turn them into VR experiences using Cardboard Camera. This is the type of program that you can either do a lot of extra programming around or make it a more passive activity.

Board Game Cafés in the Library

Supplies:

- a variety of board games to appeal to different ages and skill levels
- additional items needed for each game (pencil/paper for scorekeeping, etc.)
- a staff member who is comfortable and familiar with most of the games

This program is a great way to capture the attention of the millennials and young adult crowd that is difficult to attract to library programming but can be good for all ages. Board game cafés are increasing in popularity; however, there is usually a nominal fee associated with visiting and using a café's resources. Libraries can offer similar programming without the fee, thus attracting cost-conscious users. Librarians can also reach out to local gamers and meet a user need—oftentimes game enthusiast clubs already exist and just need somewhere to host their events. It is also important to have some staff or volunteers on hand, acting as game concierges, to show participants how to play newer games. Patrons often shy away from games they're not familiar with. Good to keep in mind that programming like this does require a strong commitment of staff resources. Final note: Do you want to target families, teens, or adult enthusiasts? Each of these groups requires different considerations, and you want to be sure to keep those in mind:

Family Cafés

Try having a lot of classic games such as Monopoly, Scrabble, and Candyland along with more modern family-friendly titles available, such as Forbidden Island, Settlers of Catan, and Apples to Apples. This allows a family to pick something they already know or get adventurous and try something new. You can also have games that are themed based on pop culture (e.g., Harry Potter themed Clue and Star Wars Monopoly) to entice children to play. In many cases, this is a more passive program as the parents take the lead on teaching and playing games with their children. The staff member should be ready to answer basic questions or help adventurous families tackle a game they've never played before.

Teen Cafés

Teens tend to be more familiar with video games and may not be avid board game players. For this reason, it can be helpful for a staff member to select a title or theme and curate the games for that particular day. We've found by selecting a particular game and advertising the event as a "Learn to Play Munchkin" or "Board Games for Those Who Love Overwatch" it will generate more interest with teens rather than having a passive program with games on tables. Having a more interactive, engaging program will encourage them to participate. We also tried this approach with other genres and formats of games and found a lot of success.

Adult Gaming Enthusiast Cafés

These folks likely have played some of the more modern titles or have heard of a particular title that they have always wanted to try playing. For this program, it is best if you can mix elements from both of the previously mentioned programs, such as making classic games available, while also having a collection of modern games that would tie in with those classic titles. You need a collection of board game titles that will appeal to them and range in complexity. You may also need to do some instruction or game setup to get them going. Listing particular games you have in the collection in your advertising for this event can be helpful to entice adult enthusiasts. Advertising the event as free to users and as a great way to meet new people will pique the interest of those looking for the social connection gaming provides. We also incorporated local game designers into our adult programs. Designers would bring in prototypes they were working on and ask participants if they were interested in trying the game and giving feedback. This kept the program fresh and also increased awareness of the local game design community.

Video Game Tournaments

Supplies:

- two or more copies of a particular videogame
- two or more consoles to play the game
- two or more televisions or screens

- multiple controllers (as many as the consoles will support)
- prizes
- a board to record matches and victories
- experienced staff member

This type of program is easy to run and usually draws large numbers, especially if it is one of the more popular tournament style games (e.g., *Smash Brothers* and *Mario Kart*). Ideally, you would have multiple copies of the game to run on multiple systems with multiple televisions. This allows more people to actively participate and fewer participants are left feeling unengaged. You could have prizes for the winners (e.g., a game store gift card) or a leaderboard in the library with the winners' names on it for bragging rights. Provide people with a code of conduct or rules of engagement as these kinds of tournaments can get rather intense. Starting points for this document would include zero tolerance for swearing and name-calling.

Depending on the game and how this event is marketed you may end up with a lot of participants. We have run a program like this on various occasions, including: a Professional Activity (PA) day for high school students, a retro game night, as part of a March Break program, and game nights for university students. As noted in the supplies section, having two or more for a lot of the supplies allows some flexibility in the program—meaning you can scale this program up or down depending on interest and capacity. Often it may be useful to have participants sign up ahead of time to gage interest and to allow you to cap the program if the need arises. What staff facilitators will do is create a round-robin type competition where players face each other and either the last player standing (e.g., in a game like *Smash Brothers*) or the one with the most wins or points (e.g., *Mario Kart*) wins. Facilitators will also need to be ready for any potential hardware/software glitches—this is especially true if you're doing anything online—and to ensure players are acting in a respectable manner. We mentioned previously that a code of conduct is a good idea and you need to enforce it.

Group Video Gaming Events

Supplies:

- two or more copies of a particular video game or access to an online gaming platform like Steam or Rainway
- two or more consoles or computers to play the game
- two or more televisions or screens
- snacks (keep in mind common dietary limitations)
- multiple controllers (as many as the consoles will support)
- a board to record matches and victories
- experienced staff member

This kind of program is very similar to a video game tournament in its structure and configuration and can draw a large number of participants. Focus on one specific game that a number of participants can play together—such as *World of Warcraft*, *Portal 2*, or one of the *Mario* franchise games. Ideally, you would have multiple copies of the game that you can run on multiple systems with multiple televisions or computers (if you are using an online gaming platform), helping make sure fewer participants are left unengaged. The point of the event is to encourage communal play and get people talking about the games, offering pointers, and creating a bit of a party atmosphere.

As with the tournament, this kind of event can draw a lot of participants. We have done similar events for game design students where 90% of the student body showed up to the library to participate. This particular setup is often referred to as a local area network (LAN) party. A LAN party is when you hook up multiple consoles or computer games to one network allowing multiple people to play together. Having participants sign up ahead of time can be essential in gauging interest and keeping participants to a reasonable number. Be prepared to think on the fly, if there are more patrons than games or consoles, perhaps introduce a board game aspect to the event. This lets everyone have a chance at both the video game and the board game. Again, having staff facilitators be prepared to troubleshoot technological issues and monitor behavior is important. This is another event to consider requiring a signed code of conduct for each participant.

Fail Game Day

Supplies:

- copies of board games that are turn based that participants can alter and take home when the program is finished

- general craft supplies

- staff member

This program is adaptable to any age group. This program is both recreational and also educational. Participants are given a chance/turn-based board game (e.g., Candyland, Monopoly, and Pay Day) and are asked to make modifications to the game to make it better. In order to achieve this, there is a discussion on player agency and the importance of choice in a game that makes it more engaging for players. If the game is entirely up to chance or luck, players quickly get frustrated as there is no way to strategize a victory. This style is typical with children's games to make it a more even playing field. You can have participants either modify the game itself (e.g., buy copies from a thrift store or yard sale) or have them create components that can be added to the game without physically altering it to make it more engaging.

The beginning of this program is a bit of a lesson in game design. Participants are told about the drawbacks of a game left entirely up to chance as it has little in the way of player agency leading to a decreased likelihood of replayability; if players cannot effect change in their outcome during play and it is all randomized, players will lose interest in playing or replaying the game. It is then explained that while games like this are usually good for small children they lack the depth to have older more experienced players enjoy playing them. Participants are then asked to think about games they've played in the past and what elements they liked about them. After some brainstorming, participants will be instructed on the importance of prototyping their ideas and playtesting. Then participants are asked to start designing their modified games so that they will be ready to be play tested. Depending on the age group, this part of the program can vary in length. At the end, participants can play each other's games—you can also modify this game so it is closer to the Game Jams program and allow for the participants to play test each other's games and allow time to incorporate feedback. We ran this program once for families and one participant added role-play elements to Monopoly, allowing people to customize their character, and each space they landed on was an adventure or task rather than a property. Another participant added constraints to Scrabble and allowed other players to add their words for bonus points if a player couldn't spell a word on their turn.

Participants come out having a deeper understanding for how games are designed and what makes a particular game more engaging over another. It also gets them to think of ways to improve other games they have or sparks their interest in doing more game design on their own after the program has ended.

Game Jams

Supplies:

- general craft supplies
- bits of "junk" (e.g., old CDs, feathers, and toilet paper tubes)
- poster board
- staff member

This program is designed to teach participants the key components of a game, how to prototype and play test a game, and how to incorporate user feedback into their creations. This program offers a lot of flexibility and can be modified to different age groups. The program can be completely open or theme based. If you want to do the program with younger children make sure that you have at least one parent per team to act as the team captain to lead them through the activity. Young children always seem to have the most unique ideas when it comes to making games. Older children and adults tend to overthink the activity, so we recommend imposing tighter constraints or providing examples.

To begin the program, the staff member goes over key components needed to create a good game: rules, components (pieces), space, goal, and mechanisms. Then participants are told to select three items of "junk" to use for the game and to use poster board if they want to create a game board. The game board can both help and hinder the ideation of the game, depending on age group. It is great for younger children allowing them tons of opportunities to contribute, whereas older children will fixate on making a board rather than a good game. Groups are given 30–45 minutes to create their first prototype. This will include creating instructions and rules. Upon completion of the prototypes, one member of the team will stay to help explain the game as members circulate to other teams and test out each other's games. Once this play testing phase is complete, teams will have additional time to work on their games and make changes based on play testing feedback. At the end of the day program, participants can reflect on the experience as a whole and talk about some of the things they liked about each other's games.

This program as written is an analog activity, but once participants understand what makes a good game mechanically, it can be adapted to a digital format for a more advanced program. If you happen to have staff members or volunteers who are familiar with some of the digital tools used to create games (e.g., Unity) you could modify the workshop to teach participants how to create these games in a digital space. This would be a good second workshop as the first provides the important context on what makes a good game mechanically and then the digital one could build on that knowledge set and teach digital design skills.

Game Night for International Students or Newcomers

Using games makes second language learning not only more approachable but also increases the abilities of international students or newcomer citizens to create friendships with domestic students or locals.[3] Here is the general setup and flow of this particular program.

Supplies:

- various board games that require use of the English language and/or digital games that do the same

- volunteers who speak English well to lead the games

- this program is very flexible and customizable depending on audience (e.g., age, mastery of the English language, interests, and background in gaming)

This program requires a lot of understanding of the patrons or participants you are serving and also a lot of trial and error. We found if you set out the games and have one leader per game, who has a high mastery of the English language, teach the game to the participants this works well versus having library staff do this. We advise this set up as it will relax the mood of the participants and make the event more enjoyable for everyone. We also found that mono language settings, where all the participants speak the same language, can be a challenge as often they will talk among each other in that language rather than practicing English. Therefore, having English-only speaking members in the group helps to encourage speaking in English. We also found some games, which we thought would be great for this program, were not, for example, Apples to Apples. This game has a lot of cultural references that did not resonate with our largely Chinese student population. We also had a similar experience with the game Word Slam, so we omitted the cultural category. This could be a good learning opportunity, but for the level of English language skills our participants had, this was far too challenging. We also tried games with elimination as the main mechanism, and the participants had a hard time eliminating each other until they were forced to do so. As mentioned, there is a lot of trial and error until you build up a collection of games that work for your group.

Themed Live-Action Clue

Supplies:

- copy of a themed Clue game (e.g., Harry Potter and Star Wars) if available
- craft supplies
- multiple rooms in the library
- prepared packages for participants
- themed decorations and snacks
- prizes
- several staff members and/or volunteers

Clue is an excellent game to adapt to live action in the library! Many people are familiar with, it allows for community involvement, and leverages many existing resources within the library. We have run this program twice with two different themes: Harry Potter and Star Wars. This type of program has a broad appeal, as it can be tailored for families, teens, or adults based on the difficulty of the puzzles and clues. You also can pick a theme that is popular at the time (e.g., we did the Star Wars themed Clue when *Force Awakens* came to movie theaters). You also can make this as big as you want or as small as you want depending on available resources. We found most teams finished in about an hour so we ran the program for three hours total.

You'll want to build out a couple of scenarios so that participants don't overhear the answer from another team; that will also allow participants to go through the game more than once. When they arrive, you hand them a themed package that includes all of the possible locations, weapons/objects, and characters. You then set up clues in the library that could be part of a scavenger-hunt type activity, or if they complete an activity in the library, they get a clue. Once the teams solve the puzzle, they can enter their names into a draw for a grand prize. We also had themed backgrounds so that team members could pose in front of a green screen and get their photos done after they solved the puzzle. The possibilities are endless (some sample activities we did for each theme are listed later). We found these activities to be very popular with many different age groups; many of the participants would come dressed up as their favorite character! We created corresponding displays of book and game resources that matched the theme of the day and noticed uptake on those items. One thing to note; when we ran the Harry Potter Clue event we got overwhelmed with participants (over 100 came during the three-hour program). We managed to still have a successful program, but learning from our mistake we had people register for the Star Wars Clue Day, which allowed us to better prepare for an influx of people.

Harry Potter:

- sorting hat activity
- build your own felt tie for your house
- planting seeds with Mrs. Sprout in herbology class
- make your own wand and test your spell-casting knowledge

Star Wars:

- test your Jedi skills with foam lightsaber battles
- train your droid (Ozzobot) to go through an obstacle course
- fly your ship (paper airplane) into the Death Star (hula hoop)

Retro Game Day

Supplies:

- retro gaming consoles (e.g., Nintendo Classic, Super Nintendo Classic, and Atari)
- screens to play the games on
- staff members who can set up the consoles and wander around during the event

Having a retro game day program in the library has never been easier with the advent of the release of several retro gaming consoles. This type of a program generally attracts Millennials or Generation X as they come to play the games they remember playing growing up. We had adults bringing their children in to play the games of their childhood, which was really fun to watch.

This is a pretty straightforward, easy program to run. When you advertise it, make sure you mention the specific systems and games you'll have to entice people to come. The more variety the better so that you have a wide draw. A skilled staff member is crucial for this event, as the adults struggled trying to remember what buttons to push (e.g., combo moves in *Street Fighter*). We occasionally partner with local museums that had original hardware and software so we were able to create a more authentic experience and have access to games you couldn't get anywhere else; this may be an option for your library if you contact local clubs or enthusiasts. If you are using older hardware be prepared to have some technological glitches—some older systems require different AV outputs than modern televisions have or, in the case of the original Nintendo Entertainment System, you need to have a curved tv monitor (such as a cathode-ray tube [CRT] television and not a flatscreen LCD TV) in order to play games like *Duck Hunt.*

Final Thoughts

Running any library program can be a bit of a gamble. We found, for the most part, programs that include gaming elements are rather popular. We did have some "flops" though, for example, we ran an "Intro to *League of Legends*" program at the library that required a lot of backend work uploading the game to the library computers, but no one attended. This is likely due to the fact that the game is "free to play" online, and most users in our area would have access to reliable Internet. In retrospect, had we been able to supply them with a "pay to play" game (e.g., *Overwatch*) they may have been more excited to come, but this would have required a lot of technical work beforehand. Another hurdle we faced was being overwhelmed with participants; our Harry Potter Clue program had 22 registrations, but we ended up with nearly 100 on the day of the program, which led to a lot of scrambling to be able to accommodate the influx. The Fail Game program had low attendance the first time, but once we changed the description of the program in the newsletter, we had better attendance the second time.

Basically, gaming programs will require a lot of trial and error. As we mentioned, these programs have been successful for us, but there are many factors that come into play: timing, weather, advertising, personal preferences and abilities, technology, and so on. This is why we have spent considerable amounts of time discussing player motivation and gamers' advisory in this book, as we want to help you make informed decisions based on your community so that you have successful programs. But even with all of this information, you may have a couple of duds and that's ok! No one wins on their first try all the time.

Notes

1. Kym Buchanan and Angela M. Vanden Elzen, "Beyond a Fad: Why Video Games Should Be Part of 21st Century Libraries," *Education Libraries* 35, no. 1–2 (Summer–Winter 2012): 15–33.

2. Jenny Levine, "Broadening Gaming Services in Libraries," *Library Technology Reports* 44, no. 3 (April 2008): 24–34.

3. Michelle Goodridge, "Conversational Gamers: Developing Language Skills and Connections through Games," in *Supporting Today's Students in the Library: Strategies for Retaining and Graduating International, Transfer, First-Generation, and Re-Entry Students*, ed. Ngoc-Yen Tran and Silke Higgins (Chicago: American Library Association, 2019).

5
User Behavior in Gaming

As with all readers' advisory services, it is important to have a good understanding of who your patrons are and what type of material they are looking for. There has been quite a bit of literature focused on video game playing styles as it relates to market share and game development, which can be used to help understand how to refer patrons to other materials. This chapter discusses some of the current literature from multiple perspectives (academics, librarians, game developers, etc.), along with a summary of how a library staff member may want to incorporate this information to gain an understanding of what their patrons' needs are. We have decided to include the discussion on user behavior in gaming because there are many theories out there, each of which offer their own unique perspective and different libraries may gravitate to one over the other.

Establishing a Player Motivation Framework

In the article "Player Types, Player Styles, and Play Complexity: Updating the Entertainment Grid," Ricardo Javier Rademacher Mena nicely encapsulates several of the frameworks that have been developed to help understand player motivation in regard to digital games; this is an excellent resource to refer to. Mena discusses two major theories and suggests combining them to create a more robust framework. One of the most pervasive and influential theories that is still being used today was that of Dr. Richard Bartle. Bartle's classification is based on player motivations in immersive online virtual worlds. Bartle breaks this down into four main categories:

1. achievers
2. explorers

3. socializers

4. killers.[1]

These four categories are placed on a set of two axes, creating four quadrants that allows for crossed axes or interest.[2] The second theory of note that gained popularity was the work of anthropologist Roger Caillois and his play taxonomy—dated from 1958; this has largely come out of favor on its own, but you may still see mention of it in the literature. As previously mentioned, Mena suggests using a combination of the two theories to form more accurate assessments of individual player styles and motivation, rather than relying on one theory that results in a more surface-level assessment.

In Chapters 7–9 of this book, we apply Bartle's four categories to describe the games listed to assist librarians in making gaming recommendations. These four categories were selected because they most succinctly describe different types of gamers across both analog and digital games without making it overly complex; do note that this is not the most detailed or comprehensive approach. You can use the remainder of this chapter to expand on our initial classifications.

In their article "Player Behavioural Modelling for Video Games," Sander Bakkes et al. provide an overview of player behavioral modeling in video games by detailing four distinct approaches. These approaches include modelling player actions, tactics, strategies, and profiling. This approach in research toward gameplay is increasing as video games increase in complexity and emphasis shifts toward developing accurate player models in order to develop a game with high player satisfaction.[3] Lastly, the Quantic Foundry Gamer Motivation Model provides an easily digestible framework for understanding and assessing what may motivate a particular gamer.[4] Quantic used data from over 450,000 gamers to create this framework and is continually building on their dataset (see figure 5.1).

Figure 5.1. Quantic Foundry Gamer Motivation Model.
Source: "Quantic Foundry Gamer Motivation Model," Quantic Foundry, accessed December 2019, https://quanticfoundry.com/#motivation-model. Used with permission.

Hybridized Gaming Genres

The gaming landscape is changing, and it is important to discuss how the gaming industry is moving away from narrow game genres to more expanded and hybridized models.[5] Michael Andreen presents a new taxonomy of choice types that are derived from research and observation to try to capture this shift in game design. Andreen also draws attention to the understanding that video games are engineered experiences. Developers and designers implement a calculated choice structure into a game—something that is contrived for any game scenario that a player might feel they have choices in. All the while they are creating worlds and characters who are relatable and believable to elicit different emotions and feelings from the players. Andreen says that because of this complex engineering games are representations and not simulations.[6]

As game genres continue to hybridize, we will likely see a lot of these models shift and change to try to adapt. This makes the job of librarians and staff to assist patrons more complex but hopefully more accurate as we continue to stay current in the trends in gaming and how this changes player motivation.

Using Digital Models for Tabletop Players

How can this relate to board games? It is often one's desire to look at discussions about game users and players and automatically assume that we are only discussing digital games. While much of the user behavior analysis is centered on the digital, it is possible to use these same models when talking about board games and other analog gaming formats. J. P. Gee states that "games can support literacy and provide tangential learning experiences";[7] however, it is the idea that games can create access points to a variety of media (digital, print, analog, etc.) that can connect digital user behavior to board games. Similar to video game player motivations, board games appeal to both avid gamers who game in other formats and the more casual gamer given their approachability.

There are also other genres and formats that may appeal to your patrons. Collectable card games, online streaming game services, mobile apps, and others may appeal to patrons for the variety of reasons already discussed. It is important to consider these models and try to apply them to other types of games so that we can understand our patrons' interests better.

Discussion of Player Appeal in a Library Context

One of the first articles to discuss the appeal of games to patrons from a library perspective was the work done by Jin Ha Lee et al. This important piece of literature is the first of its kind to use empirical evidence to try to map out why players play the games that they do. Using taxonomy gleaned from a literature review, Lee et al. asked players open-ended questions to try to identify the reasoning behind game selection. The study resulted in the identification of 16 major appeals:[8]

Narrative	Depth
Challenge	Creativity/innovation
Sensation	Expression
Fellowship	Accomplishment
Nostalgia	Competition
Fantasy	Submission
Exploration	Mastery
Mood	Learning

These 16 appeals can inform your gamers' advisory interview (more on this in Chapter 7) and be used to select relevant material for your patrons.

It is important to understand what motivates players from both a game design perspective as well as their own personal motivations for advisory, as we need to be able to reliably suggest games that our patrons might be interested in playing. As one can glean from the discussion so far, there are several existing models for understanding player behavior, which can make this a bit daunting to those who are just starting to build and support collections in this area. Thanks to the work of Jin Ha Lee, there has been some form of application of these models to library patrons specifically, but the models are still rather complex.[9]

Informed Gamers' Advisory Interviews

Games are a multifaceted media/entertainment and as such they have many different aspects that could be attracting a particular patron to them. In gamers' advisory interviews, it would be wise to connect the two platforms of games together—if a patron is discussing a video game, ask if they have ever tried a particular board game that is similar in genre or plot, and vice versa. Understanding, for instance, that Andreen's idea of how games create relatable worlds and characters can apply to board games as well as video games is an essential step in knowing you can make connections between the two types of media. Players may be attracted to a style of game play, or artwork, the type of challenges it presents, if it has a good storytelling narrative, and so many other facets that it can be a bit challenging to pinpoint an exact match—and that is ok. Just like we can suggest a particular novel to a patron based on what they enjoyed in the past, they may not like the selected book for many reasons.

As with any reference interview—especially around readers' or gamers' advisory—it is important to establish a few basic ideas: what title the patron last played, why they selected that particular title, did they like the game and why or why not, are they looking for something similar to play or would they like to try something new. If they want to try something new, this can be a good opportunity to introduce some new media: if they liked the video game *Red Dead Redemption*, perhaps they would like to try the board game Dead of Winter. Or perhaps they found something challenging about the game—this is a good time to ask them to describe that challenge. If they did not like one particular aspect of that game—puzzles for instance—you would then obviously make sure not to include any games involving puzzles in your recommendations.

Gamers are often quite knowledgeable about current and upcoming titles, which is something you can use to your advantage. If you are working with a knowledgeable patron, ask them what sorts of titles they are thinking of playing next or what they might be interested in playing and then build off those suggestions. Perhaps you have a game in your collection that is similar to something they mentioned, or you may notice that they are suggesting games all in one genre—which might lead you to believe that this patron is a particular type of gamer (an explorer), so you would know to recommend games that would appeal to that characteristic. You can also take note of any particular titles that they suggest that you can look into later, or they may have drawn a connection between two games that you hadn't thought of before. The more you work with the collection, the more knowledgeable you become; the same as with any other genre or format of collection in a library setting.

Trends in Digital Game Design

There are a few key trends that library staff need to be aware of in the digital game design world; they are persistent games, game ecosystems, player communities, and merging real and virtual worlds. "Persistent games" refers to games that have been around for a long period of time and have generated a lot of player data. Games that fall into this genre tend to be social through online game platforms (e.g., Massive Multiplayer Online Games [MMOG]). Game developers are being encouraged to think about the longevity of these games and create content that maintains player engagement over a long period of time. "Game ecosystems" refers to creating online systems that draw players in to experience multiple games within the ecosystem rather than just one (e.g., the video game company Valve created the popular game *Half Life* in 1998 and in 2013 released *Dota 2*, which has similar mechanics and references to *Half Life*). Building player communities is also a key trend in the online game development world; this includes user-generated content that is out of the control of the developers.

The ability to merge the real and virtual world is as important as ever to developers. The popularity of game walkthrough videos, online forum discussion, and other social activities players engage with outside of the game are increasingly important and can be the make or break of a game. Online communities around particular games are sometimes just as important as the game itself, and players engage with the games in ways that the developers may or may not have intended. These online communities can be of benefit for libraries as we can glean information about popularity, particular issues or challenges with a particular game and gauge overall interest, which helps us when selecting games for our collections.

The digital world is exploring ways to be more analog, while the analog world is exploring how to incorporate digital components, effectively blurring the hard lines between the two formats. Digital games are exploring ways for players to be more physically involved;[10] examples include many games for Nintendo Wii, *Dance Dance Revolution!*, and the newest game for Nintendo Switch called *Ring Fit Adventure*. These games incorporate some sort of physical device or action that is required to be able to play the digital game. In a parallel move, within the board game world, there are increasing interactions with the digital world through using Apps either during or after gameplay. By having a general understanding of where the industry is heading, library staff can be more adequately prepared to answer patron questions and build useful collections.

Artificial Intelligence in Gaming and Player Behavior

Another area where the study of player behavior and motivation has been a focus is in the field of artificial intelligence (AI). This growing aspect of gaming is devoting increased resources to being able to provide the most natural interactions to players to enhance suspension of disbelief and full immersion. Originally digital games had characters whose actions were scripted and perhaps had a few different variations that gave the game player some agency. Now with the use of AI, digital games are becoming smarter in the sense that the non-playable or computer characters that players interact with are becoming responsive rather than scripted. Within the gaming space, AI has three functions: as a companion, as a coach, or as an opponent.[11] Players interact with characters in the game that are directly responding to player actions, and these games are quickly rising in popularity given this high level of player experience.

Having AI elements within a digital game directly impacts the player motivation and interest in continuing to play. By having dynamic AI in the game, players have a new element of engagement during gameplay; some players really enjoy this and may seek out games with dynamic AI on purpose. It is important for library staff to keep an eye on this trend and use it to further shape the field of gamers' advisory, as this is likely the area with the greatest scholarship currently.

Using Personality Tests for Gamer Behavior

Lastly, there has been some discussion around using existing personality tests and frameworks (such as Myers-Briggs) to help understand players and player behavior. At this time, it has not been studied in depth, but it is important to be aware of this type of work and modelling, as it may shed light on the behavior of gamers.[12] The gaming industry is a juggernaut, and more and more companies and developers are pouring resources into understanding how gamers operate, which means libraries can tap into some of these resources and use them when appropriate to shape collections, develop programming, and offer gamers' advisory services. Although this area is less explored than some of the others, it is something that is likely to see some growth, as there is an increase in awareness of how these types of existing frameworks can be applied to gamers.

Final Thoughts

The area of gamer behavior research is being explored more and more, and it is something to note. Researchers and game developers are trying to determine how to design their games to reach specific audiences, and the research in these areas will only continue to grow given the booming growth of gaming, both in popularity and from a financial perspective.

While it can appear daunting to keep up with these trends, it is important to at least be aware so that you can use player motivation and behavior to inform all of your library's gaming-related decisions from collection development to programming to advisory services.

Notes

1. Harry Cloke, "4 Types of Gamers and Learner Engagement," eLearning Industry, September 26, 2017, https://elearningindustry.com/types-of-gamers-and -learner-engagement-4; R. Bartle, "Hearts, Clubs, Diamonds, Spades: Players Who Suit MUDs," *Journal of MUD Research* 1, no. 1 (1996).

2. Ricardo Javier Rademacher Mena, "Player Types, Player Styles, and Play Complexity: Updating the Entertainment Grid," *International Journal of Game-Based Learning* 2, no. 2 (April–June 2012): 79–85.

3. Sander C. J. Bakkes, Pieter H. M. Spronck, and Giel van Lankveld, "Player Behavioural Modelling for Video Games," *Entertainment Computing* 3, no, 3 (August 2012): 71–79.

4. Nick Yee and Nicolas Ducheneaut, "Gamer Motivation Profiling: Users and Applications," in *Games User Research*, ed. Anders Drachen, Pejman Mirza-Babaei, and Lennart E. Nacks (Oxford: Oxford University Press, 2018).

5. Michael Thomas Andreen, "Choice in Digital Games: A Taxonomy of Choice Types Applied to Player Agency and Identity," PhD Dissertation, University of Texas at Dallas, 2017.

6. Ibid., 4.

7. Gee as cited in J. H. Lee, T. Windleharth, and H. Cho, "Toward an Understanding of Cross-Media Appeals for Readers' Advisory," *Proceedings of the Association for Information Science and Technology* 54, no. 1 (2017): 241–250. doi:10.1002/ pra2.2017.14505401027

8. Jin Ha Lee, Rachel Ivy Clarke, Hyerim Cho, and Travis Windleharth, "Understanding Appeals of Video Games for Readers' Advisory and Recommendation," *Reference & User Services Quarterly* 57, no. 2 (Winter 2017): 130.

9. Ibid., 122–139.

10. Mark Owen Riedl and Alexander Zook, "AI for Game Production," Proceedings of the IEEE 2013 Conference on Computational Intelligence in Games, Niagara Falls, Canada, https://www.cc.gatech.edu/~riedl/pubs/cig13.pdf.

11. Bakkes et al., "Player Behavioural Modelling for Video Games," 71–79.

12. Ben Kirman, "Play Styles and Personality >> Computer Games Play Styles Applied to Board Gamers," Boardgamegeek.com, accessed March 2020, https://boardgamegeek.com/geeklist/18914/play-styles-and-personality-computer-games-play-st.

6
Gamers' Advisory

Beyond the examples of programming for patrons (found in Chapter 4), once you have started to engage gamers and the community as a whole with your gaming collection, you will need to effectively serve patrons and help them interact with your collection in a meaningful way. Using similar principles as those found in readers' advisory, it is important that library staff become familiar with how to go about recommending new and innovative games to patrons who are "looking for something new."

As with readers' advisory, this is not as simple as asking the patron what they read last and then grabbing the closest book on the shelf and suggesting that. Rather it is about knowing what genres the patron likes, why they liked that book, what kind of connection did they have with the book, and whether they would respond favorably to a similar book—and if not, why. In gamers' advisory, the questions are similar:

- Why did you like this game?
- Was it the genre that engaged you or the gameplay?
- Did you enjoy the competitive nature of the game or the cooperative nature?

Principles of Gamers' Advisory

There are specific principles you need to explore when working with patrons to find the right game for them. These involve asking questions about why they want to play certain games or why they did or did not enjoy some games. Once you can begin to understand their motivations in wanting a particular game, you can start recommending new and varied game titles from your collection. These principles, and the questions you need to ask, will be explored in depth throughout this chapter, but Table 6.1 outlines the basic principles behind gamers' advisory.

Table 6.1: Principles of Gamers' Advisory

Principles	Questions	Examples
Understanding player motivations	Why did you enjoy playing that game? What aspect of the game appealed to you?	A patron enjoyed playing *Grand Theft Auto*—you might discover they liked the racing aspect, but not the violence, so what could you recommend?
Understanding player intent	Do you plan to play alone or with other people? Are you planning on hosting a game night? Do you want to set up a weekly game night with some friends and need a game that will last a while? Do you want something you can play quickly?	You discover that the patron enjoys playing *World of Warcraft* online and wants to try something similar in person. So, you recommend they join the library's weekly D&D night.
Understanding player preferences	Do you prefer a specific console when playing video games? Do you like specific characters? Do you prefer certain storylines and so on?	You discover a patron enjoys board games about H. P. Lovecraft's stories, so perhaps you recommend the video game *Call of Cthulhu*.
Understanding player ability	Do you want a game you play on your own or with your whole family? Do you want a game that challenges you? What games have challenged you in the past?	You discover that a patron enjoyed how challenging the board game Blood Rage is, so you might want to consider other board games that match that level of challenge.
Understanding player comfort level	How comfortable are you with something you've never played before? Since you play a lot of video games, are you willing to try a board game based on a familiar topic or story?	You discover that a patron enjoys the Pokémon video games, but has never played the Pokémon card game, this could be a good way to engage that patron in trying something new.

Library staff need to be able to think outside the box of traditional readers' advisory questions; while different types of questions may arise in gamers' advisory, they are essential in helping patrons interact with a gaming collection.

People play games for various reasons, as we have discussed, so you will need to know what motivates your gamer as you saw in Chapter 5. It is so important to be able to understand player motivations and user behavior. For instance, do they plan to play this game alone or are they looking to play with their friends or family? You can drill down even further here and ask if they want a light game or something more involved. Do they want games to play at a party or something that will require a longer commitment and a higher degree of ability? If it is a digital game, a lot of gamers may have developed preferences for a particular gaming system (e.g., Nintendo), so they may want more titles for that system, or they may be looking to try one that they are less familiar with.

Games are complex in nature, and there are so many different motivational facets coexisting between the game and gamer that it can be a bit of a challenge to find a "perfect fit." The more you know about your patron and gaming in general, the more accurate these suggestions become. Even the most seasoned gamers sometimes suggest a game that just doesn't resonate with a player and this is ok! If you think back to some of your favorite games and the reason they are your favorites, you will start to understand the complexity. For example, maybe Monopoly is your favorite game because you played it every time your grandparents visited as a child. This is not something we can easily replicate, but we can suggest more family-friendly, party games that may create a similar experience. The biggest takeaway in gamers' advisory is that it is not an exact science despite the enormous amount of research that goes into player behavior. We can only do our best and hope that this area of research within libraries continues to grow.

Once you have a sense of the patron's experience with the game, you can start to formulate new recommendations for that individual. Thus, gamers' advisory requires a mixture of understanding about the various genres and examples of games available as well as an understanding of the users of those games.

Here are some examples of gamers' advisory interviews, which you can use as a jumping off point to engage with your patrons:

1. If the patron does not have a particular game or title in mind, you will begin asking them questions to narrow in on something that might appeal to them.

   Patron: "I am looking for a game to play."

   Staff: "Ok, great! Let me ask you a few questions to try to help you find the right game. Do you already have a title or particular game in mind?"

   Patron: "No. Just looking for something to play."

   Staff: "What games have you played in the past and liked? What did you like about those games? Are you looking for something digital or a board game type experience? Will you be playing by yourself or do you plan to play with others?"

2. You don't have the title they are looking for, so you ask follow-up questions to figure out what they might also be interested in.

   Patron: "I heard there is a new *Mario* game coming out for Nintendo Switch, do you have it or something like it?"

Staff: "Ok, what is it that you were looking to experience in that game? Did you want an open-world game? Do you like the *Mario* characters themselves? Do you want a game you can play alone or with your friends? Are you interested in trying a retro or older version that is similar?"

3. If the patron comes in with a specific idea in mind but no particular game, you ask follow-up questions about the theme.

Patron: "I just finished watching the TV show *The Witcher* and I am wondering what other games are kind of like that—either video game or board game?"

Staff: "Ok great! Was it the theme of conquering monsters that you liked? Do you want to play this with your friends? Did you enjoy the relationship between the Bard and Geralt? Have you ever tried playing Dungeons & Dragons?"

4. If you get a very general question about board games, you will need to narrow down the requirements for a proper game choice.

Patron: "I am wondering what board games you have that might be good to play with children?"

Staff: "Absolutely! What ages are the children? Will you be playing as a family or just the children by themselves? What kinds of things do your children like? Do you want something that also has learning in it or something that is strictly fun?"

These scenarios were meant to be starting points on how you might go about finding the right game for your patron. As you can see, there are a number of factors that influence why a person will want to play a particular game and even if you don't have the exact title they're looking for, you can advise them on some things they may like. Be aware though, just like with readers' advisory, these are only suggestions and sometimes we don't get it right and that is ok! Books and games are very personal experiences, and while we can do our best to make recommendations, sometimes we don't hit the mark. By providing a positive experience and an eagerness to help, you can encourage your patrons to continue to try new games and come back to the library.

Often when you recommend a new game to a patron, they may be interested in knowing more about how it is played or how to set it up. This is also the case when they are considering a game that they have never played. If they are uncomfortable with setting it up, they may avoid selecting it and go with something they know. It is the library staff member's job to make sure the patron is adequately set up to play the game, and you may even need to field gameplay related questions as part of your reference interview. Most board games will come with detailed instructions on how to set up and play the game, and you can go over them with the patron if you are not already familiar with the game itself. There are also many YouTube channels dedicated to what is called a "playthrough" that shows a person how to set up and play a particular game. There are also YouTube gamers who have made a living off of posting livestreams of them playing video games, and these can be super helpful to get someone started. Keep in mind, however, that some of these YouTube channels may not be age appropriate, so it is advised not to recommend a particular video unless you have vetted it previously. Sometimes patrons will struggle with picking up a new title, so by offering the assurance of your knowledge and other resources you can instill confidence in them to give something new a try. It might even mean you get to play a quick round with them to get them started and feel more confident with the game, which is always fun!

Here are some further questions and tools to help you in conducting a gamers' advisory interview.

Questions:

- Do you want a quick game (30 minutes or less) or something longer?
- Do you have a preference for what gaming console you want to play?
- What genres interest you? (e.g., science fiction, adventure, racing, and dexterity)
- How comfortable are you with digital technology?
- What is your favorite game and why?
- Do you enjoy playing cooperatively (as a team) or against other players?
- Do you want a game that is difficult to play and challenges you or something that is more passive or exploratory?
- Do you enjoy the social aspect of gaming or belonging to a community of gamers?
- Do you like to make a lot of customizations or build worlds when you game?
- Do you enjoy puzzles that are based on theme or more abstract?

Websites:

- Board Game Geek (https://boardgamegeek.com/)
- IGN (https://ca.ign.com/)
- GamesFAQ (https://gamefaqs.gamespot.com/)

Part II
GAMERS' ADVISORY

7
Board Games

A note on how gaming recommendations work in this volume: as spelled out in Chapter 6, we have opted to use Bartle's four categories because they most succinctly and accurately describe different types of gamers across both analog and digital games without making it overly complex; by doing this, we did simplify player behavior, but you can use the remainder of Chapter 6 to expand upon our initial classifications.

This chapter is meant to introduce some of the most common styles and mechanisms in board games to help prepare the reader to answer gaming advisory questions. This chapter outlines some key titles to help build a well-rounded collection to satisfy most player styles and motives and provides library staff with an accessible resource to refer to when recommending games.

Some of the earliest examples of games appearing in library collections include chess clubs, and during the Great Depression toy and game libraries appeared to entertain children while their parents used the resources in the library to look for employment and assistance.[1] While this is the first documented example of games entering the library, it has become clear over the years that board games never left. Games have been a part of libraries throughout the twentieth and into the twenty-first century. Although many libraries restricted games for in library use only, they have become lendable items over the last few decades. Libraries have felt comfortable providing resources toward these types of endeavors, but it was never a main feature. Julie Verstraeten used data available from BoardGameGeek.com to track the number of board games published every year and identified some major shifts that correspond to changes in the industry,[2] which is now projected to reach over $9.27 billion dollars in 2020.[3]

The rise of games published first begins in the 1950s likely correlating with the boom of the postwar era. The rise reached a pitch in and around 1995 when Settlers of Catan was published in Germany. Catan is noted as being one of the first Eurogames to popularize the genre, and within

20 years the number of board games published starts to quadruple annually and continues to grow to over 3,400 titles released in 2015. Catan was different from most of the commercially available board games at the time, as it increased player agency and strategy making it more appealing to older crowds, whereas many of (but not all) board games released previously were more geared toward family play. Other notable occurrences to propel the board game industry include when Kickstarter launched in 2009 and the launch of the *TableTop Show* with Will Wheaton, which began in 2012 and continues to educate game novices and experts alike.[4] Although a small percentage of games actually go through Kickstarter as a funding platform, it has provided a number of games the opportunity for commercial success. Each year, a large number of games are pitched through crowdfunding platforms, but only a small handful get any traction within the marketplace; however, the vast majority of games are still published through established game publishers, such as AEG Asmodee, Fantasy Flight, and Mayfair.

The seemingly fast rise of board game popularity and publishing can be somewhat intimidating to those who are not well versed in the genre. Patrons may come with titles, genres, game mechanics, publishers, or a whole host of other information when trying to locate an item they wish to play. This chapter will hopefully alleviate some of that trepidation and provide a starting point for gamers' advisory service.

In order to keep up with the rapid rate of board game production, library staff should be familiar with these key sources of information:

> **Conventions:** Conventions (or "cons") are increasing in popularity and are growing in numbers. Some of the oldest Comic Conventions have expanded rapidly to include more genres and formats of geekdom and more targeted cons have grown as a result. Some of the biggest cons for board games are Gen Con (Indiana), PAX East (Philadelphia), Origins (Ohio), and Essen Spiel (Germany). Many board game publishers and designers attend these types of events to advertise their newest offerings or announce upcoming titles. These cons are well attended by people involved in the board game industry as well as hobbyists and enthusiasts looking for the next game they may want to play.

> **Kickstarter:** Kickstarter is an online site that "helps artists, musicians, filmmakers, designers, and other creators find the resources and support they need to make their ideas a reality."[5] This platform is heavily used by board game designers to find backers to help produce their games. The backers are given incentives including extra pieces, upgraded materials used to make the game and first access to the game once it has been published. Several games have received multimillion dollar backing including Dark Souls: The Boardgame, Exploding Kittens, and most recently Kingdom Death: Monster 1.5, which received over $12,000,000 USD.[6] This is one of the best places to see what new games are coming out and which ones are getting the most excitement and attention.

YouTube Board Game Channels: The popularity of YouTube shows about board games has been steadily growing over the years. These shows offer two main benefits: first, they usually provide a demonstration of game setup and gameplay, which is helpful for those unfamiliar with a particular game, and second, they are usually given advance copies of new and upcoming games and can offer their feedback. This is beneficial for libraries for both collection development and programming, as it can quickly show a library programmer how to play a game, you can direct your patrons to it to learn a game, and you can see what new titles may suit your particular library needs. There are many of these shows in existence, but three of the more popular ones are *Dice Tower*, *TableTop*, and *Shut Up & Sit Down*.

Tabletop Controlled Vocabulary

The following is a listing of controlled vocabulary used in the board game world meant as a primer to give you a generalized understanding of board games and to be able to reference when discussing gamers' advisory with your patrons. The list includes mechanics, genres, and themes that different board games use. Some games may combine several of these definitions as they have multiple mechanics and objectives, whereas some are more straightforward and only exist within one of the definitions. This is what can make gamers' advisory somewhat challenging, as you need to determine what aspect of a game appeals to your users. As you will notice, there are some similarities between digital games and board games, which can be helpful if you are looking to recommend materials across the two platforms.

In order to be consistent, we have made ample use of Teri Litorco's *The Civilized Guide to Tabletop Gaming: Rules Every Gamer Must Live By*, Bebo of Be Bold Games's book *The Everything Tabletop Games Book*, and Simon Castle's article to craft the definitions found in Table 7.1.

Board Game Rating

Board games typically have an age range suggested on the outside of the box. This rating is not standardized in the way that video games are, but it is still important information to consider when suggesting games to people and also potentially restricting some from younger patrons (due to content or dexterity). In general, the type of considerations taken into account when putting a suggested age range onto a game include safety (e.g., could pieces be easily ingested), reading comprehension and content (e.g., language, themes, and images). Largely these are suggestions only, and there are some differing opinions on what is printed on the box versus what age range is actually appropriate. On the website Boardgamegeek.com, communities provide their suggested age ranges compared to the suggested age on the box. Sometimes these ranges are the same and other times they differ.

Table 7.1: Analog Game Vocabulary

	Definition	Examples
Dice Game or Mechanic	Uses or incorporates one or more dice as a main method of player interaction. This could include rolling dice to move around the game board (e.g., Monopoly), determining the outcome of a player's action (e.g., a health check in Dungeons & Dragons), or they are the game pieces being played (e.g., Sagrada). These games either use classic six-sided dice, various sized dice (e.g., D20), or dice that have colors, symbols, or images on them (e.g., Rory's Story Cubes).	Sagrada, Yahtzee, King of Tokyo
Drafting/ Collectible Card Game	Players pick cards to assemble a deck that they will later use to play the game. Drafting is the mechanism for assembling your deck of collectible cards where players purchase packages of cards to help build their deck versus a deck building game that includes all of the possible cards to play within the game itself. Collectible card games have "drafts" where new card packs are opened and played at an event with other players, or game players may purchase decks or individual cards on their own to build their desired deck. These types of games typically have versions, editions, or collections, and there may be rules on what edition of cards you can play during gameplay or tournament play.	Pokémon, Yu-Gi-Oh!, Magic the Gathering
Puzzle Game or Mechanic	Players are required to solve a puzzle or puzzles to play the game. These can either be a portion of the game or the entire mechanic.	DaVinci Challenge Game, Patchwork, T.I.M.E Stories
Hand Management	A game or mechanic that requires players to manage a playing hand of cards while playing the game.	Arkham Horror: The Card Game, Blood Rage, Taj Mahal, Lost Cities
Trading Game or Mechanic	A game that has a mechanism within it that allows or encourages players to trade and/ or barter with other players.	Civilization, Chinatown, Archipelago, Twilight Imperium

Table 7.1: (*continued*)

	Definition	Examples
Deck Building Game or Mechanic	Players pick cards to assemble a deck (similar to drafting games) that they will use later to play the game. Typically, all of the cards that are available to players to choose are set within the game versus a drafting game where players generally purchase packs of cards and take their chances with what they get and can always purchase more to build a better deck.	Dominion, Clank!, DC Deck Building
Pattern Building Game Mechanic	Players are required to build or identify patterns to be successful.	A Feast for Odin, Castles of Mad King Ludwig, Fuse
Party Game	Meant to be played with several people in a social setting. These games are generally high intensity with lower requirements in dexterity or strategy. These games tend to be quite popular and appeal to gamers and non-gamers alike.	Cards Against Humanity, Pictionary, How Do You Meme?
Player Elimination Mechanic	The object is to eliminate all of the other players in the game and the final player wins. These games tend to be high action with fast gameplay so eliminated players can watch entertaining gameplay until the game is over and still feel a part of the experience.	Exploding Kittens, Coup, Get Bit!
Role-play Game (RPG) or Mechanic	Players are required to act out or pretend they are another character. This typically involves character building and customization (e.g., picking a species, class, and name). These characters then go through a scenario with each player having different attributes to contribute to gameplay. These scenarios can last weeks, months, or years, which means players usually meet up regularly to play the campaign out.	Dungeons & Dragons, Pathfinder
Deduction Game or Mechanic	Players are required to use deductive logic and reasoning in order to play and/or win the game. Players are often assigned secret identities or tasks within the game, and other players may need to deduce what these secret identities and tasks are during gameplay.	Awkward Guests, Mystery Express, Chronicles of Crime, Detective
Family Game	These games can incorporate other mechanics, but they are designed in a way that is approachable to players of a variety of ages and abilities.	Apples to Apples, Monopoly, Bananagrams

(continued)

Table 7.1: (*continued*)

	Definition	Examples
Route/Network Building Game or Mechanic	Players are required to build the longest chains or connect to new areas on the game board to gather points and win.	Ticket to Ride, Settlers of Catan
Word Game	Players are required to either build, think up, or guess words and points are directly linked to their ability to do so.	Boggle, Scrabble, Word Slam
Fantasy	Games set in a fictional or speculative universe. The plot often cannot occur in the real world and involves some kind of witchcraft and magic that takes place on an undiscovered world or planet.	Gloomhaven, Mansions of Madness
Science Fiction	Games set in a science-fiction universe or world; similar to fantasy, it is not a real-world scenario.	Netrunner, Risk 2210 A.D.
Fighting Game or Mechanic	Players are required to engage in combat with other players within the fictional gaming experience. Typical close-range combat that involves one-on-one fighting or against a small number of equally powered opponents, often involving violent and exaggerated unarmed attacks.	King of Tokyo, Smash Up
Arena/Area/ Territory Control Game or Mechanic	Similar to a fighting game, but there is a set area that players must maintain control over to succeed in the game. Points are typically given to the player that controls either the largest area in the game or a specific designated area.	Dominant Species, Blood Rage, Kemet
Eurogame or German-style Game	Players indirectly interact with abstract physical components. These games have a lot of physical components, rely heavily on strategy rather than luck or chance, have an economic theme, and do not have player elimination. Players need to complete the entire game together and points are tallied at the end to determine a winner.	Tigris and Euphrates, Settlers of Catan, Carcassonne
Legacy Game	These games change over time based on outcomes of player interaction. The changes that are made are typically designed to be permanent meaning these games can typically only be played once, but they take a very long time to finish.	Pandemic Legacy, Risk Legacy, Gloomhaven
Deceit/ Deception/ Bluffing Game or Mechanic	Players are required to fool or lie to other players in order to be successful.	Coup, Sheriff of Nottingham

Table 7.1: (*continued*)

	Definition	Examples
Education Game	Designed with specific learning objectives. Typically, they are upfront with the fact that they are designed for educational purposes and tend to be created by those with an education background rather than pure game design background.	Freedom: The Underground Railroad, Wingspan
Strategy Game or Mechanic	Players are required to make calculated decisions that will directly impact the outcome of the game. Strategy games usually have multiple variables that players control meaning the game is solely up to the technique of the players rather than chance. These games usually have winning conditions along with gathering the most victory points by the end of the game.	Terra Mystica, PowerGrid, 7 Wonders, Small World
Abstract Strategy Game or Mechanic	A strategy game where the theme is not essential for the game to be played. Typically, the theme is very far removed from the gameplay itself, and if it was removed, it would not make any significant change to how the game is played.	Sequence, Azul, Chess
City Building Game or Mechanic	Players must create and/or manage a city in a predetermined way that may or may not involve efficiencies, milestones/goals, power, money/economy, etc.	&Cetera, Suburbia, Lords of Waterdeep
Worker Placement Game or Mechanic	Players move a particular piece of pawn to a spot on a board that allows you the right to do a related action. Players likely will have a pool of workers and typically these workers cannot be removed from taking the action that they have been assigned to do.	Agricola, Charterstone, Caverna
Wargames	Games that are themed around war and typically require players to engage in simulated combat with each other. The games typically have a surface board and require players to move around it. These games tend to be very strategy-oriented and create a confrontational type of gameplay.	Risk, Axis and Allies, Diplomacy
Living Card Game	A living card game (LCG) is different from a collectable card game, as there is no randomness to the cards when purchased. Both the core set and expansions come with a defined set of cards that is known ahead of time.	Arkham Horror the Card Game, Legend of the Five Rings

(*continued*)

Table 7.1: (*continued*)

	Definition	Examples
Cooperative Game or Mechanic	Players are required to work together as a team to solve a common goal or task. A subset of cooperative games are partially cooperative games where players need to not only solve a common task together but also fulfill individual objectives to win.	Pandemic, Forbidden Island, Aeon's End
Storytelling Game or Mechanic	Players are required to contribute a story based on prompts in the game.	Rory's Story Cubes, Once Upon a Time, T.I.M.E. Stories, most role-play games
Territory Building Game or Mechanic	Specific pieces or resources are used within the game to lay claim to a particular area of the game; the ultimate goal is usually to control more (or better) territory than the other players in the game. This definition is very similar to "city building" depending on the objective of the games mentioned.	Imperial Settlers, Risk, Lords of Waterdeep
Dexterity Game or Mechanic	These games tend to have simple mechanics that require players to build, stack, balance, or throw items, and they are usually also classified as party games. They can involve full body actions (e.g., Twister) or finer motor skills (e.g., Jenga) in order to play.	Jenga, Twister, Throw Throw Burrito

This is one of the largest communities of board game enthusiasts on the Internet, and this source can typically be trusted.

Games such as Cards Against Humanity or any not safe for work (NSFW) versions of games (e.g., NSFW Exploding Kittens) have adult content in the form of both graphics and language, so it is strongly suggested that if libraries are going to carry these titles that they are aware of the suggested ratings. Another area to be mindful is within the category of party games—sometimes referred to as drinking games—these are games that are meant to be played with adults and perhaps have some adult content.

Starting Collection and Reference Guide: Board Games

It is important to offer a selection of board games that will appeal to a wide audience and appeal to the different player motivations we have discussed. You will also want to consider continually updating the collection based on how quickly board games are published. The following is a suggestion for starting a well-rounded board game collection that will appeal to a broad audience. This collection could be used in academic or public libraries.

The "similar games" field is rather subjective as different players will enjoy different features in a game. Do they enjoy the theme? Cooperative play? Card games? The games that are suggested are similar in either theme, gameplay, mechanics, or user behavior, but it is best to do a proper reference interview with your users to get a true understanding as to what it is they like or are interested in playing.

Game Title: Agricola

Year published: 2007

Genre: Strategy; economic; card drafting; hand management; worker placement

Format: Board game

Available Platforms: n/a

Age: 12+

User behavior type: Achiever

Description: You are a farmer who uses improvement and occupation cards to grow and harvest your fields. This is a turn-based worker placement style game with the winner being the one with the most amount of victory points at the end.

Gameplay: 1–5 players

Series (Y or N): Yes

Other titles in the series: Many different titles within the series and expansions, including Agricola: Farmers of the Moor, Agricola: The Goodies Expansion, Agricola: All Creatures Big and Small

Similar games: Civilization, Dominant Species, Le Havre, Caylus, Caverna: The Cave Farmers

Game Title: Akrotiri

Year published: 2014

Genre: Strategy; economic; hand management; tile placement

Format: Board game

Available Platforms: n/a

Age: 13+

User behavior type: Achiever, Explorer

Description: Players are explorers in ancient Greece who are tasked with finding hidden temples. This game requires players to manage resources and place land tiles on the board to match the pieces of the map that have in hand. They then excavate temples and gather victory points. The person with the most victory points at the end of the game wins.

Gameplay: 2 players

Series (Y or N): No

Other titles in the series: n/a

Similar games: Tobago, Cafe Melange, Tsuro

Game Title: Android: Netrunner
Year published: 2012
Genre: Legacy game; bluffing; card game; science fiction
Format: Board game
Available Platforms: n/a
Age: 14+
User behavior type: Achiever, Explorer
Description: This is a living card game for two players. It is set in the cyberpunk future of Android and Infiltration that puts a megacorporation and its resources against "the subversive talents of lone runners."
Gameplay: 2 players
Series (Y or N): Yes
Other titles in the series: There are multiple card expansion sets available such as What Lies Ahead, Cyber Exodus, Trace Amount, Humanity's Shadow, True Colors
Similar games: Call of Cthulhu, Game of Thrones Card Game

Game Title: Apples to Apples
Year published: 1999
Genre: Party game; word game; cooperative
Format: Board game; card game
Available Platforms: n/a
Age: 12+
User behavior type: Socializer
Description: In apples to apples players take turns being the judge. The judge deals seven red cards to themselves and other players face down—the players then look at the hand they were dealt. The judge picks a green card from the deck and players quickly select what one of their red cards best match, The judge collects and mixes the red card submissions and proceeds to read them out loud and select the winner. The best match wins the green card and gets a point.
Gameplay: 4–10 players
Series (Y or N): Yes
Other titles in the series: Many different titles within the series and expansions, including Apples to Apples Junior, Sour Apples to Apples, Apples to Apples: Bible edition, Apples to Apples Expansion Set #1
Similar games: Dixit, Say Anything, Cranium

Game Title: Archipelago
Year published: 2012
Genre: Strategy; civilization; exploration; area control
Format: Board game
Available Platforms: n/a
Age: 14+
User behavior type: Achiever, Explorer

Description: Players explore territory, harvest resources, and build civilizations, while completing secret objectives. This is a typical German economic worker-placement type game that includes negotiation.

Gameplay: 1–2 players

Series (Y or N): Yes

Other titles in the series: Expansions and other titles available such as Archipelago: War & Peace, Frostgrave: Ghost Archipelago, Naval Battle in Archipelago

Similar games: Dead of Winter

Game Title: Arctic Scavengers

Year published: 2009

Genre: Strategy; card game; bluffing; drafting; fighting; hand management

Format: Board game

Available Platforms: n/a

Age: 13+

User behavior type: Killer, Achiever

Description: You are the leader of a small tribe of survivors who are pitted against four other tribes, fighting for survival.

Gameplay: 1–5 players

Series (Y or N): Yes

Other titles in the series: Other titles and expansions available, including Arctic Scavengers: Base Game + HQ + Recon, Arctic Scavengers: Recon, Arctic Scavengers: HQ

Similar games: Dominion, Clank!: A Deck-Building Adventure

Game Title: Arkham Horror

Year published: 2019

Genre: Adventure; fantasy; fighting; horror; cooperative; dice rolling; hand management

Format: Board game

Available Platforms: n/a

Age: 12+

User behavior type: Killer, Achiever

Description: Cooperative adventure game set on the streets of Arkham. Players upgrade the traits and skills of their characters, fighting different monsters with the goal of completing the narrative set before them while closing portals to other dimensions that are opening up around them.

Gameplay: 1–8 players

Series (Y or N): Yes

Other titles in the series: Many different titles within the series and expansions, including Arkham Horror: The Card Game, Arkham Horror: Dead of Night, Eldritch Horror, Elder Signs

Similar games: Mansions of Madness, Tales of Arabian Nights, A Touch of Evil

Game Title: Azul

Year published: 2017

Genre: Abstract; family; card drafting; pattern building

Format: Board game

Available Platforms: n/a

Age: 8+

User behavior type: Achiever

Description: Players take turns drafting colored tiles from suppliers/ center to add to their board. When the players pick up a particular color, they must pick up all the tiles of that color in that location. The goal of the game is to place the same color tiles of a particular number onto your player board, which will allow you to fill in your mosaic and score points. You gain additional points for placing tiles into your mosaic that are touching one another and completing rows or columns. Points are lost when you pick up more tiles than needed to fill a numbered row, all the additional tiles fall into a negative point overflow. The person with the most points at the end of the game wins.

Gameplay: 2–4 players

Series (Y or N): Yes

Other titles in the series: There are many expansions and titles in this series, including Azul: Stained Glass of Sintra, Azul: Summer Pavilion, Azul: Joker Tiles

Similar games: Sagrada

Game Title: Balderdash

Year published: 1984

Genre: Party; bluffing; word game

Format: Board game

Available Platforms: n/a

Age: 12+

User behavior type: Socializer

Description: This party game pits players against each other to create definitions for words having other players guess which definition they think is correct. The player with the most points at the end of the game wins.

Gameplay: 2–6 players

Series (Y or N): Yes

Other titles in the series: There are other titles in the series, including Balderdash Junior, Beyond Balderdash

Similar games: Dixit, Ex Libris

Game Title: Bananagrams

Year published: 2006

Genre: Family; word game; tile placement

Format: Board game

Available Platforms: n/a

Age: 7+

User behavior type: Socializer, Achiever

Description: The object of this game is to create a word grid or cross-word faster than your opponents. Bananagrams is a simple word game that requires little in the way of materials. The word tiles are all kept inside of a cloth banana and players spell out their words on a flat playing surface rather than a board.

Gameplay: 1–8 players

Series (Y or N): Yes

Other titles in the series: There are other titles in the series, including Bananagrams Party, Bananagrams Duel

Similar games: Scrabble

Game Title: Biblios

Year published: 2007

Genre: Family; strategy; card game; medieval; card drafting; hand management

Format: Board game

Available Platforms: n/a

Age: 10+

User behavior type: Achiever

Description: This game is set in the Medieval Age in a monastery. Players are abbots competing with each other to amass the greatest library of sacred texts. The game requires players to manage resources, acquire workers, and score victory points, which requires strategy, bluffing, and some luck.

Gameplay: 2–4 players

Series (Y or N): Yes

Other titles in the series: There is another title in the series called Biblios Dice

Similar games: Love Letter, Guillotine, Lost Cities, Citadels

Game Title: Blokus

Year published: 2000

Genre: Abstract; hand placement; tile placement; territory building

Format: Board game

Available Platforms: n/a

Age: 5+

User behavior type: Achiever

Description: This is a tactile, abstract strategy game that uses small colored pieces in a Tetris-like game play. Players place down pieces that cannot be adjacent to your other pieces, rather they have to touch a corner of a previously placed piece. Whichever player is able to place the most of their 21 pieces onto the board wins.

Gameplay: 2–4 players

Series (Y or N): Yes

Other titles in the series: There are many expansions and titles in this series, including Blokus 3D, Blokus Junior, Blokus Trigon, Blokus Dice Game, Blokus Duo

Similar games: Quads, Gemblo, Patchwork

Game Title: Blood Rage

Year published: 2015

Genre: Strategy; fantasy; fighting; card drafting; hand management; area control

Format: Board game

Available Platforms: n/a

Age: 13+

User behavior type: Achiever, Killer

Description: Each player controls their own Viking clan, which includes warriors, ships, and leader. The game occurs when Ragnarok returns signaling end of days and is the Vikings last chance to try to go down in a blaze of glory and make it to Valhalla.

Gameplay: 2–4 players

Series (Y or N): Yes

Other titles in the series: There are many expansions and titles in this series, including Blood Rage: Kickstarter Exclusives, Blood Rage: Gods of Asgard, Blood Rage: 5th Player Expansion

Similar games: Kemet, Chaos in the Old World, El Grande

Game Title: Camel Up

Year published: 2014

Genre: Family; dice game; bluffing

Format: Card game

Available Platforms: n/a

Age: 8+

User behavior type: Achiever

Description: This game is a simple, family fun game that involves betting on camel racing. Players are trying to determine which camel will race around the pyramid first. The earlier the bet is placed the more you can collect, but the camel's act in unpredictable ways so it is challenging to pick the potential winner.

Gameplay: 2–8 players

Series (Y or N): Yes

Other titles in the series: There are many expansions and titles in this series, including Camel up: Supercup, Camel Up Grand Prix of the Sahara

Similar games: Wits and Wagers

Game Title: Carcassonne

Year published: 2000

Genre: Family; city building; area/arena control; tile placement

Format: Board game

Available Platforms: n/a

Age: 8+

User behavior type: Achiever, Explorer

Description: This is a tile placement game where you place tiles out to build the walled city of Carcassonne. Whenever you play a tile, you're given the opportunity to play your meeple onto the tile in various positions or spots, each having a different way to be completed and score points. Once the scoring condition for that location is met, that location is scored, and the meeple is returned to the player. Meeples that are stuck and unable to have their scoring condition met are scored at the end of the game at a lower point value, and the player with the most points when all the tiles run out wins.

Gameplay: 2–5 players

Series (Y or N): Yes

Other titles in the series: There are many expansions within this series, including Carcassonne: Wheel of Fortune, Expansion 1—Inns & Cathedrals, Expansion 10—Under the Big Top, Carcassonne: The River

Similar games: Small World, Ticket to Ride, 7 Wonders, Castles of Mad King Ludwig, Castles of Burgundy

Game Title: Cards Against Humanity

Year published: 2009

Genre: Party game; card game; hand management

Format: Card game

Available Platforms: n/a

Age: 17+

Warnings: The cards can be quite graphic so this is not a game for children.

User behavior type: Socializer

Description: Players take turns picking a black question or fill-in-the-blank card from the top of the deck and other players use the cards in their hands to answer that question or fill in those blanks. The player holding the black card then chooses a winner and they get a point.

Gameplay: 4–12 players

Series (Y or N): Yes

Other titles in the series: Many different titles within the series and expansions, including First Expansion, 2012 Holiday Pack, The Bigger, Black Box, Fourth Expansion

Similar games: What do you meme?, Bad People, That's What She Said, Superfight

Game Title: Castles of Burgundy

Year published: 2011

Genre: Strategy; dice game; medieval; tile placement

Format: Board game

Available Platforms: n/a

Age: 12+

User behavior type: Achiever

Description: This game is set in the Burgundy region of High Medieval France. Players take on the role of an aristocrat and their goal is to build settlements, trade, and acquire resources. The object of the game is to have the most victory points after five rounds.

Gameplay: 2–4 players

Series (Y or N): Yes

Other titles in the series: There are many expansions and titles in this series, including The Castles of Burgundy: 8th Expansion, The Castles of Burgundy: The Dice Game

Similar games: The Voyages of Marco Polo, La Granja, Bora Bora

Game Title: Castles of Mad King Ludwig

Year published: 2014

Genre: Strategy; puzzle; card drafting; pattern building

Format: Board game

Available Platforms: n/a

Age: 13+

User behavior type: Achiever

Description: Players are contractors who are tasked with building an extravagant castle for King Ludwig II of Bavaria. Players also are selling their services to other players. Whoever ends up with the most castle points at the end is the winner.

Gameplay: 1–4 players

Series (Y or N): Yes

Other titles in the series: There are other titles in the series such as Between Two Castles of Mad King Ludwig and Castles of Mad King Ludwig: Secrets

Similar games: Carcassonne

Game Title: Caverna: The Cave Farmers

Year published: 2013

Genre: Strategy; economic; tile placement; fantasy

Format: Board game

Available Platforms: n/a

Age: 12+

User behavior type: Achiever, Killer

Description: This is a worker placement game where players are the head of a dwarf family who lives in a little cave in the mountains. Players cultivate the forest in front of their caves, mine, forge weapons, find water, etc. The player with the most efficiently developed farm wins. This game is a complete redesign of the game Agricola.

Gameplay: 1–7 players

Series (Y or N): Yes

Other titles in the series: There are many expansions and titles in this series, including Caverna: Cave vs. Cave, Caverna: Mini Expansion, Caverna: The Forgotten Folk

Similar games: Agricola, Civilization, Dominant Species, Le Havre, Caylus

Game Title: Clank! A Deck Building Adventure

Year published: 2016

Genre: Family; strategy; adventure; fantasy; card drafting

Format: Card game; Board game

Available Platforms: n/a

Age: 13+

User behavior type: Achiever

Description: Clank! Is a deck building game where each player is building a deck. Players are trying to sneak into an angry dragon's lair to steal its treasure.

Gameplay: 2–4 players

Series (Y or N): Yes

Other titles in the series: There are many expansions and titles in this series, including Clank!: The Mummy's Curse, Clank! Expeditions: Gold and Silk, Clank!: Dire Wolf, Clank! In! Space!

Similar games: Dominion, Arctic Scavengers, Trains, Tyrants of the Underdark

Game Title: Clue

Year published: 1949

Genre: Family; bluffing; deduction

Format: Board game

Available Platforms: n/a

Age: 8+

User behavior type: Achiever

Description: Classic detective game where players who chose a set character in the game move from room to room trying to figure out who the murderer was, what weapon was used, and what room the murder was committed in.

Gameplay: 3–6 players

Series (Y or N): Yes

Other titles in the series: There are many expansions and titles in this series such as Clue: The Card Game, Clue: Harry Potter edition, Clue: Dungeons & Dragons, Clue Jr: The Case of the Missing Cake

Similar games: Mysterium, Deception, Scotland Yard

Game Title: Codenames

Year published: 2015

Genre: Card game; deduction; party game; spies; word game

Format: Board game; card game

Available Platforms: n/a

Age: 14+

User behavior type: Achiever, Socializer

Description: Two teams compete to see who can make contact with all of their agents first by guessing words. Each team has a spymaster who know the identities of the 25 agents, and they need to give hints that are not too easy, as the other team can use them to their advantage.

Gameplay: 2–8 players

Series (Y or N): Yes

Other titles in the series: Many different titles within the series and expansions, including Codenames: Pictures, Codenames: Disney, Codenames: Undercover, Codenames: Duet, Codenames: Marvel

Similar games: Dixit, 25 Words or Less, Mysterium, Deception

Game Title: Coup

Year published: 2012

Genre: Card game; bluffing; player elimination; deduction; hand management

Format: Board game; card game

Available Platforms: n/a

Age: 10+

User behavior type: Killer, Socializer

Description: You need to manipulate and bluff your way through the game to gain power and be the last person standing while trying to avoid being victim to a coup.

Gameplay: 2–6 players

Series (Y or N): Yes

Other titles in the series: Other titles in the series include Coup: Reformation and Coup: Rebellion G54

Similar games: Bang! Bang! The Dice Game, Hoax, Citadels, Mascarade

Game Title: Cranium

Year published: 1998

Genre: Party; puzzle game; trivia; word game

Format: Board game

Available Platforms: n/a

Age: 13+

User behavior type: Achiever, Socializer

Description: Players need to successfully complete various activities in each of the four sections in order to win. The sections are Datahead (trivia), Word-Worm (unscrambling words, spelling, definitions, etc.), Creative Cat (drawing, sculpting, etc.), and Star Performer (whistling, acting, etc.).

Gameplay: 4–10 players

Series (Y or N): Yes

Other titles in the series: There are several expansions to this game, including Cranium Cariboo, Cranium Pop 5, Cranium Hoopla

Similar games: Dix-it, Say Anything

Game Title: DC Deck Building
Year published: 2012
Genre: Deck building; card drafting; hand management
Format: Board game; card game
Available Platforms: n/a
Age: 15+
User behavior type: Achiever, Killer
Description: You are trying to build the strongest deck using DC superheroes in order to be the last person in the game. The first half of gameplay is building your deck and then you play it against other players.
Gameplay: 2–5 players
Series (Y or N): Yes
Other titles in the series: There are several expansions to this game, including Forever Evil, Heroes Unite, Teen Titans, Rebirth
Similar games: Legendary (Marvel Deck Building Game), Smash Up

Game Title: Dead of Winter: A Crossroads Game
Year published: 2012
Genre: Bluffing; deduction; horror; area movement; cooperative
Format: Board game
Available Platforms: n/a
Age: 13+
User behavior type: Socializer, Explorer, Achiever
Description: You are in a postapocalyptic, zombie filled world trying to gather resources, fight off zombies, and other known and unknown enemies. Players work together to scavenge different areas trying to collect resources and find others to join the colony to fulfill the group objective, while also completing their own secret personal objectives. Players need to be quiet so as to not attract zombies, maintain high morale in the colony, and protect the other players.
Gameplay: 2–5 players
Series (Y or N): Yes
Other titles in the series: There are several expansions and other titles in the series, including Warring Colonies
Similar games: Archipelago

Game Title: Deception: Murder in Hong Kong
Year published: 2014
Genre: Party; bluffing; deduction; mystery
Format: Board game
Available Platforms: n/a

Age: 14+

User behavior type: Achiever

Description: Players take on set characters within the game and are attempting to solve a murder case; however, one of the players is the murderer and their accomplice. While the team of investigators try to find out the truth, the murderer's team is trying to mislead their investigation.

Gameplay: 4–12 players

Series (Y or N): Yes

Other titles in the series: There are other titles in the series such as Deception: Undercover Allies

Similar games: Clue, Mysterium

Game Title: Dixit

Year published: 2008

Genre: Party game; card game; storytelling

Format: Board game; card game

Available Platforms: n/a

Age: 8+

User behavior type: Socializer

Description: One player is a storyteller and looks at images in their hand, selecting one to make up a sentence. Other players then take cards from their hands that best match the sentence given. Players then vote on the best match and award the point to that player.

Gameplay: 3–6 players

Series (Y or N): Yes

Other titles in the series: There are expansions and other titles in the series such as Dixit: Jinx, Dixit: Odyssey

Similar games: Apples to Apples, Cranium, Mysterium, Codenames

Game Title: Dominant Species

Year published: 2010

Genre: Strategy; card drafting; education

Format: Board game

Available Platforms: n/a

Age: 14+

User behavior type: Achiever, Explorer

Description: Each player takes on the role of one of six major animal classes (e.g., mammals, reptile, and bird). Players then need to survive by growing their species' populations as they move through the Ice Age. The player with the most victory points wins.

Gameplay: 2–6 players

Series (Y or N): Yes

Other titles in the series: There are many expansions and titles in this series, including Dominant Species: Marine, Dominant Species: Express, Dominant Species: The Card Game

Similar games: Evolution, Wingspan, Stone Age, El Grande

Game Title: Dominion

Year published: 2008

Genre: Card game; deck building; hand management

Format: Board game; card game

Available Platforms: n/a

Age: 10+

User behavior type: Achiever

Description: Each player starts out with the same small deck and players try to buy cards from the middle to build their deck hoping to reach the most victory points by the end of the game.

Gameplay: 2–4 players

Series (Y or N): Yes

Other titles in the series: There are expansions and other titles in the series such as Evolution: Climate, Evolution: Flight, Evolution: The Beginning

Similar games: Dungeons & Dragons, Star Realms, Hero Realms, Arctic Scavengers, Clank!: A Deck Building Adventure

Game Title: Eldritch Horror

Year published: 2013

Genre: Adventure; fantasy; fighting; horror; cooperative

Format: Board game

Available Platforms: n/a

Age: 14+

User behavior type: Achiever

Description: Eldritch Horror is a cooperative horror game where players are investigators trying to solve obscure mysteries involving monsters. There are a lot of components and cards in this game making it one that can be played time and time again without repeating the outcome.

Gameplay: 1–8 players

Series (Y or N): Yes

Other titles in the series: There are many expansions and titles in this series, including Eldritch Horror: Strange Remnants, Eldritch Horror: Masks of Nyariathotep

Similar games: Forbidden Island, Arkham Horror, Robinson Crusoe, Ghost Stories

Game Title: Elysium

Year published: 2015

Genre: Strategy; card drafting

Format: Board game

Available Platforms: n/a

Age: 14+

User behavior type: Achiever

Description: Players are up and coming demigods in mythic Greece who are trying to write their own tales. The game requires players to collect combinations of cards in order to gain victory points.

Gameplay: 2–4 players
Series (Y or N): No
Other titles in the series: n/a
Similar games: 7 Wonders, Seasons, Viceroy

Game Title: Ethnos
Year published: 2017
Genre: Strategy; fantasy; card drafting; hand management
Format: Board game; card game
Available Platforms: n/a
Age: 14+
User behavior type: Achiever
Description: The fantasy land of Ethnos. Players choose six (or five if there are three players) of the 12 tribes of fantasy creatures to build the play deck. Players use these cards along with glory tokens. After three ages, the person with the most glory wins.
Gameplay: 2–6 players
Series (Y or N): No
Other titles in the series: n/a
Similar games: El Grande, Small World, Ticket to Ride

Game Title: Evolution
Year published: 2014
Genre: Strategy; card game; educational game; fighting
Format: Board game; card game
Available Platforms: n/a
Age: 12+
User behavior type: Explorer, Killer
Description: Each player focuses on creating species with over 4,000 different possibilities. It encourages players to make choices that allow for multiple paths for victory. Players fight against other animals in the ecosystem, while the ecosystem changes around them.
Gameplay: 2–6 players
Series (Y or N): Yes
Other titles in the series: There are expansions and other titles in the series such as Dominion: Seaside, Dominion: Alchemy, Dominion: Dark Ages
Similar games: Primordial Soup, Dominant Species

Game Title: Exploding Kittens
Year published: 2015
Genre: Card game; party game; hand management; player elimination
Format: Card game
Available Platforms: n/a
Age: 10+

User behavior type: Socializer, Killer

Description: The object of the game is survival. You play your hand and try to avoid drawing an exploding kitten, which can eliminate you from the game. This is a fast-paced, easy-to-learn game with humorous illustrations by The Oatmeal.

Gameplay: 2–5 players

Series (Y or N): Yes

Other titles in the series: Many different titles within the series and expansions, including Exploding Kittens: NSFW Deck, Exploding Kittens: Streaking Kittens, Exploding Kittens: Imploding Kittens

Similar games: Sushi Go, Love Letter, Coup, Catch Phrase

Game Title: Five Tribes

Year published: 2015

Genre: Strategy; fantasy; auction/bidding

Format: Board game

Available Platforms: n/a

Age: 13+

User behavior type: Achiever, Explorer

Description: The game is set in the world of 1001 Arabian Nights. The sultan of Naqala has died and control of the area is up for grabs. Players need to try to utilize the help of the Five Tribes in order to gain influence over the city. The player with the most victory points at the end wins.

Gameplay: 2–4 players

Series (Y or N): Yes

Other titles in the series: There are several expansions to this game, including The Artisans of Naqala, The Thieves of Naqala, Whims of the Sultan

Similar games: Istanbul, A Fist Full of Meeples

Game Title: Food Fighters

Year published: 2015

Genre: Family; dice game; fighting; player elimination

Format: Card game

Available Platforms: n/a

Age: 8+

User behavior type: Killer, Achiever

Description: This is a fun two-player battle game where each player controls a team of foods and is trying to win the food fight. The first player that can knock out three matching foods from the other team is the winner.

Gameplay: 2 players

Series (Y or N): No

Other titles in the series: n/a

Similar games: Star Realms, Hero Realms, Epic Card Game

Game Title: Forbidden Island
Year published: 2010
Genre: Cooperative; family; adventure; card game; fantasy
Format: Board game
Available Platforms: n/a
Age: 10+
User behavior type: Achiever, Socializer
Description: Working as a team, players must try to capture all of the treasures before the island sinks. As you play the game, tiles are removed from the board limiting your movement and escape route.
Gameplay: 2–4 players
Series (Y or N): Yes
Other titles in the series: Other games in the series include Forbidden Desert and Forbidden Sky
Similar games: Pandemic, Arkham Horror, Eldritch Horror, Spirit Island

Game Title: FUSE
Year published: 2015
Genre: Family; dice game; card drafting; cooperative
Format: Board game
Available Platforms: n/a
Age: 10+
User behavior type: Achiever, Socializer
Description: Players are members of a bomb defusal team and must act to find the 20 different bombs on the ship. Players work cooperatively and must act quickly as this is a real-time game.
Gameplay: 1–5 players
Series (Y or N): Yes
Other titles in the series: There is an expansion called FUSE: Wild Die
Similar games: Escape: The Curse of the Temple, Star Realms, Hero Realms

Game Title: The Game of Things
Year published: 2002
Genre: Party; deduction; memory
Format: Card game
Available Platforms: n/a
Age: No age given by publisher
User behavior type: Achiever, Socializer
Description: This is a party game where players write a response to a prompt on a card, and the other players have to guess who provided what answer.
Gameplay: 5–15 players
Series (Y or N): Yes

Other titles in the series: Other titles in the series include The Game of Nasty Things, The Game of Things: Travel/Expansion

Similar games: What Do You Meme?, Balderdash

Game Title: Gemblo

Year published: 2005

Genre: Abstract; strategy

Format: Board game

Available Platforms: n/a

Age: 6+

User behavior type: Achiever

Description: This is a tactile, abstract strategy game that uses hexagon pieces in unique colors for each player. Players need to get rid of all of their pieces by placing them on the board, but the pieces cannot touch previously placed pieces.

Gameplay: 2–6 players

Series (Y or N): Yes

Other titles in the series: There are many expansions and titles in this series, including Gemblo Trio, Gemblo Mini, Gemblo Woodman, Gemblo Expansion Set

Similar games: Blokus

Game Title: Gloomhaven

Year published: 2017

Genre: Eurogame; strategy; adventure; fantasy; fighting; cooperative; hand management; legacy

Format: Board game

Available Platforms: n/a

Age: 12+

User behavior type: Explorer, Achiever, Socializer, Killer

Description: This is a tactical combat game in the present world where players work together to tackle dungeons and ruins as they play. This game is played over several sessions and acts a bit like a "choose your own adventure book" as no playthrough will ever be the same.

Gameplay: 1–4 players

Series (Y or N): No

Other titles in the series: n/a

Similar games: Kingdom Death, Mage Knight, Spirit Island

Game Title: Guillotine

Year published: 1998

Genre: Family; card drafting; hand management

Format: Card game

Available Platforms: n/a

Age: 12+

User behavior type: Achiever

Description: This light card game requires players to appeal to the masses by beheading the least popular nobles. Players can interfere with other players' choices using cards that they draw and play. After three turns (or "days"), the player with the highest total wins.

Gameplay: 2–5 players

Series (Y or N): No

Other titles in the series: n/a

Similar games: Smash Up, 7 Wonders, King of Tokyo

Game Title: Hanabi

Year published: 2010

Genre: Family; card game; deduction; memory

Format: Card game

Available Platforms: n/a

Age: 8+

User behavior type: Achiever, Socializer

Description: Hanabi translates to "fireworks" in Japanese, and this game has players trying to create perfect fireworks using cards in their hands (that only the other players can see). This game has a cooperative element as players give each other clues on what card to play, since you cannot see your own cards in order to create the best firework show.

Gameplay: 2–5 players

Series (Y or N): No

Other titles in the series: n/a

Similar games: The Mind, Space Alert, Pandemic, Forbidden Island

Game Title: Imperial Settlers

Year published: 2014

Genre: Strategy; card game; city building; card drafting

Format: Board game; card game

Available Platforms: n/a

Age: 10+

User behavior type: Achiever, Killer

Description: Players play as one of these four major powers: Romans, Barbarians, Egyptians, and Japanese. Players build new buildings, extract resources, and build armies. After building up their territories, players launch attacks on other players. The game is five rounds where players draw cards and have the opportunity to take the following actions: explore new land, build buildings, trade resources, conquer enemies. The player with the most victory points wins.

Gameplay: 1–4 players

Series (Y or N): Yes

Other titles in the series: There are several expansions to this game, including Imperial Settlers: Aztecs, Imperial Settlers: Amazons, and stand-alone game Imperial Settlers: Empires of the North

Similar games: Terraforming Mars, Race for the Galaxy

Game Title: Istanbul
Year published: 2004
Genre: Strategy; dice game; economic
Format: Board game
Available Platforms: n/a
Age: 10+
User behavior type: Achiever
Description: You lead a group of a merchant and assistants to market in Istanbul and attempt to buy rubies or trade goods for rubies.
Gameplay: 2–5 players
Series (Y or N): Yes
Other titles in the series: There are expansions and other titles in the series such as Istanbul: Mocha & Baksheesh, Istanbul: Letters & Seals, Istanbul: The Dice Game, Istanbul: Big Box
Similar games: Splendor, The Ancient World, Gold West

Game Title: Junk Art
Year published: 2016
Genre: Family; party; hand management; player elimination
Format: Board game
Available Platforms: n/a
Age: 8+
User behavior type: Achiever, Socializer
Description: This is a tactile game that has 10 game modes and 60 big colorful wooden and plastic components. Players pile all of the components in the center of the table and players draw cards. Each player passes a card to the player next to them, signifying one of the components in the middle. That player must then add that component to their tower, regardless of how oddly shaped it is. Once players have finished playing their cards, whoever has the tallest work of art is the winner.
Gameplay: 2–6 players
Series (Y or N): No
Other titles in the series: n/a
Similar games: Animal Upon Animal, Go Cuckoo, Rhino Hero

Game Title: Kemet: Blood and Sand
Year published: 2012
Genre: Strategy; fighting; card drafting; hand management
Format: Board game
Available Platforms: n/a
Age: 13+
User behavior type: Achiever, Killer
Description: Players deploy troops of an Egyptian tribe using the powers of ancient Egyptian gods in the land of Kemet.
Gameplay: 2–5 players

Series (Y or N): Yes

Other titles in the series: There are other titles in this series, including Kemet: Ta-Seti

Similar games: Blood Rage, Small World

Game Title: King of Tokyo

Year published: 2011

Genre: Board game; dice game

Format: Dice game; science fiction; fighting; card drafting; player elimination

Available Platforms: n/a

Age: 8+

User behavior type: Killer, Achiever

Description: The object of the game is to have your monster become the King of Tokyo through dice rolling and "battle."

Gameplay: 2–6 players

Series (Y or N): Yes

Other titles in the series: There are expansions and other titles in the series such as King of Tokyo: Halloween, King of Tokyo: Power Up, King of New York

Similar games: Family Business, Guillotine

Game Title: Last Will

Year published: 2011

Genre: Strategy; card game; economic

Format: Board game; card game

Available Platforms: n/a

Age: 14+

User behavior type: Achiever

Description: Players all start with a set amount of inheritance, and whoever is able to spend it all in the most extravagant way possible becomes the rightful heir to the entire fortune.

Gameplay: 2–5 players

Series (Y or N): Yes

Other titles in the series: There is a follow-up title called Last Will: Getting Sacked

Similar games: Go for Broke, Viticulture

Game Title: Lords of Waterdeep

Year published: 2012

Genre: Strategy; city building; fantasy; card drafting

Format: Board game

Available Platforms: n/a

Age: 12+

User behavior type: Achiever

Description: Players take on the role of one of the masked Lords of Waterdeep who are vying for control of the city.

Gameplay: 2–5 players

Series (Y or N): Yes

Other titles in the series: There is an expansion to this game entitled Lords of Waterdeep: Scoundrels of Skullport

Similar games: Stone Age, Takenoko

Game Title: Love Letter

Year published: 2011

Genre: Family; card game; deduction, hand management; player elimination

Format: Card game

Available Platforms: n/a

Age: 10+

User behavior type: Achiever

Description: You goal is to get your love letter to the princess while deflecting the letters of the other players.

Gameplay: 2–4 players

Series (Y or N): Yes

Other titles in the series: Many themed versions, including Love Letter Premium, Love Letter: Batman, Love Letter: Star Wars, Adventure Time Love Letter, Big Love Letter

Similar games: Coup, Mascarade, Biblios

Game Title: Mansions of Madness

Year published: 2011

Genre: Exploration; fantasy; adventure; fighting

Format: Board game

Available Platforms: n/a

Age: 13+

User behavior type: Achiever, Explorer

Description: Players encounter a map and scenario when they begin to play. They will encounter challenges and monsters while acting as investigators trying to uncover mysteries.

Gameplay: 2–5 players

Series (Y or N): Yes

Other titles in the series: Many editions and expansions, including Mansions of Madness: 2nd edition, Mansions of Madness: Call of the Wild, Mansions of Madness: Forbidden Alchemy, Mansions of Madness: The Silver Tablet, Mansions of Madness: The Laboratory

Similar games: Dungeons & Dragons, Arkham Horror, Betrayal at House on the Hill, Android: Netrunner

Game Title: Monopoly

Year published: 1933

Genre: Family; economic; player elimination; trading

Format: Board game

Available Platforms: n/a

Age: 8+

User behavior type: Socializer

Description: Players purchase properties in order to control the board and collect rent from other players. Players are also able to mortgage their properties and barter/trade with each other. The object of the game is to bankrupt the other players and the last player wins. Monopoly is one of the most popular and oldest board games in North America.

Gameplay: 2–8 players

Series (Y or N): Yes

Other titles in the series: There are many themed titles in this series.

Similar games: 7 Wonders, RA, Settlers of Catan

Game Title: Munchkin

Year published: 2001

Genre: Fantasy; fighting; card drafting; dice rolling; hand management

Format: Board game; card game

Available Platforms: n/a

Age: 10+

User behavior type: Killer, Achiever

Description: You compete with other players to grab items and battle monsters. This is a card drafting style game where you build up your characters and equip them with special objects to be successful during your dungeon raids.

Gameplay: 3–6 players

Series (Y or N): Yes

Other titles in the series: Many editions and expansions, including Munchkin Quest, Munchkin Cthulhu, Star Munchkin, Super Munchkin, Munchkin Marvel, Munchkin 4: The Need for Steed, Munchkin Apocalypse, Munchkin Impossible

Similar games: Dungeons & Dragons, Cosmic Encounter, Epic Spell Wars

Game Title: Mysterium

Year published: 2015

Genre: Family; deduction; horror; family

Format: Board game

Available Platforms: n/a

Age: 10+

User behavior type: Achiever

Description: One player acts as the ghost while the other players are the mediums. The mediums work with the ghost and its memories in order to solve the ghost's murder.

Gameplay: 2–7 players

Series (Y or N): Yes

Other titles in the series: Many expansions available, including Mysterium: Secrets and Lies, Mysterium: Hidden Signs, Mysterium: The Meeple

Similar games: Codenames, Spyfall, The Resistance, Sheriff of Nottingham

Game Title: Pandemic
Year published: 2008
Genre: Cooperative; family
Format: Board game
Available Platforms: n/a
Age: 8+
User behavior type: Achiever, Socializer
Description: Players must work together leveraging their different skills and talents as particular characters in the game to stop the global outbreak of diseases by curing areas that are currently infected.
Gameplay: 2–4 players
Series (Y or N): Yes
Other titles in the series: Many expansions and other titles in the series, including Pandemic Legacy, Pandemic: Fall of Rome, Pandemic: Reign of Cthulhu, Pandemic: The Cure, Pandemic: Contagion, Pandemic: Rising Tide, Pandemic: In the Lab
Similar games: Forbidden Island, Forbidden Desert, Hanabi

Game Title: Patchwork
Year published: 2014
Genre: Abstract; family; puzzle game; card drafting
Format: Board game; card game
Available Platforms: n/a
Age: 8+
User behavior type: Achiever
Description: This two-player game has players trying to complete the most aesthetically pleasing (and high scoring) quilt on a personal game board.
Gameplay: 2 players
Series (Y or N): Yes
Other titles in the series: There are many expansions and other titles in the series, including Patchwork Express, Patchwork Doodle
Similar games: Cottage Garden, Spring Meadow, Indian Summer

Game Title: Power Grid
Year published: 2004
Genre: Strategy; economic; route building
Format: Board game
Available Platforms: n/a
Age: 12+

User behavior type: Achiever

Description: The overall goal is to supply your cities with power. Players also collect raw materials in order to build and upgrade plants, but they need to be tactile as other players can also benefit from these upgrades.

Gameplay: 2–6 players

Series (Y or N): Yes

Other titles in the series: Other titles and expansions include Power Grid: The First Sparks

Similar games: Settlers of Catan, Ticket to Ride, Civilization

Game Title: Puerto Rico

Year published: 2002

Genre: Strategy; economic; city building

Format: Board game

Available Platforms: n/a

Age: 12+

User behavior type: Achiever

Description: The object of the game is to collect victory points by trading items to Europe and constructing buildings. Each player plays on an individual board to manage their cities, plantations, and ships.

Gameplay: 3–5 players

Series (Y or N): Yes

Other titles in the series: Other titles and expansions are available, including Puerto Rico: Expansion I—New Buildings, Puerto Rico: Expansion II—The Nobles

Similar games: San Juan, Race for the Galaxy, Cuba: El Presidente, Steam

Game Title: Race for the Galaxy

Year published: 2007

Genre: Strategy; card game; economic; hand management; science fiction

Format: Board game

Available Platforms: n/a

Age: 12+

User behavior type: Achiever

Description: This is a card game where players build galactic empires.

Gameplay: 2–4 players

Series (Y or N): Yes

Other titles in the series: There are many expansions and titles in this series, including Race for the Galaxy: The Brink of War, Race for the Galaxy: Rebel vs. Imperium, Race for the Galaxy: The Gathering Storm

Similar games: Deus, Star Realms, Lost Cities, Carcassonne

Game Title: The Resistance

Year published: 2009

Genre: Party; deduction; negotiation; card game

Format: Card game
Available Platforms: n/a
Age: 13+
User behavior type: Achiever
Description: Players are either part of the resistance or imperial spies who rely on each other to carry out missions in the game. They must deduce each other's identities and gain their trust in order to have their missions approved. Based on whether the majority of missions succeed or fail, either the resistance or the imperial spies win.
Gameplay: 5–10 players
Series (Y or N): Yes
Other titles in the series: Other titles and expansions are available, including The Resistance: Avalon, The Resistance: Hidden Agenda, The Resistance: Hostile Intent, The Resistance: The Plot Thickens
Similar games: Werewolf, Shadow Hunters, Secret Hitler, Coup

Game Title: Rising Sun
Year published: 2018
Genre: Strategy; bluffing; fantasy; wargame
Format: Board game
Available Platforms: n/a
Age: 14+
User behavior type: Achiever
Description: This game is set in feudal Japan and has players leading their clans to victory. Players recruit monsters, create alliances, gather resources, and build armies.
Gameplay: 3–5 players
Series (Y or N): No
Other titles in the series: n/a
Similar games: Kemet, Blood Rage, Puerto Rico

Game Title: Risk
Year published: 1959
Genre: Family; wargame; territory building; dice rolling; player elimination
Format: Board game
Available Platforms: n/a
Age: 10+
User behavior type: Achiever, Killer
Description: Risk is one of the oldest, most popular board games. Players move around a map of the world acquiring reinforcements and taking over territories until the armies of every other player fall leaving one person the winner.
Gameplay: 2–6 players
Series (Y or N): Yes
Other titles in the series: Other titles and expansions are available, including Risk Legacy, Risk 2210 AD, Risk: The Lord of the Rings, Risk: Star Wars Original Trilogy edition, Risk Express, Risk Europe

Similar games: Axis and Allies, War! Age of Imperialism, Diplomacy, Antike, Europe Engulfed, and Conquest of the Empire

Game Title: Rory's Story Cubes
Year published: 2005
Genre: Family; party; dice game; cooperative
Format: Dice game
Available Platforms: n/a
Age: 6+
User behavior type: Socializer
Description: Pictures are printed onto large-sized dice and when you roll them you are prompted to use the pictures you get to start a story with Once upon a time... using all nine dice as a part of your story.
Gameplay: 1–12 players
Series (Y or N): Yes
Other titles in the series: Many different variants and themed versions such as Rory's Story Cubes: Scooby Doo, Rory's Story Cubes: Actions, Rory's Story Cubes: Voyages, Rory's Story Cubes: Batman, Rory's Story Cubes: Enchanted
Similar games: Dixit, Once Upon a Time: The Storytelling Card Game, Tell Tale

Game Title: Saboteur
Year published: 2004
Genre: Family; bluffing; card game; exploration
Format: Card game
Available Platforms: n/a
Age: 8+
User behavior type: Explorer, Socializer
Description: Players are dwarves who are either miners or saboteurs who are hunting for gold (your identity is secret). Miners are trying to build uninterrupted paths from the start card to the goal card, while the saboteurs are trying to prevent this without giving away their identity.
Gameplay: 3–10 players
Series (Y or N): Yes
Other titles in the series: Many expansions and other titles are available in the series, including Saboteur 2, Saboteur: The Lost Mines, Saboteur: The Duel
Similar games: Shadows over Camelot, The Castle of the Devil, The Resistance, Citadels

Game Title: Sagrada
Year published: 2017
Genre: Puzzle game; dice game; drafting game
Format: Board game
Available Platforms: n/a
Age: 14+

User behavior type: Achiever

Description: Each player builds a stained-glass window by drafting dice and using "tools of the trade." The game is visually pleasing and easy to learn.

Gameplay: 1–4 players

Series (Y or N): Yes

Other titles in the series: Expansions are available, including Sagrada: 5 & 6 Player Expansion, Sagrada: The Great Facades—Passion

Similar games: Azul, Starving Artists, Blueprints, Santorini

Game Title: San Juan

Year published: 2004

Genre: Strategy; card game; city building; economic; hand management

Format: Card game

Available Platforms: n/a

Age: 10+

User behavior type: Achiever

Description: This is a card game based on the game Puerto Rico; major differences are it is card based, and there is no trade or colonists.

Gameplay: 2–4 players

Series (Y or N): Yes

Other titles in the series: San Juan: 2nd edition

Similar games: Puerto Rico, Race for the Galaxy, The City

Game Title: Santorini

Year published: 2016

Genre: Strategy; family; tile movement;

Format: Board game

Available Platforms: n/a

Age: 8+

User behavior type: Achiever

Description: This game is fairly simple. You move your builders around the spaces and construct a building level. First player to three building levels wins.

Gameplay: 2–4 players

Series (Y or N): n/a

Other titles in the series: This game has been constantly evolving over the last 30 years, and its most current iteration came out in 2016, which is a reimagining of the 2004 version.

Similar games: Sagrada, Pagoda, Azul, Hive

Game Title: Say Anything

Year published: 2008

Genre: Party

Format: Card game

Available Platforms: n/a

Age: 13+

User behavior type: Socializer

Description: This is a simple game that begins conversations by asking your friends questions that are printed on cards. A question is asked and all players write a response and share them together, then players vote on the answer they liked best.

Gameplay: 3–8 players

Series (Y or N): Yes

Other titles in the series: Many different versions of this game, including Say Anything: Uncensored, Say Anything Family edition

Similar games: Codenames, Taboo, Wits & Wagers, Dixit

Game Title: Scotland Yard

Year published: 1983

Genre: Family; deduction; travel; cooperative

Format: Board game

Available Platforms: n/a

Age: 10+

User behavior type: Achiever

Description: One player acts as Mr. X who travels around London via taxi, but his movement is recorded secretly. Meanwhile, the other players work together to try to catch Mr. X.

Gameplay: 3–6 players

Series (Y or N): Yes

Other titles in the series: Many different titles in the series, including Scotland Yard Master, Scotland Yard: Tokyo, Scotland Yard Junior, Scotland Yard: The Dice Game

Similar games: Mister X, Nuns on the Run, Pandemic

Game Title: Scythe

Year published: 2016

Genre: Strategy; economic; fighting; science fiction

Format: Board game

Available Platforms: n/a

Age: 14+

User behavior type: Achiever, Killer

Description: Players come from different factions and have different resources available to them. They are working against each other to take over the land around the mysterious factory and complete objectives. Once one player reaches a certain number of objectives, the game ends, and the player with the most victory points wins.

Gameplay: 1–5 players

Series (Y or N): Yes

Other titles in the series: Many different versions of this game exist, including a children's version called My Little Scythe, Scythe: The Rise of Fenris, Scythe: The Wind Gambit, Scythe: Encounters

Similar games: Terra Mystica, Viticulture, Twilight Imperium

Game Title: Secret Hitler

Year published: 2016

Genre: Party; bluffing; card game; deduction; humor

Format: Card game

Available Platforms: n/a

Age: 13+

User behavior type: Achiever, Killer

Description: Secret Hitler is set in 1930s Germany, and each player is secretly assigned the role of either a liberal or a fascist; one player is Secret Hitler. The fascists are trying to install their leader, whereas the liberals must work together to find and assassinate Secret Hitler before it is too late.

Gameplay: 5–10 players

Series (Y or N): No

Similar games: Coup, The Resistance: Avalon, Werewolf, Deception: Murder in Hong Kong

Game Title: Sequence

Year published: 1982

Genre: Family; strategy; card game

Format: Card game

Available Platforms: n/a

Age: 7+

User behavior type: Achiever

Description: This game has cards and chips, and each team is trying to create rows, columns, or diagonals of chips. The game is over when a particular number of connections are made.

Gameplay: 2–12 players

Series (Y or N): Yes

Other titles in the series: Many different versions of this game are available, including Sequence for Kids, Sequence Dice, Jumbo Sequence, Sequence: States & Capitals

Similar games: Qwirkle, Tsuro, Saboteur

Game Title: Settlers of Catan

Year published: 1995

Genre: Strategy game; dice game; modular board; route/network building; trading

Format: Board game

Available Platforms: n/a

Age: 10+

User behavior type: Explorer, Achiever

Description: Players try to dominate the island of Catan by building cities and roads using resources they collect throughout the game either by territory control or through trade.

Gameplay: 1–4 players

Series (Y or N): Yes

Other titles in the series: Multiple expansions, including Catan: Cities & Knights, Catan: Seafarers, Star Trek Catan, Catan: Traders & Barbarians, and a two-player version Rivals of Catan

Similar games: Rise of Tribes, Carcassonne, Dominion, Agricola, Ticket to Ride

Game Title: 7 Wonders

Year published: 2010

Genre: Family; strategy; card game; city building; card drafting; hand management

Format: Board game

Available Platforms: n/a

Age: 10+

User behavior type: Achiever, Socializer

Description: 7 Wonders requires players to lead an ancient civilization as it evolves from being barbaric to a world power. In order to build these societies, players must build buildings, study science and technology, build armies, and so on. The game has three stages where players draw cards, choose one, and pass the remainder to the adjacent player (drafting). Players then use these cards to collect resources and interact with other players.

Gameplay: 2–7 players

Series (Y or N): Yes

Other titles in the series: Many different titles within the series and expansions are available, including 7 Wonders Duel (two-player card game version), 7 Wonders: Cities, 7 Wonders: Leaders, 7 Wonders Duel: Pantheon, 7 Wonders: Babel, 7 Wonders: Armada, 7 Wonders: Catan, 7 Wonders: Leaders Expansion

Similar games: Guillotine, Dominion, Citadels, King of Tokyo, Age of Empires

Game Title: Shadow Hunters

Year published: 2005

Genre: Party; bluffing; card game; deduction

Format: Board game

Available Platforms: n/a

Age: 13+

User behavior type: Achiever

Description: This is a survival game that is set in a devil-filled forest with groups of characters—the Shadows (creatures of the night), Hunters (humans trying to destroy supernatural beings), and Neutrals (civilians). Players belong to one of these groups, but most conceal their identity and players try to find their allies and enemies.

Gameplay: 4–8 players

Series (Y or N): Yes

Other titles in the series: There is an expansion entitled Shadow Hunters Expansion

Similar games: Werewolf, The Resistance: Avalon, Bang!, Saboteur

Game Title: Sheriff of Nottingham

Year published: 2014

Genre: Family; bluffing; card game; negotiations

Format: Board game

Available Platforms: n/a

Age: 14+

User behavior type: Achiever, Socializer

Description: Players take turns playing the sheriff who is trying to stop players from smuggling contraband to market. Players do not have to smuggle contraband and can take allowed objects to market, but they score fewer points. The game ends once everyone has had a turn playing the sheriff, and points are awarded based on what players were able to successfully take to market.

Gameplay: 3–5 players

Series (Y or N): Yes

Other titles in the series: One expansion is available, called Sheriff of Nottingham: Merry Men

Similar games: Coup, Cosmic Encounter

Game Title: Small World

Year published: 2009

Genre: Family; strategy; fantasy; fighting

Format: Board game

Available Platforms: n/a

Age: 8+

User behavior type: Achiever, Killer

Description: You play as a particular race of character and try to conquer adjacent lands, potentially destroying weaker races or letting your own race go into decline. Points are scored based on territory occupied, and each race scores differently. The player with the most points at the end of the game wins.

Gameplay: 2–5 players

Series (Y or N): Yes

Other titles in the series: There are other versions of the game available, including Small World Underground, Small World: Realms, Small World: Be Not Afraid

Similar games: Vinci, Olympos, Evo, Kemet, History of the World

Game Title: Smash Up

Year published: 2012

Genre: Strategy; card game; fantasy

Format: Card game

Available Platforms: n/a

Age: 12+

User behavior type: Achiever, Killer

Description: Players pick two themed decks and shuffle them together to make their playing deck. You then use this deck to battle over basic cards to score points.

Gameplay: 2–4 players

Series (Y or N): Yes

Other titles in the series: There are many different themes and expansions to this game, including Smash Up: The Big Geeky Box, Smash Up: Munchkin, Smash Up: Cease and Desist, Smash Up: Pretty Pretty Smash Up

Similar games: Dominion, Guillotine, Small World, Elysium

Game Title: Spirit Island

Year published: 2017

Genre: Strategy; fantasy; fighting; territory building; cooperative

Format: Board game

Available Platforms: n/a

Age: 13+

User behavior type: Achiever, Socializer

Description: Players are different spirits who have unique powers. Players act cooperatively to defend their home from colonizing invaders. The team loses if any spirit is destroyed, if the island is overrun by the blight, or if the invader deck is depleted.

Gameplay: 1–4 players

Series (Y or N): Yes

Other titles in the series: There are many expansions and titles in this series, including Spirit Island: Jagged Earth, Spirit Island: Branch & Claw, Spirit Island: Expansion Playmat

Similar games: Pandemic: Legacy, Gloomhaven, Arkham Horror, Sentinels of the Multiverse

Game Title: Stone Age

Year published: 2008

Genre: Family; strategy; dice rolling

Format: Board game

Available Platforms: n/a

Age: 10+

User behavior type: Achiever

Description: This game is set in the prehistoric, stone age. Players collect resources, trade to expand their village, and evolve their village to new levels of civilization. There are three phases in the game with players competing with each other for resources.

Gameplay: 2–4 players

Series (Y or N): Yes

Other titles in the series: Stone Age: The Expansion and My First Stone Age for children

Similar games: Champions of Midgard, Lords of Waterdeep, Russian Railroads

Game Title: Sushi Go!

Year published: 2013

Genre: Family; card drafting; hand management

Format: Card game

Available Platforms: n/a

Age: 8+

User behavior type: Achiever, Socializer

Description: Players start with seven cards, pick one and pass the hand to the next player. The object of the game is to collect sushi cards and score the most points, all the while the other players can see what type of card you are trying to collect.

Gameplay: 2–5 players

Series (Y or N): Yes

Other titles in the series: There is a party version of this game called Sushi Go Party!

Similar games: 7 Wonders Duel, Archaeology: The Card Game, Arboretum

Game Title: Takenoko

Year published: 2011

Genre: Family; farming; territory building

Format: Board game

Available Platforms: n/a

Age: 8+

User behavior type: Achiever

Description: This is a tactile, abstract strategy game that uses small colored pieces in a Tetris-like game play. Players place down pieces that cannot be adjacent to your other pieces, rather they have to touch a corner of a previously placed piece. Whichever player is able to place the most of their 21 pieces onto the board wins.

Gameplay: 2–4 players

Series (Y or N): Yes

Other titles in the series: There is one additional title in the series, Takenoko: Chibis

Similar games: The Castles of Burgundy, Tokaido, Tobago, Stone Age

Game Title: Tapestry

Year published: 2019

Genre: Strategy; civilization; dice rolling; hand management

Format: Board game

Available Platforms: n/a

Age: 12+

User behavior type: Achiever

Description: Players begin the game with nothing and advance through one of four advancement tracks (science, technology, military, and exploration). As you advance your city, build your income, and gain victory points, you also gain tapestry cards that further tell the story of your civilization.

Gameplay: 1–5 players

Series (Y or N): No

Other titles in the series: n/a

Similar games: Quads, Gemblo, Patchwork

Game Title: Terraforming Mars

Year published: 2016

Genre: Strategy; economic; territory building; science fiction

Format: Board game

Available Platforms: n/a

Age: 12+

User behavior type: Achiever, Explorer

Description: Players participate in the terraforming of Mars to make it inhabitable for humans through introducing plants and animals, building infrastructure, destroying asteroids, and more. Players complete milestones and amass wealth through production. At the end of the game, these are tabulated, and the player with the highest victory points wins.

Gameplay: 1–5 players

Series (Y or N): Yes

Other titles in the series: There are additional titles in the series, including Terraforming Mars: Colonies, Terraforming Mars: Venus Next, Terraforming Mars: Turmoil

Similar games: Imperial Settlers, Elysium, Terra Mystica, Through the Ages, Wingspan

Game Title: Terra Mystica

Year published: 2012

Genre: Strategy; civilization; fantasy; territory building; Eurogame

Format: Board game

Available Platforms: n/a

Age: 12+

User behavior type: Achiever, Explorer

Description: In the land of Terra Mystica, there are 14 groups of people who live within seven different landscapes. Players control one of these 14 groups and try to expand their territory as much as possible. Players manage resources, build dwellings, trade, build strongholds, upgrade buildings, and build the skills of your people in terraforming and with boats and rivers. Players also earn power points that can be used to cast spells. The game lasts six rounds, and the player with the most victory points wins.

Gameplay: 2–5 players

Series (Y or N): Yes

Other titles in the series: There are expansions, including Terra Mystica: Fire & Ice, Terra Mystica: Age of Innovation, Terra Mystica: Merchants of the Sea

Similar games: Terraforming Mars, Imperial Settlers, Power Grid, Scythe

Game Title: Through the Ages: A Story of Civilization

Year published: 2015

Genre: Strategy; civilization; economic

Format: Board game

Available Platforms: n/a

Age: 12+

User behavior type: Achiever

Description: This is a civilization-building game that incorporates resource management, economics, discovering technology, building a military, electing good leaders, and more.

Gameplay: 2–4 players

Series (Y or N): Yes

Other titles in the series: There are several different titles in the series, including Through the Ages: A New Story of Civilization, Roll through the Ages: The Bronze Age, Through the Ages: New Leaders and Wonders

Similar games: Terra Mystica, Imperial Settlers, Dominant Species

Game Title: Ticket to Ride

Year published: 2015

Genre: Family; trains; card drafting; hand management; route building

Format: Board game

Available Platforms: n/a

Age: 8+

User behavior type: Achiever, Explorer

Description: Players collect cards that they then use to claim railway routes on the map. The longer their route, the more points awarded. You can also score points by completing Destination Tickets.

Gameplay: 2–5 players

Series (Y or N): Yes

Other titles in the series: Other titles in the series include Ticket to Ride: Nordic Countries, Ticket to Ride: USA 1910, Ticket to Ride: Europe, Ticket to Ride: Rails & Sails, Ticket to Ride: Marklin, Ticket to Ride: Switzerland, Ticket to Ride: 10th Anniversary, Ticket to Ride: The Card Game, Ticket to Ride: Mystery Train Expansion, Ticket to Ride: New York, Ticket to Ride: First Journey

Similar games: Settlers of Catan, Carcassonne, Pandemic, Forbidden Island, 7 Wonders

Game Title: T.I.M.E. Stories
Year published: 2015
Genre: Adventure; adult; puzzle; science fiction
Format: Board game
Available Platforms: n/a
Age: 12+
User behavior type: Explorer
Description: This is a game of storytelling and narrative that has players create characters with depth and navigate through missions, time, and space.
Gameplay: 2–4 players
Series (Y or N): Yes
Other titles in the series: There are other titles in the series, including T.I.M.E. Stories: A Prophecy of Dragons, T.I.M.E. Stories: Brotherhood of the Coast, T.I.M.E. Stories: Madame
Similar games: Mansions of Madness, 2nd edition, Sherlock Holmes: Consulting Detective

Game Title: Tokyo Metro
Year published: 2018
Genre: Economic; territory building; educational
Format: Board game
Available Platforms: n/a
Age: 7+
User behavior type: Achiever
Description: The premise of Tokyo Metro is you are trying to build train lines in Tokyo in the most economically viable way. The game includes route building, investment, speculating, and area control within a realistic map of Tokyo.
Gameplay: 1–5 players
Series (Y or N): Yes
Other titles in the series: Tokyo Metro is part of the Tokyo series of games (12 total) that includes Tokyo Coin Laundry, Tokyo Game Show, Tokyo Capsule Hotel, Tokyo Jutaku
Similar games: Ticket to Ride, Power Grid

Game Title: Tsuro
Year published: 2004
Genre: Abstract; family; fantasy; hand management
Format: Board game
Available Platforms: n/a
Age: 8+

User behavior type: Achiever

Description: Tsuro is a rather quick game (about 15 minutes to play). It involves keeping your token on the board the longest, but this becomes increasingly difficult as the board fills up leaving fewer available spaces.

Gameplay: 2–8 players

Series (Y or N): Yes

Other titles in the series: Tsuro of the Seas, Tsuro of the Seas: Veterans of the Seas, Tsuro: Phoenix Rising

Similar games: Akrotiri, Indigo

Game Title: Viticulture

Year published: 2013

Genre: Strategy; hand management; economic

Format: Board game

Available Platforms: n/a

Age: 13+

User behavior type: Achiever

Description: Set in rustic Tuscany, players start with modest inherited vineyards. Players must use workers (and enthusiastic visitors) for labor to help build their vineyards with the overall goal of having the most successful vineyard in Tuscany.

Gameplay: 2–6 players

Series (Y or N): Yes

Other titles in the series: There are many expansions and titles in this series, including Viticulture: Tuscany Essential edition, Viticulture: Moor Visitors Expansion, Viticulture: Visit from Rhine Valley

Similar games: Agricola, A Feast for Odin, Russian Railroads, The Manhattan Project

Game Title: Werewolf

Year published: 1986

Genre: Party; bluffing; card game; deduction; horror

Format: Card game

Available Platforms: n/a

Age: 8+

User behavior type: Achiever, Killer

Description: Everyone playing is given a role without the other players knowing. Some are werewolves who kill the villagers, some are seers, and other just regular villagers. The point of the game is to determine who the werewolf is before everyone else is killed.

Gameplay: 8–24 players

Series (Y or N): Yes

Other titles in the series: There are many expansions and titles in this series, including One Night Ultimate Werewolf, Ultimate Werewolf Legacy, Ultimate Werewolf

Similar games: Coup, The Resistance: Avalon, Spyfall, Deception: Murder in Hong Kong

Game Title: Wingspan
Year published: 2019
Genre: Family; strategy; card game; economic; educational
Format: Board game; card game
Available Platforms: n/a
Age: 10+
User behavior type: Achiever, Explorer
Description: Wingspan is a competitive game where players are bird enthusiasts. Players need to discover and attract the best birds to your network of wildlife preserves. In order to do this, players gain food tokens, lay eggs, and draw from a deck that has hundreds of unique bird cards to play. The player with the most points after four rounds is the winner of the game.
Gameplay: 1–5 players
Series (Y or N): Yes
Other titles in the series: Wingspan: European Expansion
Similar games: Terraforming Mars

Game Title: Wits and Wagers
Year published: 2005
Genre: Party; bluffing; trivia; betting
Format: Board game
Available Platforms: n/a
Age: 10+
User behavior type: Achiever
Description: A trivia question is asked, and players write down their guesses to the question. This is placed face up on the betting mat. Then the other players bet on which answer that they think is right—the closest to the answer without going over is the winner of the round.
Gameplay: 3–7 players
Series (Y or N): Yes
Other titles in the series: Wits & Wagers Party, Wits & Wagers Family, Vegas Wits & Wagers, Wits & Wagers: Epic Geek edition, Wits & Wagers Expansion Pack 1
Similar games: Say Anything, Taboo, Codenames, Dixit

Game Title: Word Slam
Year published: 2016
Genre: Party; word game
Format: Board game; card game
Available Platforms: n/a
Age: 10+
User behavior type: Achiever

Description: Teams compete against each other to guess what hidden word their teammate has uncovered by using the clues provided; 105 explanatory cards. The player who is trying to communicate what word they have to their team only has 105 predetermined cards to do this.

Gameplay: 1–2 players

Series (Y or N): Yes

Other titles in the series: Word Slam Family, Word Slam: DSP edition, Word Slam Midnight

Similar games: Funglish, Pictionary, Dixit, Codenames

Notes

1. Scott Nicolson, "Library Trends: The Impact of Gaming on Libraries," *Library Trends* 61, no. 4 (Spring 2013): 741.

2. Julie Verstraeten, "The Rise of Board Games," Medium, April 21, 2018, https://medium.com/@Juliev/the-rise-of-board-games-a7074525a3ec.

3. Emma Bedford, "Global Board Games Market Value from 2017 to 2023," Statista, August 9, 2019, https://www.statista.com/statistics/829285/global-board-games-market-value/.

4. Verstraeten, "The Rise of Board Games."

5. "About Us," Kickstarter, accessed June 14 2019, https://www.kickstarter.com/about?ref=global-footer.

6. Frank Bergstrom, "The Top 10 Most Funded Kickstarter Board Games of All Time," Evil as a Hobby, accessed June 14 2019, https://www.evilasahobby.com/blog/the-top-10-most-funded-kickstarter-board-games-of-all-time/.

8
Video Games

Since video games were initially created in 1958, with the invention of a tennis style video game (predating Pong, which was released in 1972),[1] they have grown to become one of the largest entertainment industries worldwide. In the United States alone, sales in 2017 reached a staggering 30 billion dollars. People are playing these games at an astounding rate, and libraries need to integrate video games into their collection. By ensuring that your library not only has a video game collection but also can effectively and confidently recommend titles to users, you will be able to engage with an ever-growing diverse community of gamers!

In order to properly engage with patrons over video game titles and gameplay, it is essential to have some understanding of the various types of video games—genres and subgenres—and what kind of players are attracted to these various games. This chapter will explore some of the more common genre types of video games by discussing key titles that you should consider for your collection as well as ways to engage with patrons over recommending similar titles.

"Aesthetics are the underlying reason players return to a game."[2]

When working with patrons interested in your video game collection, keep in mind that genres are not the only qualifier in determining why a user did or did not like a game or why that user might want to select a particular game. Perhaps a gamer enjoyed the story aesthetics or the character aesthetics or some other aspect of the game that was outside the actual mechanics of the game. Thus, it is important to always consider not how the player plays the game, but the reason the player plays the game. Regardless of why the game is played, it is still essential to understand the fundamental mechanics of the various types of video games to properly assess games for your collection and eventually make recommendations for your patrons.

In order to keep up with the rapid rate of digital game production, library staff should become familiar with some key sources of information.

Conventions: Conventions (or "cons") are increasing in popularity and growing in numbers. Some of the oldest Comic Conventions have expanded rapidly to include more genres and formats of geekdom; we are even starting to see more targeted cons. Some of the biggest cons for digital games are as follows:

- EGX (United Kingdom), September 2017, 80,000 attendees
- E3 (Los Angeles), June 2019, 66,100 attendees[3] (industry professionals only)
- BlizzCon (California), 40,000 (2019)
- Tokyo Game Show (Tokyo, Japan), September 2019, 267,076 attendees[4]
- Gamescom (Germany), August 2019, 373,000 attendees[5]

Some of these cons are more focused than others (e.g., BlizzCon is only games produced by Blizzard Entertainment), whereas others are broader. Video game companies tend to make their biggest announcements during these conventions and stream video live, which makes it easier for those who can't physically be there to get new information. These cons are well attended by not only people involved in the game industry but also hobbyists and enthusiasts who are looking for the next game they may want to play.

YouTube Video Game Channels: Typically, there are two major types of video game channels: reviewers and streamers. Reviewers go over new releases, create top listings of games, test out new peripherals, and give their expert advice on playing, collecting, and enjoying video games. Popular video game reviewers include *Angry Joe Show*, *TotalBiscuit*, *PeanutButterGamer*, *IGN Entertainment*, and *MetalJesusRocks*. All of these channels have a slightly different approach—*Angry Joe Show* tends to post very in-depth videos (30–45 minutes long), whereas someone like *MetalJesusRocks* posts a lot of top listings and keeps his videos quite a bit shorter. The other type of YouTube game channel is streamers. These are players who livestream while they play digital games. Usually these are online only games, but sometimes they will stream games that are also available on consoles. These channels are incredibly popular with children and teens, and many of the top streamers have become quasi celebrities (e.g., Ninja in Fortnite). These channels are good to be aware of, but are a little less helpful when it comes to collection development and quick how-tos. It is important to note that streamers may not be age appropriate for children so before you recommend anything to younger patrons, it is a good idea to read up on them and vet the channels first.

Controlled Vocabulary

As a library develops and builds its gaming collection, librarians and library workers will begin to become familiar with various terminology and the different genres found across all video game platforms. Having this understanding can help you make great strides in developing a relationship with patrons looking to use the gaming collection. It will also help you become better at recommending games from different genres—once you are familiar with the various types of games available and have a growing understanding of the mechanics and gameplay involved, you will be better able to work with patrons looking for games in one category or hoping to find games across a spectrum of genres. As a librarian working with video games and referring titles to patrons, it is essential to have at least a basic understanding of industry-driven genre categories. Kate Berens and Geoff Howard point out that these categories mirror the industry's operations and can be seen in how retailers organize video games.

This section will help you begin to develop an understanding of those genres by defining each style of video game before we move on to looking at gaming examples. Included here are general terms and descriptions of video game genres, including some of the elements included in each video game type. By having an understanding of these elements, you can begin to see links between different games in different categories. As well, you can start to understand how some games cross categories, becoming hybrid games that incorporate multiple types of genres. New genres and concepts are being developed constantly within the video game industry, but the genres represented here are some of the primary types you will encounter (see Table 8.1).

Video Games: Rating Systems

Video games have a relatively simple rating system, put together by the Entertainment Software Rating Board (ESRB),[6] they can be an excellent way to ensure you are collecting a wide range of games for multiple audiences and gamers. The ESRB rating system is a global standard and therefore is recognizable by all gamers. Each video game will have the distinctive ESRB rating displayed prominently on the cover—usually it is found on the back, near the game's description. The rating system is broken down by letter and content description. The letter indicates the age appropriateness of the game, while the content description will give greater context to why the game has received that rating. Table 8.2 is a breakdown of the rating system to help you become better familiar with the system and feel confident in selecting the best game for your patron(s). We drew heavily on the ESRB website in drafting these descriptions. For more information about game ratings, please visit www.esrb.org/ratings.

When you are working with patrons looking for new games to play, these rating systems can be a good driving factor in making recommendations: you might want to take note of what games the patron has played and what rating they received. This can give you some indication as to what they enjoyed and what might attract them to other games. Certainly, you want to take into account the age of the patron and make sure not to give a 14 year old a game that is rated Mature.

In order to properly recommend and sustain a relationship with gamer patrons, having a range of titles across the ratings can be a good idea for libraries of all types (although, if you wanted to shy away from Adults Only,

Table 8.1: Video Game Genres

Genre	Subgenre	Description	Examples
Action Games		Action games emphasize physical challenges that require hand-eye coordination and motor skills to overcome. The player is in control of the majority of the action. These games can involve twitch gameplay that involve a player's response time, meaning that a player's reaction time becomes an important element in the gameplay.	*Grand Theft Auto*
	Platform	Although this particular genre of game has severely declined over the last 30 years, it is still one of the most well known. *Donkey Kong* is often cited as one of the first platform games and is regarded as an exemplar of this genre. As Dustin Hansen describes in his video game history *Game On!*: "Jump Man starts at one point in the game screen (the bottom left corner), and he needs to use all his skills to travel to another location (towards the princess at the tip). Along the way he has to defeat or crush enemies . . . jump over obstacles . . . climb ladders, and avoid pits—oh, and jump from platform to platform."[a]	*Super Mario Brothers U Deluxe, Donkey Kong Country: Tropical Freeze*
	Shooter	In shooter games, players use ranged weapons to participate in the action, which takes place at a distance. Most games involve violent gameplay, while some have nonviolent objectives.	*Doom* series, *Black Ops* series

Table 8.1: (*continued*)

Genre	Subgenre	Description	Examples
		There are a number of subgenres involved in the shooter genre, including: shoot 'em up, shooting gallery, light gun shooter, first-person shooter, third-person shooter, hero shooter, tactical shooter, and loot shooter. Traditionally, shooter games involve a player using a variety of weapons to achieve an overall objective, but as Tom Bissell points out, current trends in the shooter genre, and its subgenres, have morphed into "maximal mayhem supported by equally maximal technology."[b]	
	Fighting	Fighting games require players to engage in combat with other players within the fictional gaming experience. Typically, close-range combat that involves one-on-one fighting or against a small number of equally powered opponents, often involving violent and exaggerated unarmed attacks. Traditional fighter games had opponents stand toe-to-toe delivering hits back and forth, but the genre completely changed in the 1990s to include complex and unique moves for each character, often also developing storylines. This format of the genre persists today.	*Street Fighter*, *Mortal Kombat*, *Super Smash Brothers*
	Beat 'Em Up	Beat 'em up games are related but distinct from fighting games. These games put players against large number waves of opponents. Often incorporate mechanics from other action games, and multiplayers in beat 'em up games tend to be cooperative.	*Batman Arkham Asylum*

(*continued*)

Table 8.1: (*continued*)

Genre	Subgenre	Description	Examples
	Stealth	Stealthy games emphasize subterfuge and precision strikes over the more overt mayhem of shooters. Players are still able to engage in loud combat but are punished for such involvement.	*Alien: Isolation*
	Survival	Survival games start with minimal resources, in a hostile, open-world environment and require players to collect resources, craft tools, weapons, and shelter in order to survive for as long as possible. (Can include the subgenre of Battle Royale games).	*Fortnite*
	Rhythm	Rhythm games are music-themed action video games that challenge a player's sense of rhythm.	*Dance Dance Revolution* series
Action-Adventure Games		Action-adventure games combine elements of their two component genres, typically featuring long-term obstacles that must be overcome using a tool or item as leverage as well as other smaller obstacles almost constantly in the way. Tend to focus on exploration as they usually involve item gathering, simple puzzle-solving, and combat.	*Tomb Raider* series, *The Last of Us*
	Survival Horror	Survival Horror games focus on gear and attempt to scare the player via traditional horror fiction elements. A main feature is a low quantity of ammunition or number of breakable melee weapons.	*Resident Evil* series

Table 8.1: (*continued*)

Genre	Subgenre	Description	Examples
	Metroidvania	Metroidvania games feature a large interconnected world map the player can explore. Access to parts of the world is limited by obstacles that can only be opened after the player has acquired certain items. Boss Fights are a feature.	*Castelvania* series, *Hollow Knight* (2017)
	Open World	Open-world concept games feature a main storyline that can be abandoned for subordinate storylines along with large numbers of supporting characters that players have meaningful interaction with. Players can also customize their central character. Open-world games have very little objective beyond exploring, which players can do at their own pace, often completing tasks along the way.	*Grand Theft Auto* series, *Fallout* series, *World of Warcraft*, *The Elder Scrolls*
Adventure Games		Adventure games are often defined by the player taking on the role of a protagonist and working through an interactive story by exploring the world and solving various puzzles throughout. Many adventure games are often intended for single players because the design of the story and character development makes it difficult to integrate multiplayer elements. These games often draw on elements from film and literature. The first recognized adventure game is considered to be 1976's *Colossal Cave Adventure* (commonly known as just *Adventure*).[c] The popularity of games in the	*The Walking Dead: Final Season, Sam and Max Save the World, Broken Sword: The Serpent's Curse*

(*continued*)

Table 8.1: (*continued*)

Genre	Subgenre	Description	Examples
		adventure genre has waned significantly with the introduction of action-adventure games and first-person shooters. However, the genre and some of its subgenres have been making a comeback, due to nostalgia markets.	
	Text adventure and interactive fiction	Text-based adventure games (known as interactive fiction or IF) are games that have the player select actions within the game based on a set number of phrases that correspond to predetermined outcomes. This is a fairly old game mechanic that is still used today, typically is pixel style games that are created to mimic the look and feel of retro games.	*Moonlighter*
	Graphic adventure	Graphic adventure games often use graphics to convey the environment to the player and may have a variety of input types. These games will utilize a first-person or third-person perspective.	*Myst, The Walking Dead*
	Point-and-click adventure games	Point-and-click adventure games refer to games that require the player to use a mouse (or another device such as their finger in mobile games) to click or select their actions. This could be clicking where they want their player to move, selecting items, interacting with other characters, and so on. These games were very popular in early PC games and now we see them mostly in mobile app games with the occasional PC release. An example of this for consoles is *Mario Paint* for SNES.	*Broken Age, Broken Sword*

Table 8.1: (*continued*)

Genre	Subgenre	Description	Examples
	Escape the room	These are a variation on point-and-click games, where the player must figure out how to escape from an enclosed environment using the tools they have at hand while solving puzzles.	*Keep Talking and Nobody Explodes*
	Puzzle	Puzzle games in a digital context generally mean that the only major activity the player does is interact with and solve puzzles. There are some games that include puzzle elements (e.g., *Zelda: Breath of the Wild*), but they are not the main mechanic of the game, rather they are just one element.	*Myst, The 7th Guest*
	Narrative	Narrative games often have branching narratives where player choices will influence the outcome of the game by dictating what actions are available to a player. These branching dynamics often help personalize the gameplay. Games will favor narrative storytelling over traditional gameplay.	*The Walking Dead, Night in the Woods*
	Walking simulators	Walking simulators involve the players taking their time to explore their surroundings, looking for clues, objects, and general discovery through observation.	*Gone Home, Firewatch, Night in the Woods*
	Visual novels	These are hybrid games between a text and graphic game. They often feature a text-based storyline with interactive features and sprite-based visuals. They will often resemble mixed media novels.	*Doki Doki Literature Club!*

(*continued*)

Table 8.1: (*continued*)

Genre	Subgenre	Description	Examples
Role-Playing Video Games (RPVG)		Role-playing video games are at their most basic described as, "games in which players traversed elaborate worlds, gaining experience, and learning fighting techniques while completing a quest."[d] RPVGs often share much of the same characteristics as traditional role-playing games such as Dungeons & Dragons. Players interact with the game by controlling a central character, join a party or group, and explore a vast game world while completing quests and missions until they have achieved the main point to the story. These games rely on a highly developed story and setting, characters that have specific attributes that gain in strength as the player advances throughout the game. They also offer a complex level of character development and interaction than other video game genres.	*Final Fantasy* series
	Action Role-play Games	Players control a single character in real time, with a heavy emphasis on action and combat situations, while character and plot are minimized.	*Legend of Zelda, Mass Effect* series
	First-Person Party RPGs	Players lead a team of "adventurers" in first-person perspective through a labyrinth or mazelike structure.	*Elminage* series
	Massively Multiplayer Online Role-Playing Games (MMORPGs)	MMORPGs adhere to the traditional definition of RPGs, but they have a massive world to explore, and players traditionally play using one character for extensive periods of time.	*Diablo, World of Warcraft*

Table 8.1: (*continued*)

Genre	Subgenre	Description	Examples
Sandbox		Sandbox games typically allow players free movement around an open world where they can explore and build with little outside interruption. While many of these games are open, many still have mini objectives that players can do. Sandbox games can be stand-alone or a feature within the world of an existing game.	*Minecraft, No Man's Sky*
Simulation		Simulation games are a broad category of video games that often get defined as games designed to simulate a real-world environment. These games often try to copy the activities one would engage in in the real world and are often used in training situations. In the 1980s, there were a number of simulation games related to sports that were popular in the mainstream. As well, games like *Flight Simulator* (1997–2019) have been notable releases in this genre. The most popular examples of these games are found in the subgenre life simulation games. See also Sports genre.	*Cities: Skylines, Farming Simulator*
	Life Simulation	Players control one or more characters in a simulation of real life. The point of these games is to create and maintain a stable and sustainable population of organisms. To do this, players have a level of control over their "people" or creatures to sustain their lives and build their society.	*The Sims*

(*continued*)

Table 8.1: (*continued*)

Genre	Subgenre	Description	Examples
Strategy		Strategy games highlight skillful thinking and advanced planning in players' efforts to achieve victory in their quests and missions. The point of the game is often to out think one's opponent instead of defeating that opponent using advanced resources or weaponry; rather, both sides in the game have access to equal levels of weaponry.	*Civilization III*
Sports		Sports games are technically a subgenre of simulation games; however, based on sales, it continues to be one of the most popular types of video games.[e] These games attempt to model the actual gameplay of various sports by allowing players to act as team members on various teams or as athletes in different sports.	*NHL* series, *FIFA* series, *NBA* series, *Wii Tennis, MLB, Madden NFL, Mario Kart*

[a]D. Hansen, *Game On!: Video Game History from Pong and Pac Man to Mario, Minecraft and More* (New York: Macmillan, 2016), 37.
[b]T. Bissell, *Extra Lives: Why Video Games Matter* (New York: Vintage Books, 2011), 131.
[c]Mark J. P. Wolf, *Video Games FAQ: All That's Left to Know about Games and Gaming Culture* (Milwaukee, WI: Backbeat Books, 2017), 83.
[d]Ibid., 539–540.
[e]Euromonitor International, "Video Game Software in North America," *Passport*, June 2019.

that is perfectly natural). For the purposes of this volume, we have decided to omit any reference to games rated Adult Only.

Video Game Consoles

Choosing to include video game consoles as part of your gaming collection is a decision that should be made according to the needs of your community and the limitations of your budget. There are a number of options in building a video game console collection, including only offering the latest in gaming consoles or maintaining a broader range of options with old and new consoles. If you are an academic librarian supporting a game studies program, you may want to highlight nostalgia by offering classic versions of

Table 8.2: Video Game Rating System

Rating	Rating Explained	Description
EC	Early Childhood	These games are often meant for extremely young children and are commonly meant as educational games, intended for children ages three and up.
E	Everyone	These are games meant for the whole family. They might include mild or cartoon violence and some "mild language." This is a very general and broad category; you will see a large number of games falling into this rating.
E10+	Everyone 10+	These games might contain larger amounts of mild violence, mild language, and crude humor. This is not an extremely large category of games but is meant for ages 10 and up.
T	Teen	These games might contain moderate-to-mild amounts of violence, including blood, mild-to-moderate use of strong language or suggestive themes, and crude humor. This is one of the larger categories of games, currently making up 24% of all games sold.[a]
M	Mature 17+	These games include intense and/or realistic violence (blood, gore, mutilation, and depictions of death), stronger sexual themes and content, partial nudity, and more frequent use of strong language. These are games meant only for gamers over the age of 17.
AO	Adults Only 18+	These games contain mostly adult situations, including nudity, strong sexual themes, and intense violence. This is a very small category of games, making up only 1% of games sold.[b]
RP	Rating Pending	These games have not yet been rated.

[a]D. Hansen, *Game On!: Video Game History from Pong and Pac Man to Mario, Minecraft and More* (New York: Macmillan, 2016), 109.
[b]Ibid.

the Nintendo Entertainment System (NES) and the Super Nintendo Entertainment System (SNES). Regardless of how you decide to build the collection, you may want to offer a variety of consoles and game options. There is a growing shift toward having video games accessible online through cloud-based gaming. Currently there are three major online gaming platforms: Google Stadia, Steam, and Apple Arcade. For a detailed discussion on these platforms, please see Chapter 9.

There are three major gaming consoles currently available on the market:

Nintendo Switch: The Nintendo Switch debuted on the market in March 2017[7] and has become a global phenomenon. It is one of the most popular gaming systems on the market. The Switch is unique in that it can function as either a console system, allowing players to access the system on their television, or it can be a mobile gaming system, which lets users travel with the system and continue their gaming experience outside the home. The Nintendo Switch also allows users to join a larger gaming community through Nintendo Online, letting players form communities and groups to play and work through various games together. The console comes with one "Joy-con," which is the Switch controller, but additional controllers can be purchased.

The Switch does have a slightly higher price point; however, in September 2019, Nintendo released a cheaper version of the Switch—the Nintendo Switch Lite.[8] This version retails for approximately $199 (USD) compared to $369.99 (USD) for the Switch and does have some of the same features as the original console. The Lite version is designed as a handheld gaming console only, it is not able to be connected to a television. Despite this, the lower price point does make it a more attractive option for libraries to include in their collection.

Xbox One: The Xbox is Microsoft's gaming console. Xbox One S was released in 2017.[9] There are a number of game title releases developed just for the Xbox, such as the *Halo* series. The Xbox One has a number of features that make it attractive to gamers, including the ability to record and stream online gameplay, the ability to integrate satellite and cable television through the console, and an enhanced guide using the voice control.

In 2020, Microsoft released a new version of the Xbox—Xbox Series X. The console allows you to play games meant for older versions of the console, which will allow gamers the chance to upgrade their system but not give up their game collection. This will certainly be a huge benefit for libraries, as you can continue to promote your collection and even collect older games with the promise that they will work on the Xbox Series X.

PlayStation: PlayStation 4 was released by Sony in 2013 and is one of the most popular gaming consoles on the market. This version of the PlayStation places a greater emphasis on the socialization of gamers through online communities and remote play as well as the integration of other systems. The system allows players to play off consoles using other devices, such as the PlayStation Vita.

The PlayStation 4 is one of the more expensive gaming console options. Sony released a PlayStation 4 Slim, which is a smaller version of the console, as well as a more advanced version, the PlayStation 4

Pro (has 4K-TV capabilities). Although the PlayStation has a higher price point, it is regarded as a popular addition to a collection and will certainly have a lot of traction with your patrons. The PlayStation can come with various levels of storage space (500 GB or 1 TB), which is appealing to libraries looking to include digital download-able content. Keep in mind, if you're technically savvy, you can also swap out the hard drive for a larger one.

Similar to Microsoft, Sony released a new PlayStation 5 in 2020. The PlayStation 5 features backward compatibility, allowing gamers to make use of their game collection from older consoles. Like the PlayStation 4, the PlayStation 5 also includes VR capability and cloud gaming.

Other Consoles

You may want to consider including older versions of the PlayStation or Xbox, as both have a vast catalog of games that are still very popular with gamers and can easily be purchased secondhand at relatively inexpensive prices. Another good option is the still popular Nintendo Wii and Wii U, which can also be purchased secondhand and will support a greater number of games than the Switch.

Another great option to consider is the recently released classic versions of the Nintendo Entertainment Systems (NES) and Super Nintendo Entertainment System (SNES). These are self-contained devices that have all the games from these consoles preloaded onto the system. Depending on the kind of library you are working in, these will have definite appeal to all different demographics. In public libraries, both younger and older patrons will be interested in these, while in an academic setting, students in game design, game studies, or media studies may find these useful for their projects. These consoles are also excellent for programming purposes, for example, hosting retro gaming nights or a "history of video games" event. Because of the retro feel of these consoles, they are easily a major draw for users. See the Retro Gaming Systems section in this chapter for more information about retro games.

Having a variety of consoles available lets you offer several unique gaming options to patrons by allowing you to suggest something new from a different console that has similar features to what they have already been playing. Offering a variety of consoles in your library can entice a larger number of patrons and new users' groups through different library programming (e.g., Retro Games Night or a Battle of the Consoles event).

Patron Gaming Policies and Other Considerations

Once you have decided on which consoles to include in your collection, you will need to consider various loan policy elements:

- Will you allow patrons to take consoles home or will these be in library use only?

- How long should the loan period be?

- What kind of programming will you develop around these consoles?

- Will you provide additional peripherals, such as secondary controllers for multiplayer games or special controllers for specific games (e.g., the Wii Tennis Racket).

Additional factors to consider might include: when consoles are returned, will you be checking their functionality, which can be labor intensive, and will you be wiping previous player data, which again can be labor intensive.

Beyond loaning policies, you will need to consider such factors as late fees and replacement fees (for both the system and peripherals such as controllers and cables). You'll need to determine the structure of such fees—will it be replacement plus labor or will it be just the cost of replacing the items. While these kinds of policies might seem more administrative, having them in place can enable you to work with patrons on making sure they get the best gaming experience through the library. Perhaps they want to take a console home, having a strong policy statement around gaming consoles will make sure they understand what they can and can't do with that console, for example, you don't offer secondary controllers, so they know they won't be playing any multiplayer games. Deciding on the different policies around consoles can help you to better work with patrons when they are looking for gaming recommendations from the collection. It can also be important to consider that different global regions will have different preferences for consoles, so you may want to do a survey or informal ask during a gamers' advisory interview to help best accommodate patron needs.

Retro Gaming Systems

Retro gaming is a fast-rising market within the gaming community, as nostalgia has become a major player in popular culture. People who grew up in the 1980s and 1990s want to go back and play the games they "cut their teeth on," and this is evident with the rise of production of retro gaming systems. Libraries can utilize these retro gaming systems and market to a user base that is traditionally difficult to bring into the library.

Retro gaming systems with preloaded games have been around for several years, prior to the explosion of the officially licensed Nintendo Classic in 2016. They tend to look like mini versions of the original and have full-sized, wired controllers rather than the more common Bluetooth controllers that most modern gamers are used to. Sega has been releasing classic versions of their software for some time—the most recent being the Sega Genesis Classic Game Collection. To date, five collections of games—referred to as volumes by the publisher—have been released across non-Sega platforms including PlayStation and Nintendo.

In relation to retro gaming, one important bit of technology you may need to know about is a video game console emulator. This is a type of emulator that allows a computing device, such as a laptop or even the mini-consoles themselves, to emulate a particular video game console's software so that you can play the games without the original hardware. Emulation also allows for modification of gameplay, including accessing content previously only available using original hardware and also making changes to existing games (e.g., adding additional levels, cheat codes, or the ability to speed run). In order to protect their licensed content, major video game companies have decided to release their own emulated gaming systems, encouraging users to purchase their games through them rather than acquiring the games through other means (e.g., for free). Depending on the particular game and licensing, some emulators are breaking copyright law depending on the country's current legislation. This is not the case for all emulators, for example, the Internet Archive has released 14,000 of MS DOS and CD-ROM games for free on their website as these games are no longer under copyright. This can be a great free resource to keep in mind so your patrons can access free nostalgic content.[10]

Because of the popularity of these retro gaming systems, libraries will want to consider looking into purchasing them, especially for programming purposes. We recently hosted a large library event, which featured the Nintendo Classic and Super Nintendo Classic— together these were used by 80% of participants. Table 8.3 includes some of the more popular retro gaming consoles released in the last five years that your library may be interested in purchasing to have available for your patrons.

There are also ways to access retro games using modern game consoles that you may already have. Nintendo Switch has made some of the games available on Nintendo Classic and Super Nintendo Classic available for free download on the Nintendo Store. They also re-release older games (e.g., *Street Fighter*) for people to play on their modern system. Sega is one of the only video game companies to make their retro game catalog available across multiple platforms (e.g., Xbox, PlayStation, and Nintendo), which is great for users, but ended up hurting the sales of their retro gaming system as users already had readily available access to the content.

Game developers are also seeing the rise in interest for retro games so they are creating new content that emulates the style and feel of older games. The game *Tanglewood* was created in 2016 and is one of the first games to be made for Sega Mega Drive and Genesis in nearly two decades. The game was part of a Kickstarter campaign and has gone on to have a fairly successful run.[11] The lead designer for *Tanglewood*, Matt Philips, now advocates for retro game development and has given workshops at several universities. Most of these retro releases on older hardware are called "homebrew" games, as they are unlicensed titles that are limited releases on very specific, discontinued hardware.[12] This area of gaming may continue to grow, so it is good to be aware of it, but it is a difficult area to collect in.

Additionally, current systems are seeing a spike in releases that mimic the aesthetic of retro gaming. These games are commonly referred to as "Pixel Art" games because they use the art aesthetic common to older games that had pixel art graphics due to technological constraints. These games are not only popular with older gamers who played pixel art games when they were younger, but with younger gamers as the current technology allows these games to be far more sophisticated than they were in the 1980s and

Table 8.3: Popular Retro Gaming Consoles

Nintendo Classic	Released in 2016 and re-released in 2018, this console comes preloaded with 30 original Nintendo games and was the first retro console system officially released by Nintendo. The list of 30 games varies slightly between the Japanese version and the version sold in the rest of the world. Nintendo kept the cost low (under $100) and maintained two wired controllers to keep the feel of the old system; reviewers and fans have not received this decision well and have asked for Bluetooth controllers. Due to its overwhelming popularity (the first release sold out almost immediately), Nintendo decided to release the Super Nintendo Classic shortly after.
Super Nintendo Classic	Released in 2017, this Super Nintendo Classic (or SNES Classic) comes with 21 preloaded games. Similar to the Nintendo Classic, the system comes with two wired controllers, but changes were made to make the cords longer (5 feet rather than 3 feet in the Nintendo Classic). Also, similar to the Nintendo Classic, the preloaded games vary between the Japanese version and the one released in the rest of the world and had a reasonable price point of around $100.
PlayStation Classic	Released in 2018, likely after seeing the success of Nintendo's release of retro versions of their old consoles, Sony decided to follow suit and released the PlayStation Classic on the 24th anniversary of the release of the original. The PlayStation Classic has 20 preloaded games, wired controllers, and was priced at around $100. The 20 preloaded games varies between the Japanese version and the one released in the rest of the world
Sega Genesis Classic Game Console	Released in 2019, Sega's classic console has 42 games preloaded onto it, wired controllers, and is one of the cheaper retro consoles at around $80. Sega was the primary competitor of the Super Nintendo Entertainment System (SNES) in the 1990s.
Atari Flashback 8 Gold	Originally released in 2004, the first Flashback had only 20 titles preloaded onto it. Atari is no stranger to re-releasing its content and its newest retro console is the Atari Flashback 8 Gold. The Flashback 8 has 120 preloaded games, wired controllers, and sells for around $60. Atari is able to have a richer catalogue given the much smaller file size for each of the games, as it is an older technology.

1990s—so they don't notice the pixel art. The 2018 release of the dungeon crawler game *Moonlighter* is an example of this retro push in gaming.

Starting Collection and Reference Guide: Video Games

As with board games, it is essential to offer a wide selection of video games that will appeal to a broad audience and appeal to different player motivations. Due to the nearly constant release schedule of digital games, you may want to routinely update your collection, depending on the flexibility of your budget. This section provides some key suggestions for developing a well-rounded video game collection that will appeal to a broad audience and help you guide patrons in finding games depending on their needs, wants, and interests. Again, this is not an exhaustive catalog of games, but it does capture the essential titles in many of the various digital-game genres.

The "similar games" field is rather subjective, as different players will enjoy different features in a game. You will want to consider a number of questions as you begin making recommendations: Do they enjoy the theme? Can they play this game online with friends or different communities (cooperative play)? Do they like different small quests to complete along with the overall narrative quest? The games that are suggested are similar in either theme, gameplay mechanics, or user behavior—but it is best to do a proper reference interview with your users to get an understanding as to what they like or are interested in playing.

Wherever possible, we have tried to use the ratings given to games by the ESRB. Video games tend to get released as a series, the entries here will mostly reflect the most recent release in those series but will not include an entry for each game in a series. However, for series such as the Lego game catalog, we have discussed this as a series not as individual games. Video games are an ever-expanding market, so it is impossible to include a full and comprehensive list of each game in a series.

A side note here, it can be useful when building your video game collection to realize that some games are available on certain systems for free. A good example of this is *Apex Legends* (see entry). This game is available for free online play on PlayStation 4 and Xbox One and is considered comparable to games like *Overwatch* or *Fortnite*. Although it can be difficult to manage and preserve downloaded content for consoles, these kinds of games are an easy way for users and patrons to experience a wide range of digital games on numerous platforms as well as help your library increase their digital game collection with little cost upfront.

Game Title: *Animal Crossing: New Horizons* (2020)
Genre: Social simulation
Format: Digital
Available Platforms: Nintendo Switch
Age: E
Warnings: Comic Mischief
User behavior type: Achiever, Explorer, Socializer
Description: In this latest entry in the *Animal Crossings* series, players assume the role of a character who inhabits a deserted island that develops into a community of anthropomorphic animals.
Gameplay: This social simulation—open ended—game has players developing a community of animals on a deserted island. Players can decorate and enhance their island using different features and elements available throughout the game as well as customize the appearance of their main character. This includes skin color, gender,

and so on. Other notable gameplay features of this game include the introduction of a new in-game currency earned by completing various tasks, the ability to invite animals to live on their island, and the option to choose or influence where the animal constructs its home. Finally, a unique feature has the game's weather adjust according to the seasons of the Northern or Southern Hemisphere, depending on the player's real-world location.

Series (Y or N): Yes

Other titles in the series: *Animal Crossing* (2001), *Animal Crossing: Wild World* (2005), *Animal Crossing: City Folk* (2008), *Animal Crossing: New Leaf* (2012)

Similar games: The *Sims* series

Game Title: *Apex Legends* (2019)

Genre: Battle royale; first-person shooter

Format: Digital

Available Platforms: PlayStation 4, Xbox One, on Steam in 2020

Age: T

Warnings: Blood and Violence

User behavior type: Killer, Achiever

Description: This free-to-play battle royale game involves having characters arrive on an island, in teams of twenty, and having to go through various forms of combat to stay alive. Fuses traditional elements of battle royale with more narrative-based storytelling.

Gameplay: The game is played in terms of rounds, where approximately sixty players, in squads of three, skydive onto an island. One player controls where the squad lands. The teams scavenge for weapons and equipment in order to fight other players, during which time the play area is gradually constricted in size until only one squad remains and wins the match.

Series (Y or N): No

Other titles in the series: n/a

Similar games: *Fortnite* (2017)

Game Title: *Ashen* (2018)

Genre: Action; role-playing

Format: Digital

Available Platforms: PlayStation 4, Xbox One, Nintendo Switch, Steam

Age: M

Warnings: n/a

User behavior type: Explorer, Killer

Description: This is an open-world concept where the main character is searching for a place to consider as home.

Gameplay: Taking a lot of inspiration from the *Dark Souls* games, *Ashen* is a third-person perspective role-playing game where players explore an open-world concept and encounter various enemies, engaging in combat and collecting artefacts.

Series (Y or N): No
Other titles in the series: n/a
Similar games: *Underworld Ascendant* (2018)

Game Title: *Assassin's Creed: Odyssey* (2019)
Genre: Action role-playing; stealth
Format: Digital
Available Platforms: PlayStation 4, Xbox One, Google Stadia, Steam
Age: M17+
Warnings: Blood and Gore, Intense Violence, Sexual Themes, Strong Language
User behavior type: Killer, Achiever, with some Explorer aspects
Description: The most recent entry of the *Assassin's Creed* series takes place in the year 431 BC, with the backdrop of a fictional history of the Peloponnesian War between Athens and Sparta. As part of the story, players control a male or female mercenary who fights for both sides as they attempt to unite their family. The game is often praised for its world building and character development, which suggest it is good for those players who are looking for larger levels of plot in the game.
Gameplay: *Assassin's Creed Odyssey* places greater emphasis on role-playing elements than previous games in the series. The game contains dialogue options, branching quests, and multiple endings. Players are able to choose between siblings Alexios and Kassandra for the main character. The game uses a skill tree system that allows the player to unlock new abilities throughout the game.
Note: *Assassin's Creed Odyssey* includes some downloadable content. In particular, two chapters were released to continue the narrative of the main story: Legacy of the First Blade and The Fate of Atlantis.
Series (Y or N): Yes
Other titles in the series: *Assassin's Creed* (2007), *Assassin's Creed II* (2009), *Assassin's Creed Brotherhood* (2010), *Assassin's Creed Revelations* (2011), *Assassin's Creed III* (2012), *Assassin's Creed IV: Blackflag* (2013), *Assassin's Creed Rogue* (2014), *Assassin's Creed Unity* (2014), *Assassin's Creed Syndicate* (2015), *Assassin's Creed Origins* (2017)
Similar games: *Prince of Persia: The Forgotten Sands* (2010), *Hitman* (2016), *Far Cry* (2004)

Game Title: *Assassin's Creed Origins* (2017)
Genre: Action-adventure; stealth; historical fiction
Format: Digital
Available Platforms: PlayStation 4, Xbox One, Steam, Google Stadia
Age: M17+
Warnings: Violent with graphic content
User behavior type: Killer, Achiever, with some Explorer aspects[13]
Description: The game is set in Egypt, near the end of the Ptolemaic era (47 BC) and explores the fictional history of events during that

era. In particular, it explores the conflict between the Brotherhood of Assassins and The Order of the Ancient.

Gameplay: 3D person perspective, completing quests, acquiring new skills, earning experience points, overarching storylike narratives, free-roam of open-world environment, arena-based combat system, cumulative boss fight, unlocking of additional weapons and equipment, online and offline play, discovery tool to be released to create a sandbox mode with no objectives

Series (Y or N): Yes

Other titles in the series: *Assassin's Creed* (2007), *Assassin's Creed II* (2009), *Assassin's Creed Brotherhood* (2010), *Assassin's Creed Revelations* (2011), *Assassin's Creed III* (2012), *Assassin's Creed IV: Blackflag* (2013), *Assassin's Creed Rogue* (2014), *Assassin's Creed Unity* (2014), *Assassin's Creed Syndicate* (2015)

Similar games: *Prince of Persia: The Forgotten Sands* (2010), *Hitman* (2016), *Far Cry* (2004)

Game Title: *Batman: Arkham* (2009–2019)
Genre: Action; action-adventure; beat 'em up; stealth
Format: Digital
Available Platforms: Xbox, PlayStation 3, PlayStation 4, Wii U, Steam
Age: T
Warnings: n/a
User behavior type: Explorer, Killer, Achiever
Description: Ongoing series where players play as Batman, who battles against various villains in either an isolated location (Arkham Asylum) or a wider universe (Gotham). The game is an open-world concept, allowing players to explore and fight using combat moves, various weapons, and stealth. Each game focuses on at least one major villain, who has waged an assault against the whole city of Gotham, but incorporates all major Batman villains in some capacity.

Gameplay: Single player; open world. Although there is a general plot in the game, players are able to explore the open-world concept of the game by interacting with the environment and other characters (both friendlies and villains) using a variety of gadgets and tools available to Batman (including grappling guns, batarangs, Detective vision, and others). Players can also seamlessly switch between controlling Batman and his allies, Robin, Nightwing, and Catwoman. Due to the open-world concept of the game, Batman also engages in various moments of investigation—murders and other crimes— eventually leading him to the game's conclusion.

Series (Y or N): Yes

Other titles in the series: *Batman: Arkham Asylum* (2009), *Batman: Arkham City* (2011), *Batman: Arkham Origins* (2013), *Batman: Arkham Origins Blackgate* (2013), *Batman: Arkham Knight* (2015), *Batman: Arkham VR* (2016)

Similar games: *Spiderman* (2018), *Marvel Alliance: Black Order* (2019)

Game Title: *Bloodborne* (2015)

Genre: Action role-playing

Format: Digital

Available Platforms: PlayStation 4

Age: M17+

Warnings: Blood and Gore, Violence

User behavior type: Killer

Description: Follows the character, a Hunter, through a Victorian era–inspired Gothic city that has grown decrepit and fallen into ruin. Inhabitants of this world have been afflicted with a disease. The purpose of the game is to find the cause of the plague, while solving mysteries and fighting monsters.

Gameplay: This is a third-person perspective game where the players make their way through different locations, fighting enemies and collecting items that have a variety of uses—including opening shortcuts and helping the player advance through the story. The players create their character—deciding on physical attributes of the character and the class of the character. The players also engage in fast-paced and offensive combat to fight off enemies and interact with different elements of the game.

Series (Y or N): No

Other titles in the series: n/a

Similar games: *Demon's Souls* (2009), *Dark Souls* (2011), *Dark Souls: Artorias of the Abyss* (2012), *Dark Souls II* (2014), *Dark Souls III* (2016), *Dark Souls: Remastered* (2018)

Game Title: *Call of Cthulhu* (2018)

Genre: Role-playing; survival horror

Format: Digital

Available Platforms: PlayStation 4, Nintendo Switch, Xbox One, Steam

Age: M17+

Warnings: Blood and Gore, Intense Violence, Strong Language, Use of Alcohol

User behavior type: Achiever, Killer

Description: This open-world game is based on the stories of H. P. Lovecraft, in particular, Lovecraft's short story of the same name. The investigation game features themes of psychological and supernatural horror, as well as investigation elements.

Gameplay: This first-person perspective game has players controlling a private investigator as he searches for clues to solve a supernatural murder. Players must interact with a variety of characters and engage in combat against humans and Lovecraftian creatures.

Series (Y or N): No

Other titles in the series: n/a

Similar games: *The Sinking City* (2019)

Game Title: *Call of Duty*

Genre: First-person shooter

Format: Digital

Available Platforms: Microsoft Windows, OSX, Nintendo DS, Nintendo GameCube, PlayStation 2–PlayStation 4, Wii, Wii U, Xbox, Xbox 360, Xbox One, Steam

Age: M17+

Warnings: Blood and Gore, Drug Reference, Intense Violence, Strong Language

User behavior type: Killer, Achiever

Description: Originally designed as a World War II shooter game, the game has evolved into a first-person shooter in multiple different settings. General concept of the game is similar across all titles—player assumes the identity of a soldier (often an infantryman) and works through a series of objectives to accomplish a mission. Primary objective is to kill enemy targets.

Gameplay: First-person shooter with the player being in control of various firearms that are accurate for the gameplay setting

Series (Y or N): Yes

Other titles in the series: World War II games: *Call of Duty* (2003), *Call of Duty 2* (2005), *Call of Duty 3* (2006), *Call of Duty: WWII* (2017), Modern Warfare story arc: *Call of Duty 4: Modern Warfare* (2007), *Call of Duty: Modern Warfare 2* (2009), Black Ops story arc: *Call of Duty: World at War* (2008), *Call of Duty: Black Ops* (2010), *Call of Duty: Black Ops II* (2012), *Call of Duty: Black Ops III* (2015), *Call of Duty: Black Ops 4* (2018)

Similar games: *DOOM* (1993–2017), *TitanFall 2* (2016)

Game Title: *Cities: Skylines* (2015)

Genre: City-building; construction and management simulation

Format: Digital

Available Platforms: Xbox One, PlayStation 4, Nintendo Switch, also available on Steam

Age: E

Warnings: None

User behavior type: Achiever

Description: *Cities: Skylines* is a single-player, open-ended, city-building simulation where players engage in urban planning by controlling various elements of urban design, such as zoning, road placement, taxation, public services, and public transportation.

Gameplay: Players initially begin the game with a plot of land along with an interchange exit from a nearby highway and a starting amount of in-game money. The player must add roads and residential, industrial, and commercial zones and basic services like power, water, and sewage to encourage residents to move in and supply them with jobs. Throughout the game, the player unlocks new city improvements (schools, fire and police stations, health care facilities, tax and governing edicts, etc.).

Series (Y or N): No
Other titles in the series: n/a
Similar games: *Animal Crossing* series, *Tropico 6* (2019)

Game Title: *Crash Bandicoot N. Sane Trilogy* (2018)
Genre: Platform
Format: Digital
Available Platforms: PlayStation 4, Xbox One, Nintendo Switch, Steam
Age: E10+
Warnings: Cartoon Violence, Comic Mischief
User behavior type: Achiever
Description: A compilation of the remastered version of the first three games in the *Crash Bandicoot* series: *Crash Bandicoot*, *Cortex Strikes Back*, and *Warped*. These games were all developed and released for the PlayStation during the 1990s. Main narrative of the series involves, Crash Bandicoot traversing various levels in order to stop Doctor Neo Cortex from taking over the world.
Gameplay: Like many platform games, these games feature Crash Bandicoot moving from level to level dealing with different enemies and encountering various bosses using a variety of different techniques, such as spinning and jumping techniques to defeat enemies, smash crates, and collect items such as Wumpa Fruits, extra lives, and protective Aku Aku masks.
Series (Y or N): Yes
Other titles in the series: *Crash Bandicoot* (1996), *Cortex Strikes Back* (1997), *Warped* (1998), *Crash Team Racing* (1999), *Crash Bash* (2000), *Wrath of Cortex* (2001), *The Huge Adventure* (2002), *N-Tranced* (2003), *Crash Nitro Kart* (2003), *Purple: Ripto's Rampage* (2004), *Twinsanity* (2004), *Crash Tag Team Racing* (2005), *Crash Boom Bang!* (2006), *Crash of the Titans* (2007), *Mind over Mutant* (2007), *Nitro Kart 3D* (2008), *Mutant Island* (2009), *Nitro Kart 2* (2010), *Crash Team Racing Nitro-Fueled* (2019)
Similar games: *Sonic the Hedgehog* series

Game Title: *The Dark Pictures Anthology: Man of Medan* (2019)
Genre: Interactive drama; survival horror
Format: Digital
Available Platforms: PlayStation 4, Xbox One, Steam
Age: M17+
Warnings: Blood, Drug Reference, Intense Violence, Strong Language, Suggestive Themes
User behavior type: Explorer, Killer
Description: The game is structured as an unfinished story belonging to The Curator, who needs the player's help in completing the story. As the player makes different decisions throughout the game, the outcome of the story and characters is altered. The story itself is focused on a group of characters who are embarking on an underwater diving

expedition, who found themselves kidnapped and trapped on a ghost ship.

Gameplay: The game is played from a third-person perspective where players take control of five different characters, who must make decisions based on their "heart" or "heads." As characters make different choices, the game adapts and leads to one of the multiple endings.

Series (Y or N): No

Other titles in the series: n/a

Similar games: *Until Dawn* (2015), *The Sinking City* (2019)

Game Title: *Dark Souls* (2011)

Genre: Action role-playing

Format: Digital

Available Platforms: PlayStation 4, Nintendo Switch, Xbox One, Steam

Age: M17+

Warnings: Blood and Gore, Partial Nudity, Violence

User behavior type: Achiever, Killer

Description: Often considered one of the greatest video games of all time, *Dark Souls* is an open-world role-playing game where the player controls the main character, a cursed undead, locked away in an undead asylum, trapped in a world where light and dark is trapped in a cycle of dark and light. The main purpose of the game is to try to balance the two.

Gameplay: This third-person action role-playing game, which takes place in a large and continuous open-world environment, involves a great deal of exploration. Players must proceed with caution throughout the games, learning from past mistakes, or finding alternative areas to explore. A central element to the gameplay is bonfires, which are scattered throughout the world and serve as checkpoints for each level. Players can also level up and perform other functions, such as attuning magic and repairing and upgrading equipment. The other major element of the Dark Souls is combat—players must continually develop and advance their combat skills throughout the game.

Note: There is a considerable amount of downloadable content available to upgrade the game.

Series (Y or N): Yes

Other titles in the series: *Demon's Souls* (2009), *Dark Souls* (2011), *Dark Souls: Artorias of the Abyss* (2012), *Dark Souls II* (2014), *Dark Souls II: The Lost Crowns* (2014), *Dark Souls II: Scholar of the First Sin* (2015), *Dark Souls III* (2016), *Dark Souls III: Ashes of Ariandel* (2016), *Dark Souls III: The Ringed City* (2017), *Dark Souls: Remastered* (2018)

Similar games: *Star Wars: Jedi Fallen Order* (2019)

Game Title: *Death Standing* (2019)

Genre: Action

Format: Digital
Available Platforms: PlayStation 4
Age: M
Warnings: Blood, Intense Violence, Partial Nudity, and Strong Language
User behavior type: Explorer, Achiever, and partially Killer
Description: This game was one of the most anticipated games of 2019 and has received critical acclaim, including being nominated for and winning multiple gaming awards. The game is set in an apocalyptic United States, where a cataclysmic event known as the "Death Stranding" caused "Beached Things" ("BTs") to begin roaming the Earth. The focus of the game is on freelance porter Sam Porter Bridges—played by *The Walking Dead*'s Norman Reedus—who transports goods between existing colonies, known as Knot Cities. The game has an open-world concept, but players can explore this as they navigate Sam's various deliveries, encounters with BTs, and other natural and supernatural phenomena throughout the game.
Gameplay: To explore the open-world concept of the game, the player controls Sam Bridges, a porter for a company known as Bridges. The player is tasked with delivering supply cargo to various isolated cities, as well as isolated researchers and survivalists, while also connecting them to a communications system known as the Chiral Network. The player is evaluated by the company and recipients based on performance, including whether the cargo was delivered and if it is intact among other factors. These merits allow the players to level up their statistics (stability and weight capacity) and increase their standing with individual locations and characters. Players' abilities to expand the coverage of the Chiral Network allow them access to maps of areas and use of blueprints to produce consumable items and structures with the Portable Chiral Constructor, including ropes, bridges, and power generators used for charging battery-powered equipment. There is a combat element to the game as well, where the player encounters BTs and must prevent them from capturing or stealing the player's cargo.
Note: The game features quite a bit of online content that enhances the game and allows the player to advance, specifically around the social networking elements of the game.
Series (Y or N): No
Other titles in the series: n/a
Similar games: *The Last of Us* (2013)

Game Title: *Diablo* (series)
Genre: Action; role-playing; hack and slash
Format: Digital
Available Platforms: Microsoft Windows, OSX, PlayStation 3, PlayStation 4, Xbox 360, Xbox One, Nintendo Switch
Age: M17+
Warnings: Blood and Gore, Violence

User behavior type: Killer, Achiever

Description: Players are tasked with defeating Diablo—the Lord of Terror—by journeying to Hell and engaging with different challenges and combat scenarios. Players select their desired character type: Barbarian, Crusader, Demon Hunter, Monk, Necromancer, Witch Doctor, or Wizard.

Gameplay: single-player; multiplayer

Series (Y or N): Yes

Other titles in the series: *Diablo* (1996–1998), *Diablo II* (2000), *Diablo III* (2012), *Diablo III: Rise of the Necromancer* (2014), *Diablo III: The Eternal Collection* (2018)

Similar games: *Doom* (2017)

Game Title: *Donkey Kong Country: Tropical Freeze* (2014–2017)

Genre: Platform

Format: Digital

Available Platforms: Wii U, Nintendo Switch

Age: E

Warnings: Mild Cartoon Violence

User behavior type: Achiever

Description: This is the latest release in the popular *Donkey Kong Country* series, an offshoot from the original *Donkey Kong* series. It is a side-scrolling platform game where Donkey Kong and his friends travel through 10 different islands to defeat "the Snowmads," villains who have taken their home hostage.

Gameplay: Players control Donkey Kong, who is assisted by a companion who can either provide additional abilities or can be controlled by another player. Controls allow players to pick up items and stunned enemies to combat other enemies.

Series (Y or N): Yes

Other titles in the series: *Donkey Kong* has been around since 1981 and has remained one of the most popular video game titles. There have been releases for each Nintendo console. However, some of the more recent titles, available on Wii and Switch, include: *Donkey Kong Barrel Blast* (2007) and *Donkey Kong Country Returns* (2010).

Similar games: *Super Mario* games

Game Title: *Doom* (series)

Genre: First-person shooter

Format: Digital

Available Platforms: Xbox, Xbox 360, Xbox One, Nintendo Switch, PlayStation 4, Steam

Age: M

Warnings: Blood and Gore, Intense Violence, Strong Language

User behavior type: Achiever, Killer

Description: The overall series of *Doom* focuses on an unnamed Marine who is part of the Union Aerospace Corporation, the player must fight hordes of monsters and zombies.

Gameplay: In the latest installment of the game, *Doom* (2016), players engage in first-person combat against various monsters in a research facility on Mars. The game's combat is known as "push forward combat," which discourages the players from taking cover or resting. Players collect health and tools to advance their killing abilities. Game features a new function—Glory Kills—which allows players to commit execution-style kills against various enemies.

Series (Y or N): Yes

Other titles in the series: *Doom* (original release 1993, most recent re-release 2019), *Doom II* (original release 1994, re-release 2019), *Doom 3* (original release 2004, re-release 2019), *Doom 3: Resurrection of Evil* (2005), *Doom 3: BFG Edition* (2012, 2019), *Doom* (2016 and 2017), *Doom Eternal* (2020)

Similar games: *Halo Wars* (2017), *Diablo* series

Game Title: *Dragon Age: Inquisition* (2014)

Genre: Action role-playing

Format: Digital

Available Platforms: PlayStation 3, PlayStation 4, Xbox 360, Xbox One

Age: M17+

Warnings: Blood, Intense Violence, Nudity, Sexual Content, Strong Language

User behavior type: Achiever, Killer

Description: The plot of *Dragon Age: Inquisition* centers on the main character, known as the Inquisitor, as they journey to settle unrest in a fictional world, specifically to close a mysterious tear in the sky, called the Breach. The Breach unleashes demons, which the Inquisitor engages in combat with.

Gameplay: Players control the main character and any companions they meet in their journey. The game is played as a third-person perspective and gameplay includes defeating enemies with swords and magic, completing side quests, interacting with non-playable characters, and progress through the main story.

Series (Y or N): Yes

Other titles in the series: *Dragon Age: Origins* (2009), *Dragon Age II* (2011), *Dragon Age: The Dead Wolf Rises* (upcoming game, date TBA)

Similar games: *The Elder Scrolls* series, *GreedFall* (2019), *The Witcher* series

Game Title: *Elder Scrolls: Blades* (2019)

Genre: Action role-playing

Format: Digital

Available Platforms: Microsoft Windows, Xbox, Xbox One, Xbox 360, PlayStation 3, PlayStation 4, Nintendo Switch, Steam

Age: M

Warnings: Blood and Gore, Sexual Themes, Use of Alcohol, Violence

User behavior type: Achiever, Killer

Description: *Elder Scrolls* is primarily an open-world fantasy role-playing game with a focus on free-form gameplay. Games in the series have a mix between premedieval environments and high fantasy elements including magic and travel between parallel worlds.

Gameplay: Each *Elder Scrolls* game has different gameplay, but much of the overall structure is similar—players must complete tasks and demonstrate skills by either killing monsters and gaining experience points or showing off skill development and character advancement. Skill advancement helps players level up throughout the game.

Series (Y or N): Yes

Other titles in the series: *The Elder Scrolls: Arena* (1994), *The Elder Scrolls II: Daggerfall* (1996), *An Elder Scrolls Legend: Battlespire* (1997), *The Elder Scrolls III: Morrowind* (2002), *The Elder Scrolls IV: Oblivion* (2006), *The Elder Scrolls V: Skyrim* (2011), *The Elder Scrolls V: Skyrim—Special Edition* (2016), *The Elder Scrolls: Legends* (2017), *The Elder Scrolls: Skyrim VR* (2017)

Similar games: *The Legend of Zelda: Breath of the Wild* (2017)

Game Title: *Fallout* (1997–2018)

Genre: Action; role-playing

Format: Digital

Available Platforms: Windows, Mac OS and OSX, PlayStation 2, PlayStation 3, PlayStation 4, Xbox, Xbox 360, Xbox One, Nintendo Switch, Steam, as well as mobile platforms

Age: T

Warnings: n/a

User behavior type: Achiever

Description: *Fallout* is a series of games that take place in a post-apocalyptic landscape where players interact with the landscape and use technology to survive. Game relies on a post–World War II/1950s aesthetic of technological hope and nuclear paranoia. Each game in the series builds on this concept—with players saving remnants of humanity. It also includes spin-off board games.

Gameplay: First-person game where the player must complete tasks to earn rewards. The players' actions and decisions dictate the game's story and eventual outcome. As players encounter enemies, they engage in turn-based combat to advance the game's narrative.

Series (Y or N): Yes

Other titles in the series: *Fallout 1* (1997), *Fallout 2* (1998), *Fallout 3* (2008), *Fallout 4* (2015)

Similar games: *Skyrim* (2011)

Game Title: *FIFA* series (1994 through 2020)

Genre: Sports; simulation

Format: Digital

Available Platforms: PlayStation, PlayStation 2, PlayStation 3, PlayStation 4, PlayStation Portable, PlayStation Vita, Nintendo DS,

Nintendo 3DS, Wii, Wii U, Nintendo Switch, Microsoft Windows, Xbox 360, Xbox, Xbox One, various mobile platforms

Age: E

Warnings: n/a

User behavior type: Achiever

Description: Sport simulation game based on the FIFA world soccer league—released annually since the 1990s. Released in 18 languages and 51 countries.

Gameplay: Simulation—players play as individual soccer personalities on a variety of worldwide teams.

Series (Y or N): Yes

Other titles in the series: 1990s: *FIFA International Soccer, FIFA 95, FIFA 96, FIFA 97, FIFA: Road to World Cup 98, FIFA 99*; 2000s: *FIFA 2000, FIFA 2001, FIFA Football 2002, FIFA Football 2003, FIFA Football 2004, FIFA Football 2005, FIFA 06, FIFA 07, FIFA 08, FIFA 09*; 2010s: *FIFA 10, FIFA 11, FIFA 12, FIFA 13, FIFA 14, FIFA 15, FIFA 16, FIFA 17, FIFA Mobile, FIFA 18, FIFA 19, FIFA 20*

Similar games: *Club Soccer Director* (2020), *Score! Hero!* (2015)

Game Title: *Final Fantasy XV* (2016 and 2018)

Genre: Role-playing

Format: Digital

Available Platforms: Microsoft Windows Phone, Nintendo DS and 3DS, Nintendo Switch, PlayStation 4, Xbox One, Xbox 360, Steam, and multiple mobile platforms

Age: Most entries in the series are for teens and older

Warnings: T

User behavior type: Achiever, Explorer

Description: All entries of the series have a stand-alone story but generally revolve around a group of heroes who have to battle a great evil that is threatening their home. The games usually also include elements where the characters explore internal and external struggles between themselves. Titles in the main *Final Fantasy* series often do not include subtitles, instead numbering 1 through 15.

Gameplay: *Final Fantasy* games are often seen as an interactive novel where players must make choices that will allow them to explore new areas of the game environment. As players advance through the environment, they must either travel or engage in a variety of battle sequences.

Series (Y or N): Yes

Other titles in the series: (released between 1987 and 2019): *Final Fantasy, Final Fantasy I, Final Fantasy II, Final Fantasy III, Final Fantasy IV, Final Fantasy V, Final Fantasy VI, Final Fantasy VII, Final Fantasy VIII, Final Fantasy IX, Final Fantasy X, Final Fantasy XI, Final Fantasy XII,* Final Fantasy XIII, *Final Fantasy XIV, Final Fantasy XV*

Similar games: *Dragon Quest XI* (2019), *Secret of Mana* (1993), *The Last Remnant* (2008)

Game Title: *Fortnite* (2017)

Genre: Survival; battle royale; sandbox

Format: Digital (online only)

Available Platforms: PlayStation 4, Xbox

Age: T

Warnings: Violence

User behavior type: Explorer, Killer

Description: *Fortnite* is an online video game with three distinct game mode versions that otherwise share the same general gameplay and game engine.

Gameplay: While each of the three games share similar characteristics in gameplay and game engine, the three modes do have specific elements that make them unique. *Fortnite: Save the World* is a cooperative shooter-survival game (up to four players) to fight off zombie-like creatures and defend objects with fortifications they can build. *Fortnite Battle Royale* is a free-to-play battle royale game where up to 100 players fight to be the last person standing. And *Fortnite Creative* gives players freedom to create worlds and battle arenas.

Note: *Fortnite* is exclusively available online through various platforms and consoles, so it will not be possible to purchase a physical copy of the game; however, loading the game onto one of your PlayStations or Xboxes or gaming laptops can be beneficial, as this is a hugely popular game. In fact, *Fortnite Battle Royale* is a free-to-play game, which is appealing to library budgets and gaming patrons alike.

Series (Y or N): No

Other titles in the series: n/a

Similar games: *Minecraft* (2009), *Apex Legends* (2019)

Game Title: *Forza Horizon 4* (2018)

Genre: Racing

Format: Digital

Available Platforms: Xbox One

Age: E

Warnings: n/a

User behavior type: Achiever

Description: An open-world racing game based in a fictionalized version of Great Britain.

Gameplay: The game allows players to create their own races, as well as taking place in a synchronized shared world, with each server supporting up to 72 players. The game features a dynamic weather program to simulate different weather systems, increasing the game's difficulty level.

Series (Y or N): Yes

Other titles in the series: *Forza Motorsport* 1–7 (2005–2017), *Forza Horizon* 1–4 (2012–2018)

Similar games: *Gran Turismo Sport* (2017), *DiRT Rally 2.0* (2018)

Game Title: *Gears of War* (2005)

Genre: Third-person shooter

Format: Digital

Available Platforms: Xbox One, Xbox 360, Microsoft Windows

Age: M17+

Warnings: Blood and Gore, Intense Violence, Strong Language

User behavior type: Killer

Description: The *Gear of Wars* series centers on a conflict between humanity, an underground reptilian race (Locust Horde), and groups of mutated humans and reptiles (the Lambent and the Swarm). Players engage in battle missions to try to advance the war toward humanity's favor.

Gameplay: Third-person shooter with an emphasis on the "over the shoulder" perspective

Series (Y or N): Yes

Other titles in the series: *Gears of War* (2005), *Gears of War 2* (2008), *Gears of War 3* (2011), *Gears of War Judgement* (2013), *Gears of War 4* (2016), *Gears of War 5* (2019)

Similar games: *Call of Duty* series

Game Title: *God of War* (2018)

Genre: Action-adventure; hack and slash

Format: Digital

Available Platforms: PlayStation 4, Steam

Age: M

Warnings: Blood and Gore, Intense Violence, Strong Language

User behavior type: Killer

Description: The latest entry in the *God of War* series, which is loosely based on Nordic mythology, is set in ancient Norway in the land of Midgard. The game has two protagonists, Kratos and Alterus—the key objective is to reach the highest peak of the nine realms and spread the ashes of Kratos's second wife.

Gameplay: In this single-player, third-person perspective action-adventure game, which features an over-the-shoulder camera, players must navigate through the game's world to reach the objective. Players play as Kratos and to a limited extent Alterus. The game features combat-style gameplay and occasional puzzles that the player must solve to advance and gain advantages.

Series (Y or N): Yes

Other titles in the series: The *God of War* series is developed only for the PlayStation consoles, titles include: *God of War* (2005), *God of War II* (2007), *God of War: Betrayal* (2007), *God of War: Chains of Olympus* (2008), *God of War III* (2010), *God of War: Ghost of Sparta* (2010), *God of War: Saga* (2012), *God of War: Ascension* (2013), *God of War: Call from the Wilds* (2018)

Similar games: *Uncharted* series, *Diablo* series

Game Title: *Grand Theft Auto* series (1997–2013)

Genre: Action-adventure

Format: Digital

Available Platforms: Game Boy Advance and Color Mac OS, Microsoft Windows, Nintendo DS, PlayStation, PlayStation 2, PlayStation 3, PlayStation 4, PlayStation Portable, Xbox, Xbox 360, Xbox One, Steam

Age: M

Warnings: Extreme Violence, Sexuality, Nudity

User behavior type: Killer, Achiever

Description: Player engages in missions, while the player attempts to advance as part of the criminal underworld of the game; missions and side activities include: car-jacking, first-person shooter activities, driving, and other such activities.

Gameplay: Open world

Series (Y or N): Yes

Other titles in the series: *Grand Theft Auto* (1997), *Grand Theft Auto: London 1969* (1999), *Grand Theft Auto: London 1961* (1999), *Grand Theft Auto 2* (1999), *Grand Theft Auto III* (2001), *Grand Theft Auto: Vice City* (2002), *Grand Theft Auto: San Andreas* (2004), *Grand Theft Auto Advance* (2004), *Grand Theft Auto: Liberty City Stories* (2005), *Grand Theft Auto: Vice City Stories* (2006), *Grand Theft Auto IV* (2008), *Grand Theft Auto IV: The Lost and Damned* (2009), *Grand Theft Auto: Chinatown Wars* (2009), *Grand Theft Auto: The Ballad of Gay Tony* (2009), *Grand Theft Auto V* (2013)

Similar games: *Watch Dogs 2* (2016), *Saints Row IV* (2013), *Sleepy Dogs* (2012)—all are open-world concepts that deal with some aspects of criminal lifestyles and protagonists pushing against that lifestyle

Game Title: *Halo Wars 2* (2017)

Genre: First-person shooter

Format: Digital

Available Platforms: Xbox, Xbox One, Xbox 360, Microsoft Windows, OSX, Steam, various mobile platforms

Age: T

Warnings: Mild Blood, Mild Language, Violence

User behavior type: Achiever and Killer

Description: This is a science-fiction first-person shooter game that centers on an interstellar war between humans and an alien alliance known as the Covenant. Players assume the identity of human soldiers—members of a super-soldier group named Spartans and are tasked with working to help end the interstellar war.

Gameplay: Primarily first-person shooter

Series (Y or N): Yes

Other titles in the series: *Halo: Combat Evolved* (2001), *Halo 2* (2004), *Halo 3* (2007), *Halo: Reach* (2010), *Halo 4* (2012), *Halo 5: Guardians* (2015), *Halo Wars 2* (2018), *Halo: Fireteam Raven* (2018), *Halo Infinite* (2020)

Similar games: *Destiny 2* (2017), *Titanfall 2* (2016), *DOOM* (1998)

Game Title: *Happy Words* (2019)
Genre: Word games
Format: Digital
Available Platforms: Nintendo Switch, Steam, Google Play
Age: Everyone
Warnings: n/a
User behavior type: Achiever
Description: This is an online-based multiplayer board game where you are given a set of words and must use those to create new ones.
Gameplay: This game can be played with one to four players and follows a similar mechanic to Scrabble, where players must create words and attempt to collect the highest number of points.
Series (Y or N): No
Other titles in the series: n/a
Similar games: *Scrabble Online*

Game Title: *Horizon Zero Dawn* (2017)
Genre: Action-adventure; role-playing
Format: Digital
Available Platforms: PlayStation 4, Steam
Age: T
Warnings: Blood, Drug Reference, Language, Mild Sexual Themes, Violence
User behavior type: Killer, Explorer
Description: The plot for this action role-playing game follows a hunter in a world overrun by machines, who sets out to uncover her past. Although there is a direct narrative for the game, it is an open-world concept and includes a number of side quests that the players must engage in as they progress.
Gameplay: Players guide the hunter Aloy through the open world, engaging in combat with a variety of enemies and using various weapons and tools. Players must also uncover different elements and objects throughout the environment.
Series (Y or N): No
Other titles in the series: n/a
Similar games: *The Legend of Zelda: Breath of the Wild* (2017)

Game Title: *Injustice* II (2017)
Genre: Fighting
Format: Digital
Available Platforms: PlayStation 3, PlayStation 4, PlayStation Vita, Wii U, Xbox 360, Xbox One, Steam, Microsoft Windows, iOS, Mobile platforms
Age: T

Warnings: Blood, Language, Suggestive Themes, Use of Tobacco, Violence

User behavior type: Killer

Description: This is a fighting game based in the DC comics universe, where Superman has become a tyrant. The player selects which side to play and chooses various characters to engage in combat with. The objective is to knock out the opponent. It builds on and takes inspiration from games like *Mortal Kombat.*

Gameplay: single-player, multiplayer

Series (Y or N): Yes

Other titles in the series: *Injustice: Gods among Us* (2013), *Injustice 2* (2017)

Similar games: *Mortal Kombat XI* (2019), *Batman: Arkham* series

Game Title: *Inside* (2016)

Genre: Puzzle-platform; adventure

Format: Digital

Available Platforms: Xbox One, PlayStation 4, Nintendo Switch

Age: M17+

Warnings: Blood and Gore, Violence

User behavior type: Achiever

Description: This puzzle-platform game takes place in a surreal and monochromatic environment where a young boy must move through this environment, solving puzzles and overcoming obstacles to try to save this world.

Gameplay: In this third-person game, the player controls the main character—Boy—who explores an environment, uses objects, and solves puzzles to progress through the game. The boy gains various abilities to control bodies to advance in the game.

Series (Y or N): No

Other titles in the series: n/a

Similar games: *Limbo* (2010)

Game Title: *Keep Talking and Nobody Explodes* (2015)

Genre: Puzzle

Format: Digital

Available Platforms: PlayStation 4, Xbox One, Nintendo Switch, Steam

Age: E10+

Warnings: Mild Violence

User behavior type: Achiever, Explorer, Socializer

Description: In this video game, designed for two people, one player must disarm a procedurally generated bomb with the assistance of the other player who is reading a manual containing instructions on how to successfully complete their task.

Gameplay: The game is designed to be played with at least two players: one player is the bomb "Defuser," playing the game on a device, with the remaining players as the bomb "Experts" reading the bomb defusal manual. Defusers cannot look at the manual and must rely on the Experts to instruct them; meanwhile, the Experts cannot see the bomb, and must rely on the Defuser to describe the bomb to them. Bombs will vary in style, with multiple modules and features.

Series (Y or N): No

Other titles in the series: n/a

Similar games: *Little Big Planet* series (2004–2014), *I Expect You to Die* (2016)

Game Title: *The Last Guardian* (2016)

Genre: Action-adventure

Format: Digital

Avalable Platforms: PlayStation 4

Age: T

Warnings: Blood, Fantasy Violence

User behavior type: Explorer, Killer

Description: This third-person perspective, action-adventure game follows a young boy, along with his huge birdlike companion, Trico, as they explore a ruined landscape and solve puzzles to complete the game.

Gameplay: This game combines action-adventure and puzzle elements, allowing the player, controlling an unnamed boy, to cooperate with a birdlike creature to solve puzzles and explore areas. The boy is able to climb on structures, carry objects such as barrels, and operate mechanisms such as levers as well as occasionally control Trico in particular situations.

Series (Y or N): No

Other titles in the series: n/a

Similar games: *Horizon Zero Dawn* (2017)

Game Title: *The Last of Us* (2016)

Genre: Action-adventure; survival horror

Format: Digital

Available Platforms: PlayStation 4

Age: M

Warnings: Blood and Gore, Intense Violence, Sexual Themes, Strong Language, Use of Alcohol

User behavior type: Achiever, Killer

Description: This action-adventure survival game takes place in a postapocalyptic world where players control Joel, a smuggler tasked with escorting Ellie across a destroyed United States.

Gameplay: The game is played from a third-person perspective where players use firearms and other weapons, as well as stealth, to defend against hostile human and cannibalistic creatures. There is also an option to play in an online multiplayer mode with up to eight players and engage in cooperative and competitive gameplay.

Series (Y or N): Yes

Other titles in the series: *The Last of Us* (2013), *The Last of Us Part II* (2020)

Similar games: *Uncharted: The Lost Legacy* (2017), The *Tomb Raider* series (1997–2018).

Game Title: *The Legend of Zelda: Breath of the Wild* (2017)

Genre: Action-adventure

Format: Digital

Available Platforms: Nintendo Switch, Wii U

Age: E10+

Warnings: Mild Suggestive Themes

User behavior type: Explorer, Achiever

Description: A recent, and extremely popular, release in *The Legend of Zelda* franchise depicts the series main protagonist, Link, awakening Roma's hundred-year sleep to defeat Calamity Ganon before it can destroy the kingdom of Hyrule.

Gameplay: The game relies on the open-world concept where players can freely explore the environment around them while completing both minor and major quests and tasks. Tasks include collecting items to aid in objectives and solving puzzles or side quests for rewards. The world is largely unstructured and is meant to reward experimentation and exploration. The game and narrative are meant to be completed in a nonlinear fashion.

Note: The *Legend of Zelda* series has crossed a number of different Nintendo Platforms, from the NES, Super NES, GameCube, Wii, and Wii U—while you will want to collect the most recent titles in most series, it can also be beneficial to think about retro gaming, which will appeal to various demographics that your library may serve.

Series (Y or N): Yes

Other titles in the series: *The Legend of Zelda* (1986), *The Adventure of Link* (1987), *A Link to the Past* (1991), *Link's Awakening* (1993), *Ocarina of Time* (1998), *Majora's Mask* (2000), *The Wind Waker* (2002), *Twilight Princess* (2006), *Skyward Sword* (2011), *A Link between Worlds* (2013), *Link's Awakening* (2019)

Similar games: *Final Fantasy* Series

Game Title: *The Legend of Zelda: Link's Awakening* (2019)

Genre: Action-adventure

Format: Digital

Available Platforms: Nintendo Switch

Age: E

Warnings: Mild Fantasy Violence

User behavior type: Explorer

Description: Remake of the 1993 game for Game Boy, it retains the top-down perspective and features a retro modern art style. The purpose of the game is to help Link escape Koholint Island.

Gameplay: This single-player game has the player explore an open-world concept, collecting eight instruments to help Link escape the island. The player is tasked with exploring dungeons, solving puzzles, and fighting bosses to achieve the task.

Note: The *Legend of Zelda* series has crossed a number of different Nintendo Platforms, from the NES, Super NES, GameCube, Wii, and Wii U—while you will want to collect the most recent titles in most series, it can also be beneficial to think about retro gaming, which will appeal to various demographics that your library may serve.

Series (Y or N): Yes

Other titles in the series: *The Legend of Zelda* (1986), *The Adventure of Link* (1987), *A Link to the Past* (1991), *Link's Awakening* (1993), *Ocarina of Time* (1998), *Majora's Mask* (2000), *The Wind Waker* (2002), *Twilight Princess* (2006), *Skyward Sword* (2011), *A Link between Worlds* (2013), *The Legend of Zelda: Breath of the Wild* (2017)

Similar games: *Final Fantasy* series

Game Title: *Limbo* (2010)

Genre: Puzzle; platform

Format: Digital

Available Platforms: PlayStation 4, Xbox One, Nintendo Switch, Steam

Age: T

Warnings: Animated Blood, Mild Violence

User behavior type: Achiever

Description: This 2D side-scroller incorporates a physics system that governs environmental objects and the player character. The player acts as an unnamed boy, navigating dangerous environments and traps. The game expects the player to fail the various puzzles before finding the correct solution. This is referred to by the game's developers, as "trial and death."

Gameplay: Limbo is quite typical of most two-dimensional platform games in which the player can run left or right, jump, climb onto short ledges or up and down ladders and ropes, and push or pull objects. The game also features mechanical puzzles and traps, many of which are not apparent until triggered, often killing the boy. The player can restart at the last encountered checkpoint, with no limits placed on how many times this can occur. The player will likely encounter numerous deaths before they solve each puzzle and complete the game.

Series (Y or N): No—although an earlier version of the game was released in 2007

Other titles in the series: n/a

Similar games: *Alto's Adventure* (2015), *INSIDE* (2016)

Game Title: *Little Big Planet* (2008)

Genre: Puzzle-platform; sandbox

Format: Digital

Available Platforms: Playstation 3, PlayStation 4

Age: E

Warnings: Comic Mischief, Mild Cartoon Violence, Tobacco Reference

User behavior type: Explorer

Description: The primary purpose of the game is to allow players, either alone or with groups of others—online or on the same console—to create new content using the in-game creation tools and share creations and discoveries online with other players.

Gameplay: The game revolves around the player's control of a small character, known as a "Sackboy," in a variety of platforming levels. The game features pre-built levels for the player to explore, as well as a customizable nature where players build entirely new objects and levels, and share and play them online with other players as part of the Little Big Planet community.

Note: *Little Big Planet 3* is playable on PlayStation 4.

Series (Y or N): Yes

Other titles in the series: *Little Big Planet 2* (2011), *Little Big Planet 3* (2014)

Similar games: *Tearaway* (2013), *Minecraft* (2011)

Game Title: *Marvel Ultimate Alliance 3: The Black Order* (2019)

Genre: Action; role-playing; hack and slash

Format: Digital

Available Platforms: Nintendo Switch

Age: T

Warnings: Mild Blood, Mild Suggestive Themes, Violence

User behavior type: Achiever, Explorer, Killer

Description: This is the latest installment in Marvel's *Ultimate Alliance* game series and the first major Marvel game developed for the Nintendo Switch.

Gameplay: The game includes some features of a top-down dungeon crawler but is mostly third-person perspective with an emphasis on cooperative play. Up to four players can play at a single time, and players can play online with friends. Players choose four characters from various Marvel franchises to work through linear scenes, fight enemies, and defeat major bosses.

Series (Y or N): Yes

Other titles in the series: *Ultimate Alliance* (2006), *Marvel's Ultimate Alliance 2* (2009)

Similar games: *Spiderman* (2017), *Batman: Arkham* series

Game Title: *Metal Gear* (2018)

Genre: Action-adventure; stealth

Format: Digital

Available Platforms: GameCube, Microsoft Windows, various mobile platforms, Nintendo 3DS, Mac OS X, PlayStation, PlayStation 2, PlayStation 3, PlayStation 4, PlayStation Portable, Wii, Xbox, Xbox 360, Xbox One, Steam

Age: M

Warnings: n/a

User behavior type: Killer, Achiever

Description: Originally developed in 1987, *Metal Gear* is an alternative history game that centers on various military units, and individual characters within those units, as they work to solve civil, social, governmental, and political crises across the globe—often focuses on CIA and U.S. military bodies.

Gameplay: Overhead military; first-person shooter; various with each installment

Series (Y or N): Yes

Other titles in the series: *Metal Gear* (1987), *Snakes Revenge* (1990), *Metal Gear 2: Solid Snake* (1990), *Metal Gear Solid* (1998), *Metal Gear: Ghost Babel* (2000), *Metal Gear Solid 2: Sons of Liberty* (2001), *Metal Gear Solid: The Twin Snakes* (2004), *Metal Gear Solid 3: Snake Eater* (2004), *Metal Gear Acid* (2004), *Metal Gear Acid 2* (2005), *Metal Gear Solid: Portable Ops* (2006), *Metal Gear: Portable Ops Plus* (2007), *Metal Gear Solid Mobile* (2008), *Metal Gear Solid 4: Guns of the Patriots* (2008), *Metal Gear Online* (2008), *Metal Gear Solid Touch* (2009), *Metal Gear Solid: Peach Walker* (2010), *Metal Gear Solid: Social Ops* (2012), *Metal Gear Rising: Revengeance* (2013), *Metal Gear Solid V: Ground Zeroes* (2014), *Metal Gear Solid V: The Phantom Pain* (2015), *Metal Gear Survive* (2018)

Similar games: *Call of Duty* series

Game Title: *Minecraft* (2011)

Genre: Sandbox; survival

Format: Digital

Available Platforms: Microsoft Windows, MacOS, Xbox 360, PlayStation 3, PlayStation 4, Wii U, Nintendo Switch, Steam

Age: E

Warnings: n/a

User behavior type: Achiever, Explorer

Description: This incredibly popular game allows players to build digital worlds using a variety of sized blocks. Beyond the building or creation feature of the games, players can also explore the digital worlds of Minecraft, create and procure resources to survive within that world, do crafting, and engage in combat with other players.

Gameplay: This game is primarily a sandbox game, which means there is no end objective to the game, giving players the freedom to explore and manipulate the game as they desire. However, there are various other gameplay features for the game: survival, where players gather natural resources to craft particular items; creative, where players have the freedom to create and construct without restraint; adventure, where players are required to complete specific tasks or missions; spectator, where players can watch the gameplay without interacting; and multiplayer, where players can interact with each other in a single world.

Series (Y or N): Yes

Other titles in the series: *Minecraft Story Mode* (2015), *Minecraft Earth* (2019), *Minecraft Dungeons* (2019)

Similar games: The *Lego* series is a similar concept, especially the more sandbox version of those games.

Game Title: *Mortal Kombat 11* (2019)

Genre: Fighting

Format: Digital

Available Platforms: Nintendo 64, Nintendo Switch, PlayStation 1, PlayStation 2, PlayStation 3, PlayStation 4, Steam, Windows, various mobile platforms

Age: M17+

Warnings: Blood and Gore, Strong Violence

User behavior type: Killer, Achiever

Description: Fantasy-themed fighting game, known for extreme levels of graphic violence. Originally developed as a 2D combat game, with fighters pairing off, attempting to defeat each other using special moves (original to the *Mortal Kombat* series), but later evolved into a 3D fighting game that featured storylines, puzzles, and quests. The game is most known for its grisly "deaths" of characters at the end of each match.

Gameplay: The game is structured as a versus game, with players fighting as one of two characters against each other using a variety of attack moves, special moves, and trademark finishing moves.

Series (Y or N): Yes

Other titles in the series: *Mortal Kombat* (1992), *Mortal Kombat II* (1993), *Mortal Kombat 3* (1995), *Ultimate Mortal Kombat 3* (1995), *Mortal Kombat Trilogy* (1996), *Mortal Kombat Mythologies: Sub-Zero* (1997), *Mortal Kombat 4* (1997), *Mortal Kombat Gold* (1999), *Mortal Kombat Special Forces* (2000), *Mortal Kombat Advance* (2001), *Mortal Kombat: Deadly Alliance* (2002), *Mortal Kombat Tournament Edition* (2003), *Mortal Kombat: Deception* (2004), *Mortal Kombat: Shaolin Monks* (2005), *Mortal Kombat: Armageddon* (2006), *Mortal Kombat: Unchained* (2006), *Ultimate Mortal Kombat* (2007), *Mortal Kombat vs. DC Universe* (2008), *Mortal Kombat* (2011), *Mortal Kombat Arcade Kollection* (2011), *Mortal Kombat: Komplete Edition* (2012), *Mortal Kombat X* (2015), *Mortal Kombat XL* (2016), *Mortal Kombat 11* (2019)

Similar games: *Street Fighter* series, *Injustice* series

Game Title: *NBA Live '19* (2018)

Genre: Sports

Format: Digital

Available Platforms: Most recent entries in the series—Microsoft Windows, Playstation, PlayStation 2, PlayStation 3, PlayStation 4, Xbox, Xbox 360, Xbox One, Wii, Steam, mobile platforms

Age: E

Warnings: n/a

User behavior type: Achiever

Description: Basketball simulation game where players can select different teams and players.

Gameplay: Players can create their own avatars to compete in games, they are able to complete full NBA seasons as well as build franchises. The game cam be played in either single-player or multiplayer modes.

Series (Y or N): Yes

Other titles in the series: *NBA Live 95* (1994) through *NBA Live 18* (2017)

Similar games: *NBA 2K* series

Game Title: *NHL* (series)

Genre: Sports

Format: Digital

Available Platforms: Most recent entries in series—Microsoft Windows, PlayStation, PlayStation 2, PlayStation 3, PlayStation 4, Xbox, Xbox 360, Xbox One, Wii

Age: E

Warnings: n/a

User behavior type: Achiever

Description: Hockey simulation game where players can select different teams and players.

Gameplay: Players can create their own avatars to compete in games, and they are able to complete full NHL seasons as well as build franchises. The game can be played in either single-player or multiplayer modes.

Series (Y or N): Yes

Other titles in the series: *NHL Hockey* (1991) through *NHL 19* (2018)

Similar games: If players enjoy this series, they might also enjoy other sports games, such as the NBA series.

Game Title: *No Man's Sky* (2018)

Genre: Action-adventure; survival

Format: Digital

Available Platforms: PlayStation 4, Xbox One, Steam

Age: T

Warnings: Fantasy Violence

User behavior type: Achiever, Explorer

Description: In this game, players are cast as "The Traveler," who awakes on an alien planet, must find and rebuild his spacecraft, and journey to the center of the galaxy to restart an alien mechanism called the Atlas. The Atlas functions as a way to either end the game or completely restart the game with a new version of the traveler—in this way, players can continue to play and redo certain actions from earlier game attempts.

Gameplay: This game is played from a first- or third-person perspective that allows players to engage in four principal activities: exploration, survival, combat, and trading.
Series (Y or N): No
Other titles in the series: n/a
Similar games: *Astroneer* (2019)

Game Title: *Octopath Traveller* (2018)
Genre: Role-playing
Format: Digital
Available Platforms: Nintendo Switch, Steam
Age: T
Warnings: Blood, Fantasy Violence, Mild Language, Suggestive Theme, Use of Alcohol
User behavior type: Explorer, Achiever
Description: The game's central narrative involves having the player follow the stories of eight heroes as they journey through Orsterra, a world created by 13 deities before 12 were forced to seal the fallen god Galdera, who refused to relinquish what they created, within the afterworld. The story of the game involves tasking these eight heroes with fighting Galdera and ensuring he does not escape from his prison.
Gameplay: This role-playing game puts players in the role of one of eight adventurers, each of whom begins their journey in different ways. Each character comes from different parts of the world, with different jobs or attributes, and each has a unique Path Ability command that can be used when interacting with other characters. The game also features turn-based battles where the player can attack using different kinds of weapons or elemental attacks, as well as use abilities and items.
Series (Y or N): No
Other titles in the series: n/a
Similar games: *Xenoblade Chronicles 2* (2017), *The Legend of Zelda: Breath of the Wild* (2017)

Game Title: *Overcooked 2* (2018)
Genre: Simulation; family
Format: Digital
Available Platforms: PlayStation 4, Xbox One, Nintendo Switch, Steam
Age: E
Warnings: n/a
User behavior type: Achiever
Description: This is a cooperative cooking simulation game where up to four players cooperatively prepare and cook orders in absurd restaurants.

Gameplay: In this game, players chop and cook ingredients, combine them on plates, and serve dishes via a conveyor belt. The game becomes overwhelming and challenging due to the level of coordination and multitasking players must accomplish. Players must create new recipes and overcome increasingly strange obstacles to succeed in the game.

Series (Y or N): Yes

Other titles in the series: *Overcooked* (2016)

Similar games: *Gangbeats* (2014)

Game Title: *Overwatch* (2016)

Genre: First-person shooter

Format: Digital

Available Platforms: PlayStation 4, Xbox One, Nintendo Switch

Age: T

Warnings: Blood, Use of Tobacco, Violence

User behavior type: Achiever, Killer

Description: This is a multiplayer first-person shooter where players are assigned to teams, each character has a unique fighting style. The main plot centers on the international task force—Overwatch—which combats global threats and restores order to a fictionalized earth.

Gameplay: *Overwatch* features a number of different game modes, all of which are designed around squad-based combat of opposing teams (each of six players). Players select from 24 premade Hero characters from three types: Damage Heros, Tank Heros, and Support Heros. Players can change their hero throughout the game. Players can either engage in casual play or competitive play—engaging lets players gain experience points.

Series (Y or N): No

Other titles in the series: n/a

Similar games: *Fortnite* (2017), *Apex Legends* (2019)

Game Title: *Pokémon: Let's Go, Pikachu! and Let's Go, Eevee!* (2018)

Genre: Role-playing

Format: Digital

Available Platforms: Nintendo Switch

Age: E

Warnings: n/a

User behavior type: Achiever

Description: This is the first Pokémon game released for a home console, a remake of the 1998 Game Boy game *Pokémon Yellow*, and is a role-playing game with common elements to traditional Pokémon games—collecting and battling Pokémon characters. The game also features connectivity to the popular mobile game *Pokémon Go* and features a new controller for the Switch, the Poke Ball Plus.

Gameplay: While the game does feature common elements of the main series, such as battling non-player character Pokémon Trainers and Gym Leaders with caught Pokémon creatures, the game's battles do not function in a similar manner. Instead, the game uses a mechanic based on *Pokémon Go*, where players throw Poke Balls at wild Pokémon by using motion controls.

Series (Y or N): Yes

Other titles in the series: The majority of Pokémon games have been released on mobile game platforms, including Game Boy and Nintendo 3DS—you may want to consider whether your library can support offering games and mobile console. Popular titles include *Pokémon Black and White* (2010), *Pokémon Black 2 and White 2* (2012), *Pokémon Omega Ruby and Alpha Sapphire* (2014), *Pokémon Sun and Moon* (2016), and *Pokémon Ultra Sun and Ultra Moon* (2017).

Similar games: *Minecraft* (2009)

Game Title: *Pokémon: Sword* and *Pokémon: Shield* (2019)
Genre: Role-playing
Format: Digital
Available Platforms: Nintendo Switch
Age: E
Warnings: Comic Mischief, Mild Cartoon Violence
User behavior type: Achiever
Description: Each game (*Sword* or *Shield*) chronicles the journey of a young Pokémon trainer in a fictionalized version of Great Britain. The game's main objective is to dethrone the Pokémon League Champion, Leon, in a tournament that various other Gym Leaders also take part in. *Sword* and *Shield* introduce 81 new Pokémon alongside 13 regional variants of preexisting Pokémon, a number of new functionalities that change the Pokémon in specific ways, and the Wild Area, which is a large, open-world area with free camera movement that contains co-op raid battles.

Gameplay: Contains elements of previous Pokémon games, including *Pokémon Go*, as well as introducing some new elements—such as the open area for players to explore and engage in combat within.

Series (Y or N): Yes

Other titles in the series: The majority of Pokémon games have been released on mobile game platforms, including Game Boy and Nintendo 3DS—you may want to consider whether your library can support offering games and mobile console. Popular titles include *Pokémon Black and White* (2010), *Pokémon Black 2 and White 2* (2012), *Pokémon Omega Ruby and Alpha Sapphire* (2014), *Pokémon Sun and Moon* (2016), *and Pokémon Ultra Sun and Ultra Moon* (2017), and *Pokémon: Let's Go, Pikachu! and Let's Go, Eevee!* (2018).

Similar games: *Monster Strike* (2013), *Fortnite* (2017)

Game Title: *Portal 2* (2011)
Genre: Puzzle-platform
Format: Digital
Available Platforms: PlayStation 3, Xbox 360, Steam
Age: E10+
Warnings: Fantasy Violence, Mild Language
User behavior type: Explorer, Achiever
Description: A puzzle-based game where players solve puzzles by placing portals and teleporting between them. The sequel to the immensely popular Portal, added such features as tractor beams, lasers, and other elements to enhance gameplay.
Gameplay: This is a first-person puzzle game where the player takes the role of Chell in the single-player campaign or as one of two robots in the cooperative campaign or as a simplistic humanoid icon in the community-developed puzzles. The characters explore and interact with their environment with the overall objective is to explore the Apertune Science Laboratory completing puzzles.
Series (Y or N): Yes
Other titles in the series: *Portal* (2007)
Similar games: *Minecraft* (2009), *Half Life 2* (2007)

Game Title: *Quantum Break*
Genre: Action-adventure; third-person shooter
Format: Digital
Available Platforms: Xbox One, Steam
Age: M17+
Warnings: Blood, Intense Violence, Strong Language
User behavior type: Killer, Achiever
Description: The game focuses on Jack Joyce, who has time manipulation powers after a failed time-machine experiment. The main narrative plot of the game details Joyce's conflict with former friend Paul Serene over how to deal with an apocalyptic "End of Time." Game features platform game elements in less action-oriented segments, as well as having a tie-in with a live-action television show.
Gameplay: As Jack Joyce, players can manipulate time making everything freeze except Joyce, while facing a variety of enemies deploy different tactics and strategies in order to defeat them. Throughout the game, players may be shifted to different characters, acting out major plot points and moving the narrative along.
Note: The game features a live-action television series as a tie into the plot of the game, episodes are available online, but this can be a good way for users to experience an immersive experience into a game. It might be beneficial to include information on the TV series along with the game itself.
Series (Y or N): No
Other titles in the series: n/a
Similar games: *Alan Wake* (2012, 2014)

Game Title: *Rayman's Legends* (2013)

Genre: Platform

Format: Digital

Available Platforms: Wii U, PlayStation 4, Xbox One, Nintendo Switch, Steam

Age: E10+

Warnings: Cartoon Violence, Comic Mischief

User behavior type: Achiever

Description: The primary plot of the game centers on Rayman and his friends (the primary protagonists of the series) as they battle a series of nightmares and villains, called "Dark Teensies," to save their world.

Gameplay: This platform game allows up to four players to simultaneously make their way through various levels, defeating enemies, unlocking levels, and collecting various important objects.

Note: Other games in the *Rayman* series have been re-released on current consoles.

Series (Y or N): Yes

Other titles in the series: *Rayman* (1995), *Rayman 2: The Great Escape* (1999), *Rayman 3: Hoodlum Havoc* (2003), *Rayman Origins* (2011)

Similar games: *Little Big Planet 3* (2017)

Game Title: *Red Dead Redemption II* (2018)

Genre: Action-adventure

Format: Digital

Available Platforms: PlayStation 4, Steam, Xbox One

Age: M

Warnings: Blood and Gore, Intense Violence, Nudity, Sexual Content, Strong Language, Use of Drug and Alcohol

User behavior type: Killer, Achiever

Description: A sequel to the original *Red Dead Redemption* (2010). An open-world, third-person perspective western action-adventure game set in 1911 and follows outlaws Arthur Morgan and John Marston, a member of the Van der Linde gang. The game details his attempts to survive government forces, rival gangs, and other adversaries. The story also follows John Marston, who was the protagonist in the original *Red Dead* game.

Gameplay: The game is played from either a first-person or third-person perspective where the player controls Marston to complete missions, linear scenarios with particular objectives to advance through the story. Beyond the missions, players can freely roam the game's environment, engage various enemies using a variety of weapons, and use horses or trains as a means of transportation. The game can be played as a single-player or multiplayer online.

Series (Y or N): Yes

Other titles in the series: *Red Dead Revolver* (2004), *Red Dead Redemption* (2010),

Similar games: *Call of Juarex: Gunslinger* (2013)

Game Title: *Rocket League*

Genre: Sports

Format: Digital

Available Platforms: PlayStation 4, Xbox One, Nintendo Switch, Steam

Age: E

Warnings: Mild Lyrics

User behavior type: Achiever

Description: An action racing game where players drive futuristic cars while engaging in games of soccer.

Gameplay: Players commonly control a rocket powered car and use it to manipulate a soccer ball across a large field to score goals. Players' cars can jump, gain speed, as well as destroy their own car, or those of other players to gain small advantages.

Series (Y or N): Yes

Other titles in the series: *Supersonic Acrobatic Rocket-Powered Battle-Cars* (2008)

Similar games: *Grand Theft Auto* (1997)

Game Title: *Scribblenauts Showdown*

Genre: Sandbox; party; puzzle-platform

Format: Digital

Available Platforms: Nintendo Switch, Steam

Age: E10+

Warnings: Cartoon Violence, Crude Humor

User behavior type: Explorer

Description: The main point of this game is for players to engage in a variety of tasks and mini-games using a selection of words, actions, modifiers, and characters.

Gameplay: With each new game or puzzle, players interact with the game by typing in random nouns and adjectives to create different word combinations that trigger comical scenarios. Some games or tasks prompt players to use "cartoony" weapons to deplete the health meters of other characters. Each mini-game can have its own unique style of interaction.

Series (Y or N): Yes

Other titles in the series: *Scribblenauts* (2009), *Super Scribblenauts* (2010), *Scribblenauts Remix* (2011), *Scribblenauts Unlimited* (2012), *Scribblenauts Unmasked: A DC Adventure* (2013, 2018), *Scribblenauts: Fighting Worlds* (2014 and 2016)

Similar games: *Drawn to Life* (2007)

Game Title: *Sea of Thieves* (2018)
Genre: Action-adventure
Format: Digital
Available Platforms: Xbox One, Steam
Age: T
Warnings: Crude Humor, Use of Alcohol, Violence
User behavior type: Achiever
Description: This Xbox exclusive game is a first-person perspective game where players take the role as a pirate in either a solo adventure or as part of a four-person crew and embark on sailing adventures in a fantasy world.
Gameplay: Players travel and explore an open world via a pirate ship, assuming different roles (steering, hoisting sails, navigation, and firing cannons), and embark on quests, collect loot, and engage in combat with other players. Importantly, *Sea of Thieves* is a shared game world where groups of players encounter each other regularly throughout their adventures.
Note: There is an expansion for the game called *Sea of Thieves: Forsaken Shores*, but this can be purchased online.
Series (Y or N): No
Other titles in the series: n/a
Similar games: *Red Dead Redemption II* (2018)

Game Title: *The Sinking City* (2019)
Genre: Action-adventure; third-person shooter; survival horror
Format: Digital
Available Platforms: PlayStation 4, Nintendo Switch, Xbox One, Steam
Age: M17+
Warnings: Blood and Gore, Suggestive Themes, Violence
User behavior type: Killer, Achiever
Description: This detective game, based on the stories of H. P. Lovecraft, is centered on a private investigator who is looking into a series of strange and supernatural events happening in the fictional town of Oakmont.
Gameplay: The game is a third-person perspective mystery that features an investigation system where the outcome is defined by how observant the players are when investigating different clues and pieces of evidence. The players have a number of tools and weapons available to them, as well as sanity, which is used to build up investigative powers.
Series (Y or N): No
Other titles in the series: n/a
Similar games: *Call of Cthulhu* (2018)

Game Title: *Spider-Man* (2017)
Genre: Action-adventure

Format: Digital
Available Platforms: PlayStation 4
Age: T
Warnings: Some Violence and Mild Language
User behavior type: Achiever
Description: Based on the Marvel Comics character, this hugely popular PlayStation title's main narrative includes Spider-Man's attempt to protect New York City from an attack by Mister Negative while achieving other missions and tasks.
Gameplay: Presented in the third-person perspective, with a focus on Spider-Man and his various abilities. As Spider-Man, the player can move freely around New York City, interacting with various characters from the comic book series, completing missions, and unlocking new gadgets and suits while progressing through the main story and tasks. Combat requires players to make use of the environment as well as using Spider-Man's various abilities.
Series (Y or N): No
Other titles in the series: n/a
Similar games: *Batman Arkham* series (2007–2016)

Game Title: *Splatoon* 2 (2017)
Genre: Third-person shooter
Format: Digital
Available Platforms: Nintendo Switch
Age: E10+
Warnings: Cartoon Violence
User behavior type: Achiever, Killer
Description: This sequel to the popular 2015 *Splatoon* game is a third-person shooter game where players, playing as either Inklings or Octolings, engage in combat using colored ink as ammunition. Characters can morph between humanoid into squid form, where they can swim through ink of their own color.
Gameplay: This third-person, single-player or multiplayer game casts players as either Inklings or Octolings, who use a variety of weapons and defense mechanisms. It features a number of modes, including Turf War, where players are part of four-player teams. League Battles allow players to form teams with friends through online interaction.
Series (Y or N): Yes
Other titles in the series: *Splatoon* (2015)
Similar games: *Super Smash Brothers Ultimate* (2017), *Super Mario Odyssey* (2017)

Game Title: *Star Link: The Battle for Atlas* (2018)
Genre: Action-adventure
Format: Digital
Available Platforms: PlayStation 4, Xbox One, Nintendo Switch

Age: E10+

Warnings: Fantasy Violence

User behavior type: Achiever, Killer

Description: The main narrative of the game focuses on the player, as a member of a star fighter group, having to rescue their commanding officer from the Forgotten Legion, the game's main antagonist. The Nintendo Switch version of the game features a crossover with the popular *Star Fox* franchise.

Gameplay: In this third-person perspective game, players pilot star-fighters and transverse different parts of the galaxy—mostly the Atlas system—while encountering alien races, forming alliances, and engaging in combat to achieve their ultimate goal of rescuing their commanding officer and stopping the Forgotten Legion.

Series (Y or N): No

Other titles in the series: n/a

Similar games: *Star Fox Zero* (2016)

Game Title: *Star Wars: Battlefront II* (2017)

Genre: First-person shooter; third-person shooter

Format: Digital

Available Platforms: PlayStation 2, PlayStation 4, Xbox, Xbox One, Steam

Age: E10+

Warnings: May contain Violence, Suggestive Themes, Crude Humor, Minimal Blood, Simulated Gambling, and/or infrequent use of Strong Language

User behavior type: Achiever, Killer

Description: This is a series of video games based on the *Star Wars* film franchise. Players assume the identity of soldiers in either the Rebellion or the Empire throughout the time period of the *Star Wars* franchise.

Gameplay: Games in the series take place on various maps across the *Star Wars* galaxy, with battle zones varying in theme and size. The objective of the game is to eliminate all of the opponent's reinforcements.

Series (Y or N): Yes

Other titles in the series: *SW: Battlefront* (2004), *SW: Battlefront II* (2005), *SW: Battlefront: Renegade Squadron* (2007), *SW Battlefront: Elite Squadron* (2008), *SW: Battlefront: Mobile Squadrons* (2009), *Star Wars Battlefront* (2015)

Similar games: *Star Wars Old Republic* (2011), *Star Wars Jedi Knight* (2003)

Game Title: *Star Wars: Jedi Fallen Order* (2019)

Genre: Action-adventure

Format: Digital

Available Platforms: PlayStation 4, Xbox One, Steam

Age: T
Warnings: Mild Language, Violence
User behavior type: Explorer, Achiever
Description: Set between the third and fourth movie episodes of the popular *Star Wars* franchise, the game follows Jedi Cal Kestis as he fights to escape persecution from the Galactic Empire and Inquisitors.
Gameplay: The game is played from a third-person perspective. Players control the main character, Cal Kestis, who traverses alien landscapes, killing or destroying enemies.
Series (Y or N): No
Other titles in the series: n/a
Similar games: Other games in the *Star Wars* franchise

Game Title: *Street Fighter* series (most recent releases: *Street Fighter V* and *Streetfighter 30th Anniversary*)
Genre: Fighting
Format: Digital
Available Platforms: Available on most major systems, including Nintendo Switch, PlayStation 4, Xbox One, Steam
Age: T
Warnings: Mild Blood, Mild Language, Suggestive Themes, Violence
User behavior type: Killer, Achiever
Description: This is a very traditional fighting game, for one or two players. Players choose particular characters to battle, building strength and using special unique attacks to defeat their opponents. Newer versions of the game have introduced story modes and new characters—commonly through downloadable content for the game.
Gameplay: The game series utilizes the traditional 2D fighting gameplay where two fighters use a variety of attacks and special abilities to knock out their opponent. Recent entries into the series often feature an EX strength gauge, which builds as the player lands attacks and can be used to either power up special moves or perform super combos.
Series (Y or N): Yes
Other titles in the series: Main series games: *Street Fighter* (1987), *Street Fighter II* (1991), *Street Fighter Alpha* (1995), *Street Fighter EX* (1996), *Street Fighter: Crossover* series (1996), *Street Fighter III* (1997), *Street Fighter IV* (2008), *Street Fighter V* (2016). Other Entries: *Street Fighter 2010: The Final Fight* (1990), *Super Puzzle Street Fighter II Turbo* (1996), *Street Fighter Anniversary Collection* (2004), *Street Fighter 30th Anniversary Collection* (2018)
Similar games: *Mortal Kombat* series, *Injustice* series

Game Title: *Sunset Overdrive* (2014)
Genre: Action-adventure; third-person shooter
Format: Digital
Available Platforms: Xbox 360, Xbox One, Steam

Age: M17+

Warnings: Blood and Gore, Drug References, Sexual Themes, Strong Language, Violence

User behavior type: Killer, Achiever, Explorer

Description: This action-adventure shooter game is set in a fictional metropolis called Sunset City where the player controls an employee of FizzCo, who has to fight off the OD, short for Overcharge Drinkers: humans who have turned into mutants after drinking FizzCo's energy drink beverage.

Gameplay: Players have the option of customizing their protagonist's character, including gender, body type, and other physical characteristics. Players can explore the game's open world, utilizing a fast travel system to reach different locations and navigate the world quickly. The game features a main campaign with story elements and side missions, which are triggered automatically when players enter certain locations in the city. Beyond this main campaign, players encounter ODs and must regularly engage in combat with these characters.

Series (Y or N): No

Other titles in the series: n/a

Similar games: *Marvel's Spiderman* (2018), *Grand Theft Auto* series

Game Title: *Super Smash Bros: Ultimate* (2018)

Genre: Fighting

Format: Digital

Available Platforms: Nintendo 64, Wii, Nintendo 3DS, Wii U, Nintendo Switch

Age: E10+

Warnings: Cartoon Violence, Comic Mischief, Suggestive Themes

User behavior type: Killer, Achiever

Description: This is a crossover fighting game featuring characters from multiple video game and pop cultural properties.

Gameplay: This is a fighting game for up to eight players fighting and various characters trying to knock each other out of an area.

Series (Y or N): Yes

Other titles in the series: This is the latest installment of the *Smash Brothers* series, but other titles include *Super Smash Brothers* (1999), *Super Smash Brothers: Melee* (2001), *Super Smash Brothers: Brawl* (2008), *Super Smash Brothers* for 3DS and Wii U (2014)

Similar games: *Street Fighter* series, *Mortal Kombat* series

Game Title: *Tomb Raider* (series)

Genre: Action; action-adventure

Format: Digital

Available Platforms: Xbox, PlayStation 3, PlayStation 4, Steam

Age: M17+

Warnings: n/a

User behavior type: Explorer; Achiever

Description: In most of the *Tomb Raider* entries, players play as Lara Croft, attempting to uncover lost artifacts, solving mysteries, and battling against the nefarious corporation Trinity. Players solve puzzles and mysteries to unlock rewards and challenges to ultimately complete the game.

Gameplay: This single-player game requires you to play as protagonist Lara Croft in exploring dangerous environments, solving puzzles, engaging in combat with the ultimate goals of finding lost treasure or stopping her enemies from stealing rare and valuable artifacts.

Series (Y or N): Yes

Other titles in the series: *Tomb Raider* (1996), *Tomb Raider 2* (1997), *Tomb Raider 3* (1998), *The Lost Revelation* (1999), *Tomb Raider Chronicles* (2001), *Curse of the Sword* (2001), *The Prophecy* (2002), *The Angel of Darkness* (2003), *Legend* (2006), *Anniversary* (2007), *Underworld* (2008), *Lara Croft and the Guardian of Light* (2010), *Tomb Raider* (reissued 2013), *Lara Croft and the Temple of Osiris* (2014), *Lara Croft: Relic Run* (2015), *Lara Croft Go* (2015), *Rise of the Tomb Raider* (2015), *Shadow of the Tomb Raider* (2018)

Similar games: *The Last of Us* (2013)

Game Title: *Tropico 6* (2019)

Genre: City builder; construction and management simulation; government simulation

Format: Digital

Available Platforms: Xbox One, PlayStation 4, Nintendo Switch, Steam, Google Stadia

Age: T

Warnings: Drug Reference, Mild Language, Violence

User behavior type: Achiever

Description: In this city-building simulation game, players take on the role of a president of the Caribbean Island, Tropico. The game progresses through four different eras: Colonial, the World Wars, the Cold War, and the Modern era.

Gameplay: Players, taking on the role of "El Presidente" of the island Tropico, work to build up the islands and other smaller islands of an archipelago. Players are also able to build bridges between the islands, customize their own El Presidente palace, and deal with fully simulated citizens who will react to player choices throughout the game.

Series (Y or N): Yes

Other titles in the series: *Tropico* (2001), *Tropico: Pirate Cove* (2003), *Tropico 3* (2009), *Tropico 4* (2011), *Tropico 5* (2014)

Similar games: *Animal Crossing* series, *Cities: Skylines* (2015)

Game Title: *Unravel 2* (2018)

Genre: Puzzle; platform

Format: Digital

Available Platforms: PlayStation 4, Xbox One, Nintendo Switch
Age: Everyone
Warnings: Mild Fantasy Violence
User behavior type: Achiever, Explorer
Description: The game's plot centers on two "Yarnys"—small anthropomorphic creatures made of yarn—as they navigate a small island in an attempt to return to their original homeland.
Gameplay: This game features both single-player and multiplayer modes, a third-person perspective, where players must work together to solve puzzles and manipulate the world around them to achieve their goal. The game features increasingly difficult levels as the player progresses through the challenges.
Series (Y or N): Yes
Other titles in the series: *Unravel* (2016)
Similar games: *The Witness* (2016), *ABZU* (2016)

Game Title: *Until Dawn* (2015)
Genre: Survival horror; interactive drama
Format: Digital
Available Platforms: PlayStation 4
Age: M17+
Warnings: Blood and Gore, Intense Violence, Sexual Themes, Strong Language
User behavior type: Killer, Explorer, Achiever
Description: In this interactive drama game, players play as eight young adults who have to survive in an isolated location on Blackwood Mountain as they are pursued by a masked killer.
Gameplay: Gameplay consists of a combination of cut scenes and third-person exploration in which characters interact with a linear environment and find clues and items. To progress through the game, players collect totems to uncover what has happened throughout the game's narrative. Interestingly, the game also features a butterfly effect system where the decisions that players make have significant consequences throughout the game.
Series (Y or N): Yes
Other titles in the series: *Until Dawn: Rush of Blood*, a Virtual Reality Game (2016)
Similar games: *The Last of Us* (2013), *The Dark Pictures: Man of Medan* (2019)

Game Title: *Watch Dogs* (2014)
Genre: Action-adventure
Format: Digital
Available Platforms: PlayStation 3, PlayStation 4, Xbox One, Wii U, Steam, Stadia (upcoming release)
Age: M17+

Warnings: Blood, Intense Violence, Nudity, Strong Language, Strong Sexual Content, Use of Drugs and Alcohol

User behavior type: Achiever, Killer

Description: Overall plot of the game involves the player controlling the main character, Aiden Pearce, a hacker, as he plots and takes revenge on those people responsible for the murder of his niece. The plot also revolves around a series of hacking jobs and their consequences.

Gameplay: This third-person, action-adventure game has the player controlling hacker Aiden Pearce, who uses his smartphone to control city infrastructure, infiltrate security systems, jam cell phones, and access private citizen information, while emptying their bank accounts. The hacking element of the game involves the solving a variety of puzzles. The game is set in an open-world environment, which permits free roaming and has a day–night cycle and dynamic weather system, which changes the behavior of non-player characters. Players must also engage in combat throughout the game, using a variety of weapons.

Series (Y or N): Yes

Other titles in the series: *Watch Dogs 2* (2016), *Watch Dogs: Legion* (2020)

Similar games: *Grand Theft Auto* series, *Sleeping Dogs* (2012), *Tom Clancy's Splinter Cell* series

Game Title: *The Witcher III: Fallen Hunt* (2015 and 2019)

Genre: Action role-playing

Format: Digital

Available Platforms: Xbox One, PlayStation 4, Nintendo Switch, Steam

Age: M17+

Warnings: Blood and Gore, Intense Violence, Nudity, Strong Language, Strong Sexual Content, Use of Alcohol

User behavior type: Explorer, Killer, Achiever

Description: This action-adventure game follows Geralt of Riva, a monster hunter—a witcher—who is searching for his missing daughter. The game follows Geralt as he moves through the environment, fighting monsters with a variety of weapons.

Gameplay: In this third-person perspective game, players navigate through various elements in the game's world—fighting human enemies and supernatural elements. The game focuses on narrative, which allows players to make different decisions, leading to a variety of different endings.

Series (Y or N): Yes

Other titles in the series: *The Witcher* (2007), *The Witcher 2: Assassins of Kings* (2011)

Similar games: *Assassin's Creed* series

Game Title: *Wolfenstein: Youngblood* (2019)

Genre: First-person shooter

Format: Digital

Available Platforms: PlayStation 4, Nintendo Switch, Xbox One, Steam, Stadia

Age: M17+

Warnings: Blood and Gore, Intense Violence, Strong Language

User behavior type: Achiever, Killer

Description: In this installment of the Wolfenstein series, events take place 20 years after 2017's *Wolfenstein II: The New Colossus*, and follows a group of American spies trying to infiltrate Nazi-occupied Europe.

Gameplay: In this first-person perspective shooter game, players assume control of either Jessie or Zofia Blazkowicz as they complete various missions, unlock new gear and abilities. As part of an optional cooperative multiplayer mode, players can complete the game with another player or with an artificial intelligence substitute.

Series (Y or N): Yes

Other titles in the series: *Castle Wolfenstein* (1981), *Beyond Castle Wolfenstein* (1984), *Wolfenstein 3D* (1992), *Wolfenstein Spear of Destiny* (1992), *Wolfenstein: Return to Castle Wolfenstein* (2001), *Wolfenstein: Enemy Territory* (2003), *Wolfenstein: RPG* (2008), *Wolfenstein* (2009), *Wolfenstein: The New Order* (2014), *Wolfenstein II: The New Colossus* (2017), *Wolfenstein: Cyberpilot* (2019)

Similar games: *Rage 2* (2019), *Call of Duty: Modern Warfare* (2019)

Lego Series

One of the larger collections of video game titles belongs to the Lego brand. The Lego franchise covers a great number of genres (platform, sandbox, action-adventure, and puzzle) and are available for a variety of age groups. Although the majority of games are rated safe for all age groups, there are certain games aimed at younger audiences, such as *Lego My Style Preschool & Kindergarten* (2000).

Lego games primarily incorporate popular film, comic book, and television franchises, adding unique puzzle and sandbox elements into commonly known narratives, allowing players to engage in a level of interactivity with their favorite characters. In the popular *Lego Star Wars* games (2004, 2007, and 2017), players are able to experience the entire *Star Wars* story by building and constructing the characters and environments known to that universe. In addition to creating games based on popular franchises, Lego has also created a number of video games based on their own toys, including *Lego Bionicle* (2001), *Lego Battles: Ninjago* (2011), *Lego City Undercover* (2013), *Lego Friends* (2013), and *Lego Legends of Chima Online* (2013). The majority of these games function as action-adventure, with a number of puzzle and sandbox elements.

Other Lego games, such as *Lego Worlds*, have greater sandbox elements. In this particular game, players are able to build constructions without the constraints of missions or quests. Below is a representative list of popular Lego games, as well as a general description of the gameplay—gameplay is generally consistent across all titles. You might find that many different user types (across all ages) will want to engage with the Lego title series. Titles run across a wide number of consoles with many titles being duplicated on each console; the *Lego Star Wars* games, for instance, are available on many Nintendo systems, as well as PlayStation and Xbox. These titles can be a good way to diversify your collection and offer something to a number of different users.

Entries for the Lego franchise follow, including a list of all the recent games available.

Game Title: *Lego* series

Genre: Action-adventure; puzzle; sandbox

Format: Digital

Available Platforms: PlayStation 1, PlayStation 2, PlayStation 3, PlayStation 4, Xbox, Xbox One, Xbox 360, Nintendo Switch, Wii, Wii U, Microsoft Windows, MacOS, various mobile platforms

Age: E

Warnings: None

User behavior type: Achiever, Explorer

Description: Lego-based adaptations of many popular pop cultural properties where the player experiences that specific universe by building and creating different aspects key to the plot of the movie, TV show, or comic book. Players normally need to collect artifacts key to the gameplay, for example, in *Lego Star Wars: The Complete Saga*, players need to collect golden bricks to advance levels. Other games, such as *Lego Worlds*, players are engaged in a sandbox game that allows them to build constructions without the constraints of missions or quests. These games can be very popular with individuals wanting to interact with their favorite pop culture universes or enjoy sandbox games.

Gameplay: Various gameplays. In certain games, players advance through levels by completing missions, quests, or puzzles to get to the next stage of the game (*Lego Star Wars* or *Lego DC Super-Villains*), while others have a more combat and creation building aspect to the gameplay (*Lego Worlds* or *The Lego Movie 2 Videogame*).

Titles within various franchises: *Lego Creator: Harry Potter* (2001), *Lego Creator: Harry Potter and the Chamber of Secrets* (2002), *Lego Star Wars: The Video Game* (2005), *Lego Star Wars II: The Original Trilogy* (2006), *Lego Star Wars: The Complete Saga* (2007), *Lego Indiana Jones: The Original Adventures* (2008), *Lego Batman: The Video Game* (2008), *Lego Indiana Jones 2: The Adventure Continues* (2009), *Lego Harry Potter: Years 1–4* (2010), *Lego Universe* (2010), *Lego Star Wars III: The Clone Wars* (2011), *Lego Pirates of the Caribbean: The Video Game* (2011), *Lego Harry Potter: Years 5–7* (2011), *Lego Batman 2: DC Super Heroes* (2012), *Lego Lord of the Rings* (2012), *Lego Marvel Super Heroes* (2013), *The Lego Movie Videogame* (2014), *Lego*

The Hobbit (2014), *Lego Batman: Beyond Gotham* (2014), *Lego Star Wars: Microfighters* (2014), *Lego Jurassic World* (2015), *Lego Marvel's Avengers* (2016), *Lego Star Wars: The Force Awakens* (2016), *The Lego Batman Movie Game* (2017), *Lego Marvel Super Heroes 2* (2017), *Lego The Incredibles* (2018), *Lego DC Super-Villains* (2018), *Lego Cube* (2018), *The Lego Movie 2 Videogame* (2019), *Lego Star Wars: The Skywalker Saga* (2020)

Sandbox games: *Legoland* (2000), *Lego Creator: Knights' Kingdom* (2000), *Lego Island 2: The Brickster's Revenge* (2001)

Other: *Lego Racers* (1999), *Lego Rock Raiders* (1999), *Lego My Style Preschool & Kindergarten* (2000), *Lego Alpha Team* (2000), *Lego Stunt Rally* (2000), *Lego Racers 2* (2001), *Lego Bionicle* (2001), *Galidor: Defenders of the Outer Dimension* (2002), *Football Mania* (2002), *Island Xtreme Stunts* (2002), *Drome Racers* (2002), *Bionicle: Matoran Adventures* (2002), *Bionicle* (2003), *Lego Knights' Kingdom* (2004), *Bionicle: Maze of Shadows* (2005), *Bionicle Heroes* (2006), *Lego Battles* (2009), *Lego Rock Band* (2009), *Lego Battles: Ninjago* (2011), *Lego City Undercover* (2013), *Lego City Undercover: The Chase Begins* (2013), *Lego Friends* (2013), *Lego Legends of Chima Online* (2013), *Lego Legends of Chima: Laval's Journey* (2013), *Lego Legends of Chima: Speedorz* (2013), *Lego Minifigures Online* (2014), *Lego Ninjago: Nindroids* (2014), *Lego Legends of Chima: Tribe Fighters* (2015), *Lego Ninjago: Shadow of Ronin* (2015), *Lego Worlds* (2017), *The Lego Ninjago Movie Video Game* (2017)

In 2015, Lego released a unique action-adventure game called *Lego Dimensions* that utilized the toy-to-life feature to interact with the video game. The toy-to-life function requires users to purchase a physical action figure to fully play and interact with the video game. There is usually some form of interactive technology—commonly, a port—through which the action figure plugs into the game. There are a number of video games that make use of this (*Skylander*, Nintendo Labo), with *Lego Dimensions* building a large collection of action figures from a variety of popular culture franchises. Significantly, all action figures and the toy-to-life port had to be built by the player. Although *Dimensions* was primarily action-adventure, it did incorporate puzzle and sandbox elements as well.

Dimensions, although no longer produced, can be acquired quite cheaply from different sources—online, secondhand, and so on. And while it may be problematic to sign out both the base set for the game, as well as the various minifig action figures to interact with the game, there are still some opportunities for programming within the library. This might include a *"Lego Dimensions* Night," where patrons are encouraged to bring their own sets or build one to then play with each other. Here is an entry for *Dimensions* as well as a list of the various titles you can find for the game:

Game Title: *Lego Dimensions* (2015)
Genre: Action- adventure
Format: Digital

Available Platforms: PlayStation 3, PlayStation 4, Wii U, Xbox One, Xbox 360

Age: E

Warnings: None

User behavior type: Explorer, Achiever

Description: The game features the toy-to-life format where the player has a Lego minifig and a constructed toy that gets plugged into the game, which then becomes the player's character for the game. Game features over 30 different popular culture franchises, including *Star Wars*, *Batman*, *Doctor Who*, *Ghostbusters*, *Powerpuff Girls*, and *The Wizard of Oz*. Plot of the game revolves around saving the Lego universe.

Gameplay: Players control Lego minifigs, based on a popular franchise, and using their character's abilities to solve puzzles, defeat enemies, and attempt to reach the level's end.

Series (Y or N): No—but does include multiple story and character packs

Other titles in the series: *Lego Dimensions Starter Pack* (2015), *Ghostbusters Story Pack* (2016), *Fantastic Beasts and Where to Find Them Story Pack* (2016), *The Lego Batman Movie Story Pack* (2017), *Back the Future Level Pack* (2015), *Portal 2 Level Pack* (2015), *The Simpsons Level Pack* (2015), *Doctor Who Level Pack* (2015), *Ghostbusters Level Pack* (2016), *Midway Arcade Level Pack* (2016), *Adventure Time Level Pack* (2016), *Mission: Impossible Level Pack* (2016), *Sonic the Hedgehog Level Pack* (2016), *The Goonies Level Pack* (2017), *Jurassic World Team Pack* (2015), *Scooby-Doo Team Pack* (2015), *Lego Ninjago* (2015), *DC Comics Team Pack* (2016), *Adventure Time Level Pack* (2016), *Harry Potter Team Pack* (2016), *Gremlins* (2016), *The Powerpuff Girls Team Pack* (2017), *Teen Titans Go! Team Pack* (2017), plus various fun packs (2015–2017)

Similar games: *Skylander* series (2011–2018)

The *Super Mario* Franchise

The *Super Mario* franchise is one of the most popular and numerous game series in video game history, with Mario appearing in over 200 games across various genres.[14] Originally, Mario started as the character "Jumpman" in the *Donkey Kong* arcade game but quickly morphed into one of the most successful game series in the history of video games.[15] Because of the popularity of this series, it is worthwhile to make sure you include some representation of Mario in your collection. As well, because of the multitude of genres represented by various Mario games, you will be able to recommend a number of titles to patrons looking for something specific. This volume is certainly unable to list all the Mario games; however, we have included a number of listings of the most popular and recent games available on current console systems.

Game Title: *Super Mario U Deluxe* (2012–2019)

Genre: Platform

Format: Digital
Available Platforms: Wii U, Nintendo Switch
Age: E
Warnings: None
User behavior type: Achiever
Description: As with most *Super Mario* games, this is 2.5D side-scrolling platform game where players move across various maps, completing levels and defeating bosses to eventually rescue Princess Peach.
Gameplay: Using controllers, or the Wii U's screen, players move Mario and other characters across various levels to reach the goal flag at the end of each stage while avoiding enemies and hazards, defeating bosses, and progressing each level until defeating Bowser at the final level.
Series (Y or N): No—this is a stand-alone *Mario* game. But it would be worthwhile to collect *Mario* games, as it is one of the most popular video game series.
Other titles in the series: n/a
Similar games: *Super Mario Galaxy* (2010), *Super Mario Maker 2* (2019), *Super Mario Odyssey* (2017)

Game Title: *Mario Kart 8 Deluxe* (2017)
Genre: Racing
Format: Digital
Available Platforms: Wii U, Nintendo Switch
Age: E
Warnings: None
User behavior type: Achiever
Description: This is a series of go-kart style racing games featuring popular characters from various *Mario* games and other Nintendo franchises.
Gameplay: Continues traditional gameplay from previous *Mario Kart* entries where players race against other characters and players and attempt to hinder their opponents or improve their own performances using various tools found in item boxes. The game includes different difficulty levels and features unique car designs and various tracks themed after various levels from different *Mario* video games.
Series (Y or N): Yes
Other titles in the series: *Super Mario Kart* (1992), *Mario Kart 64* (1996), *Mario Kart: Super Circuit* (2001), *Mario Kart Double Dash* (2003), *Mario Kart DS* (2005), *Mario Kart Wii* (2008), *Mario Kart 7* (2011), *Mario Kart Arcade GP VR* (2017)
Similar games: *Dirt Rally* (2015), *Sonic & All-Stars Racing* (2012)— there are not many equivalent games, as one of the many draws of *Mario Kart* is the integration of so many familiar *Mario* characters in the game mechanic.

Game Title: *Mario Tennis Aces* (2018)
Genre: Sports

Format: Digital
Available Platforms: Nintendo Switch
Age: E
Warnings: Mild Cartoon Violence
User behavior type: Achiever
Description: Part of the *Mario Tennis* series, this is a sports game where various characters from the *Super Mario* franchise engage in playing tennis tournaments against one another.
Gameplay: Strongly utilizes the hardware for the Nintendo Switch—the Joy-Cons—players engage in various tournaments and matches, unlocking different characters with each match they play.
Series (Y or N): Yes
Other titles in the series: *Mario Tennis* (1995–2013), *Mario Power Tennis* (2004, 2009), *Mario Tennis: Power Tour* (2005, 2014), *Mario Tennis Open* (2012), *Mario Tennis Ultra Smash* (2015)
Similar games: *Mario Sports Superstars* (2017)

Game Title: *Super Mario Odyssey* (2018)
Genre: Platform; action-adventure
Format: Digital
Available Platforms: Nintendo Switch
Age: E10+
Warnings: Cartoon Violence, Comic Mischief
User behavior type: Explorer, Achiever
Description: In this platform game, players follow Mario and Cappy, a sentient hat that allows Mario to control other characters and objects, as they journey across various worlds to save Princess Peach from Mario's nemesis Bowser. Unlike more traditional *Mario* games, this features a more open-world concept, allowing players to explore more freely in the game's world.
Gameplay: Taking advantage of the 3D open-world concept, this game allows players to manipulate Mario as he and his companions travel across various worlds. Many functions are the same as previous installments—allow Mario to jump, attack, run, and so on. The game also features some 2D sections, rendering the game more familiar to players of the *Mario* franchise.
Series (Y or N): Yes
Other titles in the series: See other entries in this section
Similar games: See other entries in this section

Game Title: *Yoshi's Crafted World* (2019)
Genre: Platform; side-scrolling
Format: Digital
Available Platforms: Nintendo Switch
Age: E
Warnings: Mild Cartoon Violence
User behavior type: Explorer, Achiever

Description: In this entry into the *Yoshi* spin-off series of the *Mario* franchise, Yoshi must attempt and stop Baby Bowser from stealing articles located in his home, Yoshi Island.

Gameplay: In this single-player or multiplayer side-scrolling platform 3D characters are moved on a 2.5D plane, and players are able to move and interact in a third dimension. Players also have the ability to travel forward and backward in sections of levels, as well as the ability to throw eggs at scenery and other elements of the foreground and background. The gameplay is similar to prior *Yoshi* games where the player may use Yoshi's tongue to eat enemies or other objects, turn them into eggs, and throw them outwardly into the level.

Series (Y or N): Yes

Other titles in the series: *Yoshi Island* (1995, 2002), *Yoshi's Story* (1997), *Yoshi's Universal Gravitation* (2004), *Yoshi Touch & Go* (2005), *Yoshi's Island DS* (2006), *Yoshi's New Island* (2014), *Yoshi's Woolly World* (2015)

Similar games: *Super Mario* franchise entries

Game Title: *Captain Toad: Treasure Tracker*

Genre: Action; puzzle

Format: Digital

Available Platforms: Wii U, Nintendo 3DS, Nintendo Switch

Age: E

Warnings: Cartoon Violence

User behavior type: Achiever

Description: In this puzzle, action-adventure game, which builds off games in the *Super Mario* franchise, players work with Toad as he travels across worlds, solving puzzles and collecting treasures.

Gameplay: In this third-person perspective game, players control Captain Toad, a Toad, and his companion Toadette into safely navigating through various obstacles to reach a gold star at the end of each level. Players can control the camera to give different perspectives throughout the game.

Series (Y or N): Yes

Other titles in the series: See other entries in this section on *Super Mario*

Similar games: *Super Mario Bros U* (2012)

Game Title: *Luigi's Haunted Mansion 3* (2019)

Genre: Action-adventure

Format: Digital

Available Platforms: Nintendo Switch

Age: E

Warnings: Comic Mischief, Mild Cartoon Violence

User behavior type: Explorer, Achiever

Description: In this fixed third-person perspective game, players control Luigi as they capture ghosts across a hotel setting.

Gameplay: The game can be played in either single-player story or multiplayer game mode. Players stun ghosts with Luigi's flashlight, snag them with his Poltergust, and then weaken their health down to 0 in order to capture them. Game also includes some puzzle-solving quests.

Note: The 2015 release *Luigi's Mansion Arcade* is not available for home release; it was released as an arcade game only.

Series (Y or N): Yes

Other titles in the series: *Luigi's Hammer Toss* (1990), *Mario is Missing!* (1992), *Luigi's Mansion* (2001), *Luigi's Mansion: Dark Moon* (2013), *New Super Luigi U* (2013), *Dr. Luigi* (2013, 2014), *Luigi's Mansion Arcade* (2015)

Similar games: See *Super Mario* series

Game Title: *Super Mario Maker 2* (2019)

Genre: Level editor; platform

Format: Digital

Available Platforms: Nintendo Switch

Age: E

Warnings: Mild Cartoon Violence

User behavior type: Explorer, Achiever

Description: This is a side-scrolling platform and level creation game where players are able to create their own courses and levels using elements found across a variety of titles in the *Super Mario* franchise.

Gameplay: In the game, players choose from a selection of prior *Super Mario* games to base their course's visual style and gameplay on (*Super Mario Bros.*, *Super Mario Bros. 3*, *Super Mario World*, *New Super Mario Bros. U*, and *Super Mario 3D World*). Gameplay mechanics and enemy behaviors can vary between the styles, with some elements being limited to specific styles.

Series (Y or N): Yes

Other titles in the series: *Super Mario Maker* (2015)

Similar games: *Minecraft* (2011), the *LEGO* series of games

Nintendo Switch's Labo for the Nintendo Switch

One of the recent additions to the Nintendo Switch is the introduction of the award-nominated Nintendo Labo,[16] an interactive construction set that allows users to build a variety of toys and other devices for use with the system. Kits include a robot kit, a vehicle kit, a VR kit, and a variety kit. The variety kit, for instance, allows users to build remote-controlled cars, a fishing rod, a toy piano, and so on. The devices are operated by inserting one or both of the system's joy-cons into the device and then operating them through the touch screen of the Switch's console. The variety kit also allows users to build a toy motorbike, which can be used to interact with *Mario Kart 8 Deluxe*. Various other titles also have the ability to interact with the Labo system.

This particular system is incredibly popular; however, the major down-side to these kits is their one-time use. Once the kits have been built, they can be used to interact with games but cannot be disassembled and reassembled. Because of this, libraries may not find it cost-effective to offer the Labo system on a regular basis. However, a number of sites provide templates for the various titles in the Labo system. It is advised that you purchase the original kit(s) at least once to understand their construction before using the templates to replicate, replace, or repair. Because of the number of sites that can prove a template, libraries may want to explore the Labo system for programming needs, such as a "Build Your Own Labo Piano event." Using the popular Labo system can engage users of multiple ages, drawing in children as well as parents and teachers. This can be a unique addition to your library's gaming collection.

WarHammer Video Games

The popular miniature tabletop gaming series, WarHammer, created and produced by UK-based Games Workshop, has a number of video and digital game titles that tie in with their tabletop counterparts. While some of these games are playable on console systems, most of them are playable only on PC desktops or gaming laptops.

Although a great many of the video games are produced by the Game Workshop, none of the games are actually situated in traditional WarHammer settings. A number of third-party video game producers have also created games broadly based on the franchise.

If you are going to include any of the miniature tabletop gaming versions of WarHammer, it might be beneficial for you to consider incorporating some of the video games into your collection as well. This can be especially useful if you plan any programming around WarHammer—such as gaming nights or paint your own miniatures night. Having the digital games can ensure you attract interested patrons to these events. Finally, if you have novice WarHammer players who find themselves enjoying these games, being able to direct their attention to the digital games can help you to draw attention to that collection.

Here are a few examples of console-based *WarHammer* games:

Game Title: *Space Hulk: Deathwing* (2018)
Genre: First-person shooter
Format: Digital
Available Platforms: PlayStation 4
Age: M17+
Warnings: Blood and Gore, Intense Violence
User behavior type: Killer
Description: This first-person shooter game is based upon the turn-based strategy of the tabletop miniatures board game Space Hulk. It expands the gameplay environment beyond the narrow mazelike corridors of the original board game to include massive spaceship interiors.

Gameplay: The player takes on the role of a Librarian of the Dark Angels 1st company of Space Marine, with the objective of preventing their ship, The Space Hulk, from being taken over by Genestealers and losing the artifacts they have collected prior to invasion.

Series (Y or N): Yes

Other titles in the series: See other entries in this list

Similar games: See other games in *WarHammer* section

Game Title: *Warhammer: Vermintide 2*

Genre: Action

Format: Digital

Available Platforms: PlayStation 4 and Xbox One

Age: M17+

Warnings: Blood and Gore, Intense Violence

User behavior type: Killer

Description: This first-person, cooperative game is set in the Warhammer universe, players battle cooperatively against the Chaos army and a race of rat-men known as the Skaven.

Gameplay: Players can choose from five different characters, each with a unique and customizable set of abilities. Players also choose from 15 different missions, collecting loot and engaging in combat throughout the game. Players can also set the difficulty level for the game—one of three versions.

Note: There are a number of expansions for this particular game, these expansions either open up new missions, weapons, enemies, characters, or levels of difficulty.

Series (Y or N): Yes

Other titles in the series: See other entries in this list

Similar games: See other games in *WarHammer* section

Game Title: *Blood Bowl 2* (2015)

Genre: Sports; turn-based strategy

Format: Digital

Available Platforms: Xbox One, PlayStation 4, Steam

Age: T

Warnings: Alcohol Reference, Blood and Gore, Language, Mild Suggestive Themes, Violence

User behavior type: Achiever, Killer

Description: A sequel to the 2009 *Blood Bowl* video games, this series features a fantasy version of American Football and is adapted from the popular Blood Bowl Board game. The game features a number of playable races, including Humans, Orcs, Dwarfs, Skaven, High Elves, Dark Elves, Bretonnians, and Chaos.

Gameplay: Gameplay here replicates the rules of American Football, with a number of fantastical twists. For instance, the game is played between two teams of up to 16 players, each team fielding up to 11 players at a time. Scoring includes touchdowns, which are scored by taking the ball into the opposition's end zone, and a team can win either by scoring the most touchdowns or by violently eliminating the other team's entire roster. Along with various features of the original Blood Bowl, the sequel features a number of new and unique modes, such as the Campaign Mode, where the player must help a defeated team return to their glory. It should be noted that Blood Bowl is known for its extreme violence.

Series (Y or N): Yes

Other titles in the series: *Blood Bowl* (2009)

Similar games: Other sports games, such as *NFL* games, to capture the sports element of the game. But if users are more interested in the fantastical elements of the game, they can look to other games in the *Warhammer* franchise, or other fantasy or sci-fi video games.

Notes

1. "This Month in Physics History: October 1958: Physicist Invents First Video Game," *American Physical Society* 17, no. 9 (October 2008), https://www.aps.org/publications/apsnews/200810/physicshistory.cfm.

2. Shawn M. Doherty et al., "Recategorization of Video Game Genres," *Proceedings of the Human Factors and Ergonomics Society Annual Meeting* 62, no. 1 (September 2018): 2100.

3. Eddie Makuch, "E3 2019 Attendance Falls Compared to Last Year," Gamespot, September 16, 2019, https://www.gamespot.com/articles/e3-2019-attendance-falls-compared-to-last-year/1100-6467795/.

4. Tom Ivan, "Tokyo Game Show 2019 Attendance Declines, 2020 Event Dated," VGC, September 16, 2019, https://www.videogameschronicle.com/news/tokyo-game-show-2019-attendance-declines-2020-event-dated/.

5. "Gamescom Wiki Guide: Attendance and Stats," April 16, 2020, https://www.ign.com/wikis/gamescom/Attendance_and_Stats.

6. Entertainment Software Ratings Board, "Ratings Guide," 2019, https://www.esrb.org/ratings-guide/.

7. "Nintendo Switch System Launches Worldwide," Free Library, 2017, https://www.thefreelibrary.com/NINTENDO+SWITCH+SYSTEM+LAUNCHES+WORLDWIDE-a0510556297.

8. Michael Andronico, "The $199 Nintendo Switch Lite Is a Dedicated Handheld with a Smaller Screen, Longer Battery Life," Toms Guide, July 10, 2019, https://news.yahoo.com/199-nintendo-switch-lite-dedicated-122018150.html.

9. James Wright, "Xbox One S Release Date, Specs and Price Confirmed for Microsoft's Slim HDR Ready Console," *Daily Star*, September 26, 2019, https://www.dailystar.co.uk/tech/gaming/xbox-one-release-date-specs-17085516.

10. "Classic PC Games," Internet Archive, accessed February 2020, https://archive.org/details/classicpcgames.

11. "Tanglewood," *Tanglewoodgame.com,* accessed March 2020, https://tanglewoodgame.com/index.html.

12. Andrew Webster, "These Are the Developers Creating New Games for Old Consoles," The Verge, May 9, 2017, https://www.theverge.com/2017/5/9/15584416/new-games-retro-consoles-nes-snes-sega-genesis-famicom.

13. Thorsten Quanat and Sonja Kröger, eds., *Multiplayer: The Social Aspects of Digital Gaming* (New York: Routledge, 2013).

14. Mark J. P. Wolf, *Video Games FAQ: All That's Left to Know about Games and Gaming Culture* (Milwaukee, WI: Backbeat Books, 2017), 145.

15. Ibid., pp. 145.

16. Stefanie Fogel, "'God of War,' 'Red Dead 2' Lead BAFTA Game Awards Nominations," *Variety*, March 15, 2019, https://variety.com/2019/gaming/news/british -academy-games-awards-2019-nominees-1203163369/.

9
Online Video Game Platforms

While it is essential to include physical video games and video game consoles as part of your collection, there is a rising trend in gaming that libraries may also want to consider—online gaming. Online gaming has existed as long as the Internet has been in existence, since the 1990s,[1] and with the development of 3D graphics and increasingly stronger resolution of images online, online games continue to evolve and improve. There are different genres of online gaming, and you may already be familiar with some of the terminology. Massive Multiplayer Online (MMO) is a general phrase used to describe any online game that has large numbers of players playing together in a particular setting or world. Since 2004, one specific genre has been seen as an industry leader within the online gaming world: Massive Online Role-Playing Games (MORPGs).[2] MORPGs, such as *World of Warcraft* (2004) (hereinafter referred to as *WoW*) and *Final Fantasy XIV Online* (2010), draw millions of gamers a year and continue to be a major draw for gamers. Alongside MORPGs is the growing world of mobile gaming, available through smartphones, with games such as *Pokémon Go* (2016). The playing field for gamers to transition online continues to grow. In fact, globally, the online gaming market size is expected to reach $79 billion (USD) by 2025.[3] Because of the number of gamers who involve themselves in online gaming, as well as the unique possibilities it provides to people interested in trying new games, libraries should be taking online gaming into consideration.

One of the most attractive elements around online gaming is the abundance of games that have become free to play or download from online sources. This naturally has some excellent benefits for a library looking to set up a gaming collection by having a dedicated laptop with an abundance of games loaded to either check out to users or plan programming around. One of the most popular free-to-play titles is *League of Legends*. However, the downside to free-to-play games are the number of in-game purchases that players are expected to make in order to progress through the game.[4] Henry Tucker describes this phenomenon in relation to Electronic Arts' game *Battlefield Heroes*, where "the idea is that you have your soldier and you earn points in the game, which you can then use to customize your character to make them unique to you. However, if you don't have much time in which to do this, you can buy upgrades using real money to help you progress faster."[5] These in-game purchases, commonly referred to as microtransactions, have unfortunately become an industry standard. Microtransactions may cause a number of problems for libraries as there may be no way to monitor and prevent users from making purchases within the game. Nonetheless, being aware of online gaming is essential because of the inherent social aspect gamers find within these games.

Players flock to online gaming platforms and games in part for the ease of access but also for the socialization aspect. For instance, in speaking about the development of social skills and language skills for English as a second language learners, Sarah Pasfield-Neofitou explains, "By combining social and game aspects, game worlds provide opportunities to participate in interaction which is both supportive and social, as well as authentic and goal-driven."[6] Pasfield-Neofitou is speaking directly on the subject of online games—such as *WoW*—and the way these games create a sense of community for players—which we will discuss later.

Online gaming systems have become a recent major trend in video games through such platforms as Steam, Google Stadia, and Apple Arcade. Because of the number of gamers who are now flocking to online gaming, and the ease with which games are available through such platforms, libraries need to consider how they might best utilize these systems and resources.

This chapter will explore various online games as well as introduce some of the more popular online platforms for gaming, including some suggestions for library programming for both categories. It will also address the all-important question for libraries: to subscribe or not to subscribe?

Online Role-Playing Games

Currently, MORPGs and Massive Multiplayer Online Role-Playing Games (MMORPGs) are the most predominant type of online games. Since their appearance in 1997, with the introduction of *EverQuest* (1997),[7] MORPs and MMORPGs have become a multimillion-dollar gaming genre. While early MMORPGs were certainly popular with gamers online, it was the introduction of *WoW* in 2004 that really saw the genre skyrocket in popularity. As Nick Yee points out, *WoW* had more than 6 million subscribers by 2006, and by 2013 it broke the 12 million subscriber mark—making it one of the most successful online games in history.[8]

There are a number of elements that define this genre, including:

- a player assumes the identity of just one character for the majority of the game play,

- multiple players are able to interact with each other, and

- the game has a persistent world (hosted by the game's publisher) that continues to exist and evolve even while the player is offline.

In particular, MMORPGs are commonly regarded as games where players must go on missions, quests, and raids, and complete tasks in order to achieve rewards—all within the rules and confines of the game.[9] These games also have a large social aspect, as gamers must build groups—or guilds—of players they engage with in their adventures throughout the game. The players form strong attachments to their team members who count on them in order to complete particular tasks; however, one possible downside is when team members are located around the world, in different time zones. Thus, these games appeal to players because of the world they create, the communities they build, and the emotional attachment they can promise gamers.

Programming with Online Gaming

While online gaming—specifically online role-playing games—exists primarily online and is often subscription based, libraries should look at the value of adding this resource to their collection, as it does provide for some unique programming opportunities. Here are a few examples of programs that work very well with this platform:

Build-a-Guild Workshops: This could be an event targeted at younger or inexperienced players, where a librarian (or community member) experienced in *WoW* or other MMORPGs walks attendees through establishing a character and either creating or joining a guild. You might want to use a library computer room or invite users to bring their own devices, walk the attendees through signing up and how to create a character suitable for them. It is a good idea to include some active time in the game to help those new to playing become familiar with the controls and functions of the game.

In-game Event Celebrations: Many MMORPGs include in-game events or even holidays, for instance, *WoW* hosts such holidays as "Love is in the Air" in February and the Cataclysm Timewalking Dungeon Event every April.[10] These events can happen annually or be a one-time event and often include: small free-for-all skirmishes (usually with the intent of finding treasure or rewards), worldwide friendly celebrations, and ongoing military campaigns. Keeping track of these kinds of events and organizing programming around them can be beneficial to your library and gaming collection. Perhaps, for instance, you will host a pseudo Valentine's Day program focusing on the "Love is in the Air" event, encouraging users to join a campaign and play in the library.

Online Consoles and Gaming Platforms

The genres of online gaming are becoming increasingly complex with the advent of online console gaming. In the beginning, online games were typically played by purchasing a CD-ROM version of the game and purchasing a monthly subscription. Then games shifted to being hosted on online platforms such as Steam, and more recently online games are available across multiple platforms. Players can now play the game using their online gaming accounts and their computer or they can play using their PlayStation or Xbox by purchasing the game title and an online subscription through the consoles.

To Subscribe or Not to Subscribe

Video games are no longer confined to being played on the console. As the discussion on online role-playing games has clearly indicated, video games have increasingly become an online fixture.

Given that there will be an interest from patrons for the ability to game online, libraries must weigh the pros and cons of offering such services. This discussion is quite similar to the one we had in Chapter 2 when we discussed end-user license agreements (EULAs), managing online accounts, and subscription-based gaming. Depending on a variety of factors, libraries may wish to proceed with online consoles and online gaming platforms to provide this service to their patrons either for programs online or create some sort of borrowing/loan system. We encourage you to go back and read Chapter 2 and use that discussion to help formulate your plan if you wish to offer this service. Online gaming—specifically online consoles or gaming platforms—can take a variety of forms:

- Each major console system now offers an online store where games can be purchased and later downloaded onto the player's console.

- The major consoles systems—Nintendo, PlayStation, and Xbox—all have an online platform where you can play older games from previous iterations of those gaming systems. These platforms are commonly a subscription-based service where the user can determine the fee structure they want. For example, Nintendo offers Nintendo Switch Online where users can sign up to play games available on the original Nintendo Entertainment System and the Super Nintendo Entertainment System.

- Platforms also offer online gaming options to allow for friends to play games together, this is especially valuable for multiplayer games. Again, these are mostly subscription based, and while there is the opportunity for a group account, libraries may find this option difficult to maintain and supervise.

Cloud Gaming

This section will outline each of the three major services—Steam, Google, and Apple—as well as talking about some of the smaller services, in order to help libraries decide if they want to consider signing up for these services. Because of the cost-effective nature of these services (e.g., Google Stadia is approximately a third of the cost of purchasing a Nintendo Switch or a PlayStation 4), they can be very appealing to libraries as a gaming option. But some consideration needs to be made here as to how to include this option in your collection. Will you provide log-in information for patrons? Or will you simply download the software only to your computers and require patrons to have their own account to play their own games? Will you circulate the controllers? Or will you use these systems purely for programming purposes?

Recently, a new trend has started to develop in online gaming—cloud gaming or online gaming platforms. These new systems—the major ones offered by Apple, Google, and Valve Corporation—allow users to either download a game directly onto their PC or play that game directly through their service. Along with the major services, there are a number of small, but equally unique services, such as Nvidia and RainWay.

These systems offer a range of unique opportunities for gamers and for libraries, including providing greater access to games, providing a cost-effective gaming option, and providing greater connectivity to gaming communities. The majority of these systems also include a gaming controller unique to their systems; however, the controller and cost of games can be remarkably less expensive than investing in one or more of the consoles.

Below are descriptions of each service, along with some discussion as to potential avenues of exploration around programming for libraries to consider when developing a gaming collection or working with patrons looking for their next gaming adventure.

Stadia

This is a fairly new addition to the gaming console environment, having been released by Google in 2019, as a new alternative in gaming. This is a cloud-based streaming gaming service that allows users to access a large catalogue, provided users are using a high-speed internet connection.[11]

Users purchase a Stadia gaming controller through Google, which includes a Google Chromecast that allows you to connect to the Stadia store and link your controller to your TV, laptop, or mobile device. You are also able to connect wirelessly through a network, rather than the device you are playing on, which limits problems around connectivity. In order to play games, however, users log onto the Stadia catalogue and purchase individual games to stream and play, which is not dissimilar to more traditional consoles. At the time of writing, Google has made approximately 50 (and growing) games available for purchase and play on Stadia, with pricing ranging between $30 and $60. Some of the titles include: *Tomb Raider: Definitive Edition*, *Red Dead Redemption II*, *Marvel's Avengers*, *Final Fantasy XV*, and *Assassin's Creed: Odyssey*.

Although Stadia is a fairly new way of playing console games, it does have some unique possibilities for library gaming collections and programming. You will want to consider a couple options:

- **Lending out the Stadia controller and Chromecast**. This option presents some specific issues—will patrons be buying their own games? What happens once they return the device? How will they access and play games they bought for themselves? This also presents the question of whether you will be wiping patron data from the system each time the controller has been returned. It is essential to consider this to ensure the privacy of a patron's information.

- **Set up a dedicated account, with a variety of games**. This option also presents some problems— will you be purchasing the same game over multiple consoles? Will the patron have to log-in to your account, possibly allowing them to make purchases on their own?

- **Having the Stadia be a dedicated "for use in library only" console**. This option means you can control not only what games are being purchased for the system but also you prevent patrons from having to spend a great deal of their own money. This way you can arrange and organize different types of programming around the Stadia. Perhaps developing a special afternoon gaming time, where patrons can connect the Stadia to their own devices and play, rather than require the additional use of a TV or other screen to play— which is a limitation with more traditional consoles and library programming.

Although this is a brand-new form of technology for gaming and is thus far untested in the library environment, there are some really interesting possibilities for this kind of technology. For instance, this may be a good alternative if a library's budget does not allow for multiple expensive consoles and games.

Steam

Steam originally was created and debuted in 2003 by Valve Corporation[12] as a tool for the company to provide updates to their games, but it quickly became a unique online platform and store for games. Steam currently has over 30,000 games available to play and purchase (this does not include downloadable licensed content (DLCs) or software).[13] Steam has transitioned from being a cloud-based warehouse for games and a community of gamers[14] into an actual online cloud-based gaming platform.

At the most basic level, Steam acts as a space to play games. Unlike Stadia, Steam will connect using most available Bluetooth game controllers, including: the PlayStation Dualshock 4 controller, the Xbox One controller, and others. Using the Steam app, users connect to the system (using PC- or Apple-based option, smart TV option, or various mobile versions) and play the game of their choice.

Steam is synonymous with online gaming and has some of the most popular titles including *Counterstrike: Global Offensive, Dota 2, Tom Clancy's Rainbow Six Siege, Team Fortress 2, Destiny 2, and Monster Hunter: World*, among others and routinely has over 16 million active users playing games at any given time.[15]

Steam also offers support for game developers, referred to as Steam Workshops and Steamworks, which offer developers tools and a community and services to both create and eventually publish their games.[16] The workshops are primarily intended as "a hub that lets community item creators show off their creations so that they can be rated by other players."[17]

There are a number of ways in which libraries can engage with Steam. You may opt not to create a subscription account for the library, but you can explore other ways to engage with the service (e.g., evenings devoted to the Steam Workshop program, where patrons can work on aspects of different games and work through the various workshops available through the platform).

Another feature of Steam is the *Tabletop Simulator* (2015), a video game that is designed to mimic particular tabletop board games, as well as being a sandbox that allows users to create their own board games in a virtual space. Up to ten players can engage in play of a number of preloaded games: chess, checkers, and poker. Users can mix up games, change game content, or create new games and game elements. The producers of *Tabletop Simulator* have also partnered with various game publishers to offer virtual versions of different games, such as Tiny Epic Galaxy, Boss Monster, and Scythe.[18]

Because of the creator element of the *Tabletop Simulator*, libraries might find this an interesting option when exploring programming as users can create and customize both pieces of games and create new games. These new creations are then supported and shared using Steam Workshop. Libraries might want to capitalize on this functionality by holding Creator Nights, where patrons can engage with *Tabletop Simulator* and create new games, or try some of the unique offerings available through Steam. Or, if a library does not have access to a particular physical board game that a patron wants to try, they might want to try using the Simulator.

As discussed earlier in the book, many libraries are experimenting with having Steam accounts in the library. Typically, these accounts are tied to a particular computer that users can access in the library rather than giving out passwords to accounts. It is important to read the section on online game licensing in Chapter 2 before you consider adding this particular platform for your patrons, as there are some important considerations to take into account (e.g., EULAs, software and hardware requirements, technical support, and ongoing costs). In our experience, the libraries that have provided this service to their patrons have largely been successful.

Apple Arcade

Apple recently introduced their own online subscription cloud-based gaming system, accessible only through their mobile systems, computers, Apple TV, and other Apple systems. There are a number of unique factors around the Apple Arcade platform, including the ability to use either Apple Arcades own controller or most other Bluetooth-enabled controllers with the system. Currently, there are over a hundred games available on the system,[19] all of which are generally unique to Apple Arcade. Games include: *Lego Brawls* (2019), *Sayonara: Wild Hearts* (2019), *Ocean Horn 2: Knights of the Lost Realm* (2019), *Sonic Racing* (2019), and *Kings of the Castle* (2019). Some games like *Shantae 5* (2019) can also be found on Nintendo Switch.

The subscription service does not use streaming, rather users will need to download the games they want to play. Apple promotes the system as free of any microtransactions or in-game ads, rather promising a "highly curated service [that] features premium games that are untainted by in-app purchases and ads."[20]

Because of the proprietary nature of the Apple Arcade, libraries may find there are few ways to engage with this system unless they have a large collection of Apple computers or mobile devices, such as iPads. Nonetheless, libraries might find Apple Arcade beneficial when hosting group gaming events or video game tournaments.

Other Online Gaming Platforms

While Steam is a juggernaut of online gaming, with Apple and Google gaining traction, there are other services outside of these three major players. In the online gaming platform environment, there are a large number of smaller, but no less powerful, online services. These services include, but are not limited to:

Remotr

Rainway

Nvidia GameStream

Jump

GeForce Now

Shadow by Blade

Playkey

Parsec.

Uplay

Origin

GOG.com

Battle.net

These services offer a variety of ways for users to access their gaming collection and discover new and independent games. Rainway, for instance, offers users with a platform or dashboard, through which users can access games from a variety of different platforms and vendors, including Steam, Epic Games, and RockStar Games.[21] Rainway, then, allows users to access games from their account(s) and play them across multiple screens.

Libraries can utilize some of these other systems by downloading the platforms' software onto library computers—or those computers the library has dedicated to gaming—and allow users to log into their own accounts and play games saved there. This can also be a good way for libraries to engage in video game tournaments, as they can provide the space and the technology for patrons, but ask that patrons or users join the tournament with their own copies of the game.

Starting Collection and Reference Guide: MORPGs and MMORPGs

Below you will find a select few MORPGs and MMORPGs. Keeping in mind that these games are online-based subscriptions, if you find that *WoW* events, for instance, are proving popular with patrons and gamers, you might want to look at incorporating some of the novelizations and strategy guides for that game into your collection. When dealing with users who express interest in games like *WoW*, it will be important to know of other titles in the genre to refer to them.

Game Title: *Elder Scrolls Online*

Year: 2014

Genre: Massive Multiplayer Online Role-Playing Game; action

Format: Digital (online)

Available Platforms: Microsoft Windows, MacOS, PlayStation 4, Xbox One, Steam, Google Stadia online only—available for play through desktop and laptops, PlayStation 4, and Xbox One. Also available through Steam and Google Stadia.

Age: M17+

Warnings: Blood and Gore, Sexual Themes, Use of Alcohol, Violence

User behavior type: Killer, Achiever, Explorer, Socializer

Description: The online version of *Elder Scrolls*, which is directly connected with other entries on the series (see the section on Video Games), takes place on the fictional continent of Tamriel and is an open-world game that allows players to explore the game's environment, engage in quests, events, and socialized adventure. Although the game does not feature any single-player offline features, it does allow gamers who prefer solo playing ample opportunity in the online environment.

Gameplay: Player initially designs their character (avatar) by selecting a class, gender, race, and crafting skill. The player can also opt to select a creature (vampire or werewolf) as their avatar. The player then can either join groups of other players, or engage on solo adventures as they explore the expansive environment of the game.

Series (Y or N): Yes

Other titles in the series: *Elder Scrolls Online: Tamriel Unlimited* (2015), *Elder Scrolls Online: Gold Edition* (2016), *Elder Scrolls Online: Morrowind Expansion* (2017), *Elder Scrolls Online: Summerset Expansion* (2018), *Elder Scrolls Online: Elsweyr Expansion* (2019), *Elder Scrolls Online: Greymoor Expansion* (2020)

Similar games: See other games in this section

Game Title: *EVE Online*
Year: 2003
Genre: Massive Multiplayer Online Role-Playing Game; Science Fiction; Action-adventure
Format: Digital (online)
Available Platforms: Microsoft Windows, MacOS, Steam
Age: T
Warnings: Violence
User behavior type: Killer, Achiever, Explorer, Socializer
Description: This is a spaced-based, persistent world MMORPG, which is known for its complex, single-shared game world where players engage in unscripted economic competition, warfare, and political schemes with other players.
Gameplay: There are some unique features to *EVE Online*, for instance, players start the game by either selecting a previously created character or by creating a new one, selecting race and other definable characteristics of that character. Also, *EVE Online* is a single-universe game, which means there are not numerous copies of the game running at once. The primary push of the game is exploration, in that players explore space, flying around and visiting various stations and engaging in combat in real time. Players progress in the game by training skills, which is a passive process, so that it continues when the player is logged out.
Series (Y or N): No
Other titles in the series: n/a
Similar games: See other games in this section

Game Title: *EverQuest*
Year: 1999–2003
Genre: Massive Multiplayer Online Role-Playing Game; fantasy
Format: Digital (online)
Available Platforms: Microsoft Windows, MacOS, Steam
Age: T
Warnings: Suggestive Themes, Use of Alcohol, Violence
User behavior type: Achiever, Killer
Description: This 3D fantasy-themed MMORPG had players create a character and navigate an open-concept medieval fantasy world, Norrath, encountering monsters and other enemies to gain both treasure and experience points as well as mastering trade skills. The game, like other MMORPGs, heavily relies on role-play by having players join guilds and interacting with other players as either allies or enemies. Subsequent sequels to the game expanded upon the original and allowed players to continue evolving and exploring in the game.
Gameplay: Players start by creating their character—avatar—by deciding on gender, race, class, occupation, and physical appearance. Players advance in levels by gaining experience points, which they receive

by fighting monsters, learning skills, and completing quests. Players can engage in player versus player combat but only in specific zones designated to that kind of play. The game is divided up into more than 500 zones, which represent a variety of geographic features.

Note: It is important to note that *EverQuest* faced massive competition from *WoW*, which dominated the MMORPG market and made it increasingly difficult for *EverQuest* to secure more players. In 2015, there was a release to celebrate the 16th anniversary of the game, which saw a small uptake in popularity. Finally, in 2019, an online free Emulated *EverQuest* Server started giving players the opportunity to play the original game again, which caused a massive uptake due to the nostalgic quality of this option.

Series (Y or N): Yes

Other titles in the series: Expansions include: *The Ruins of Kunark* (2000), *The Scars of Velious* (2000), *The Shadows of Luclin* (2001), *The Planes of Power* (2002), *The Legacy of Ykesha* (2003), *Lost Dungeons of Norrath* (2003), *Gates of Discord* (2004), *Omens of War* (2004), *Dragons of Norrath* (2005), *Depths of Darkhollow* (2005), *Prophecy of Ro* (2006), *The Serpent's Spine* (2006), *The Buried Sea* (2007), *Secrets of Faydwer* (2007), *Seeds of Destruction* (2008), *Underfoot* (2009), *House of Thule* (2010), *Veil of Alaris* (2011), *Rain of Fear* (2012), *Call of the Forsaken* (2013), *The Darkened Sea* (2014), *The Broken Mirror* (2015), *Empires of Kunark* (2016), *Ring of Scale* (2017), *The Burning Lands* (2018), *Torment of Velious* (2019)

Similar games: See other games in this section

Game Title: *Final Fantasy XIV*

Year: 2013

Genre: Massive Multiplayer Online Role-Playing Game; Fantasy; Action-adventure

Format: Digital (online)

Available Platforms: Microsoft Windows, MacOS, PlayStation 4, Xbox One, Steam, PlayStation 3

Age: T

Warnings: Alcohol Reference, Animated Blood, Mild Language, Suggestive Themes, Violence

User behavior type: Achiever, Killer, Explorer

Description: This MMORPG takes place in the fictional land of Eorzea, the player character escapes the devastation of an apocalyptic event, caused by the primal dragon Bahamut by time traveling five years into the future. As Eorzea recovers and rebuilds, the player must deal with the impending threat of invasion by the Garlean Empire from the north. The game is very similar to other MMORPGs with the creation of a character, the choice of a class, the choice of a server (realm), and open-world exploration to engage in quests or campaigns to gain experience and increase the character's level.

Gameplay: *Final Fantasy XIV* features an ever-evolving environment in which players can interact with it and each other. Initially, players create and customize their characters for use in the game by selecting name, race, gender, facial features, and starting class. Players improve their characters by gaining experience points (EXP). There are four primary sources of experience points: completing quests, exploring instanced dungeons, participating in Full Active Time Events, and slaying monsters. Characters use a variety of weapons to engage in combat with monsters and fight in battles—which form the major element of action (party play) in the game. The game also includes its own economy, which players can interact with by selling items in the game and conducting microtransactions.

Series (Y or N): Yes

Other titles in the series: See entry for *Final Fantasy XV* in the Key Starting Collection Suggestion: Video Games Section

Similar games: See other games in this section

Game Title: *Guild Wars 2*

Year: 2012

Genre: Massive Multiplayer Online Role-Playing Game; Action-adventure

Format: Digital (online)

Available Platforms: Microsoft Windows, MacOS, Steam

Age: T

Warnings: Blood, Mild Language, Use of Alcohol, Violence

User behavior type: Killer, Achiever, Explorer, Socializer

Description: In this sequel to an immensely popular *Guild Wars* (2005), players encounter an open-world concept where they must reunite members of a disbanded guild who are the only chance to defeat a group of dragons that have caused havoc to the game's setting: Tyria. The game is unique in that the storyline is responsive to player actions—a rare feature in multiplayer games.

Gameplay: Players initially create a character by deciding on their race, gender, class, and profession—which can then determine the kinds of skills a player can access throughout the game. The game uses skill-based combat, where players select a limited series of skills—some predetermined, some chosen by the player, and then engage in combat. There are two types of combat present in *Guild Wars* 2, a smaller-scale, tactical combat or a "World versus World" combat, which takes place in a persistent world.

Series (Y or N): Yes

Other titles in the series: Original Game: *Guild Wars* (2005). *Guild Wars 2* expansions have been released between 2013 and 2017. These expansions develop a story called The Living World 1–4. Notable titles include: *Dragon Bash* (2013), *Guild Wars 2: Sky Pirates of Tyria* (2013), *Guild Wars 2: Bazaar of the Four Winds* (2013), *Guild Wars 2: Cutthroat Politics* (2013), *Guild Wars 2: Super Adventure Box: Back to School* (2013). *Guild Wars 2: Hearts of Thorns* (2015), *Guild Wars 2: Out of its Shadows* (2016), *Guild Wars 2: Path of Fire* (2017).

Similar games: See other games in this section

Game Title: *League of Legends*
Year: 2009
Genre: Massive Multiplayer Online Role-Playing Game; Action-adventure; Fantasy
Format: Digital (online)
Available Platforms: Microsoft Windows, MacOS, Steam
Age: T
Warnings: Blood, Mild Language, Use of Alcohol and Tobacco, Fantasy Violence, Mild Suggestive Themes
User behavior type: Killer, Achiever, Explorer, Socializer
Description: *League of Legends (LoL)* is free to play online but is supported through microtransactions, which can be costly for the player. The main purpose of the game is for players to assume the role of a "champion" and battle against a team of other players—or computer-controlled champions. Players must destroy the opposing team's "Nexus," a structure that lies at the heart of a base protected by defensive structures.
Gameplay: *LoL* is a multiplayer online battle arena game. In the game, players must compete in matches that last between 20 and 50 minutes. Players must work together in teams to achieve victory. Notably, each match is discrete, with all champions starting off relatively weak but increasing in strength by accumulating items and experience over the course of the game.
Series (Y or N): No
Other titles in the series: n/a
Similar games: See other games in this section

Game Title: *Star Wars: The Old Republic*
Year: 2011
Genre: Massive Multiplayer Online Role-Playing Game; Science Fiction; Action-adventure
Format: Digital (online)
Available Platforms: Microsoft Windows, Steam
Age: T
Warnings: Blood and Gore, Mild Language, Sexual Themes, Violence
User behavior type: Explorer, Achiever, Killer
Description: This MMORPG takes place in the Star Wars universe and takes place at a time of peace between the Sith Empire and the Galactic Republic. The game is often considered one of the fastest-growing MMORPGs with millions of subscribers mere days after its launch.[22] As with other MMORPGs, players must design their avatar, deciding on their class and other customizable options. The game is open world but has a number of instanced elements where players complete specific quests to increase their level. The game is set during a Cold War where the Jedi Order and Galactic Republic are struggling to maintain control of core worlds while the Sith plot their downfall and the expansion of the Sith Empire. There is a significant focus on

the storyline, and the various classes available to players are focused on a three-act storyline that progresses as each character levels up.

Gameplay: Players join the games as members of either the Galactic Republic or the Sith Empire, each individual player may possess morality at any point along the light/dark spectrum—which can force the player to become either Jedi or Sith. Players advance by completing missions, exploring, and defeating enemies. New skills are unlocked with each by level and are taught by trainers and can be learned at a multitude of locations. There are various missions that can be played in a multiplayer format, which requires the cooperation of multiple players to complete objectives. Players' choices can permanently open or close storylines and affect players' non-player character (NPC) companions. The game provides greater levels of context for characters' missions than other MMORPG. Each player receives a starship, and engages in space combat, which is intended to feel very much like a cinematic experience. Finally, like other MMORPGs, the game features dungeons and raids.

Series (Y or N): Yes

Other titles in the series: Expansions include *Rise of the Hutt Cartel* (2013), *Galactic Starfighter* (2014), *Galactic Strongholds* (2014), *Shadow of Revan* (2014), *Knights of the Fallen Empire* (2015), *Knights of the Eternal Throne* (2016), *Onslaught* (2019)

Similar games: See other games in this section

Game Title: *World of Warcraft*

Year: 2004

Genre: Massive Multiplayer Online Role-Playing Game; Fantasy; Action-adventure

Format: Digital (online)

Available Platforms: Microsoft Windows, MacOS, Steam

Age: T

Warnings: Blood and Gore, Crude Humor, Mild Language, Suggestive Themes, Use of Alcohol, Violence

User behavior type: Achiever, Killer, Explorer

Description: The game takes place within the Warcraft world of Azeroth and is an open-world concept game where players create unique character avatars from a range of character types, join a guild, and engage in campaigns and adventures to earn rewards and increase the level and abilities of their character—currently the level cap for the game is 120. The game is known for its socialization elements in which players interact with each other through their avatars, the ever-evolving and updating environment in which the characters play, and the degree of microtransactions that players may have to purchase throughout their experience in the game. Important to note that for players to get the full experience of *WoW*, they must purchase a subscription—players can sign up for a trial subscription, but they are limited in gameplay and can only advance to level 20.

Gameplay: *WoW* has a generally simple gameplay—initial stages include creating your avatar (including race and what faction you want to belong to) and selecting a server (realm). Each realm is an individual copy of the game world, is organized by language, and falls into one of two categories:

- **Normal:** Where the gameplay is mostly focused on defeating monsters and completing quests, with optional player-versus-player fights and role-play

- **Role-play (RP):** Works the same as a "Normal" realm but focuses on players role-playing in-character

    As characters become more developed, they gain various talents and skills, requiring the player to further define the abilities of that character. To become more developed, players must engage in and complete quests. Quests are usually available from non-playable characters (NPCs) and will reward the player with some combination of experience points, items, and in-game money as well as new skills and abilities and the ability to explore new areas. Quests are the game's primary narrative tool through the quest's text and scripted NPC actions. Quests involve killing creatures, gathering resources, finding objects, speaking to various NPCs, visiting specific locations, interacting with objects in the world, or delivering an item to gain experience and treasures.

Series (Y or N): Yes

Other titles in the series: Prior to *WoW*, the series was referred to as *Warcraft*: *Warcraft: Orcs & Humans* (1994), *Warcraft II: Tides of Darkness* (1995), *Warcraft II: Beyond the Dark Portal* (1996), *Warcraft II: Battle.net Edition* (1999), *Warcraft III: Reign of Chaos* (2002), *Warcraft III: The Frozen Throne* (2003). There have been a number of expansions to the original *WoW* game: *World of Warcraft* (2004), *World of Warcraft: The Burning Crusade* (2007), *World of Warcraft: Wrath of the Lich King* (2008), *World of Warcraft: Cataclysm* (2010), *World of Warcraft: Mists of Pandaria* (2012), *Hearthstone* (2014), *World of Warcraft: Warlords of Draenor* (2014), *World of Warcraft: Legion* (2016), *World of Warcraft: Battle for Azeroth* (2018), *World of Warcraft Classic* (2019), *Warcraft III: Reforged* (2020), *World of Warcraft: Shadowlands* (2020)

Similar games: See other games in this section

Notes

1. Nick Yee, *The Proteus Paradox: How Online Games and Virtual Worlds Change Us—and How They Don't* (New Haven, CT: Yale University Press, 2014), 15.

2. Ibid., 17.

3. "Online Gaming Market to Grow at 10% CAGR to Hit $79 Billion by 2025—Global Insights on Share, Size, Growth Drivers, Value Chain Analysis, Investments

Plans, Key Stakeholders and Business Opportunities: Adroit Market Research," Globenewswire, February 14, 2020, https://www.globenewswire.com/news-release /2020/02/14/1985063/0/en/Online-Gaming-Market-to-grow-at-10-CAGR-to-hit -79-billion-by-2025-Global-Insights-on-Share-Size-Growth-Drivers-Value-Chain -Analysis-Investments-Plans-Key-Stakeholders-and-Business-.html#.

4. Euromonitor, "Free to Play and In-game Purchases Are Preferred," *Country Report: Video Games in the US*, June 2019.

5. Henry Tucker, "Gaming Online," *ITNow* 53, no. 5 (September 2011): 13.

6. Sarah Pasfield-Neofitou, "Language Learning and Socialization Opportunities in Game Worlds: Trends in First and Second Language Research," *Language and Linguistics Compass* 8, no. 7 (2014): 271–284.

7. Yee, *The Proteus Paradox*, 16.

8. Ibid., 17.

9. G. Crawford, V. Gosling, and B. Light, "The Social and Cultural Significance of Online Gaming," in *Online Gaming in Context*, ed. G. Crawford, V. Gosling, and B. Light (New York: Routledge, 2011), 8.

10. "World Events," Wowhead, accessed February 21, 2020, https://www.wowhead .com/events.

11. Paul Tassi, "Google Stadia Launch Review: A Technical, Conceptual Disaster," *Forbes*, November 18, 2019, https://www.forbes.com/sites/paultassi/2019/11/18 /google-stadia-launch-review-a-technical-conceptual-disaster/#28dc629e5ec7.

12. "About Us," Valve Corporation, accessed February 23, 2020, https://www .valvesoftware.com/en/about.

13. Jonathon Bolding, "Steam Now Has 30,000 Games," PC Gamer, January 13, 2019, https://www.pcgamer.com/steam-now-has-30000-games/.

14. Tucker, "Gaming Online," 14.

15. "Steam & Game Stats," Steam, accessed February 20, 2020, https://store .steampowered.com/stats/.

16. "Build & Distribute Your Games on Steam," Steamworks, accessed February 24, 2020, https://partner.steamgames.com/.

17. Tom Senior, "Team Fortress 2: The Best of the Steam Workshop." PC Gamer, October 19, 2011, https://www.pcgamer.com/team-fortress-2-the-best-of-the-steam -workshop/.

18. Berserk Games, "Games: Tabletop Simulator," accessed April 1, 2020, https:// www.tabletopsimulator.com/games?fbclid=IwAR22mGrGKppdsmGrN6hIIv4C wag8vNHRyaVlmV0503m3rwcAYJ4pdknaLA0.

19. Apple Arcade, accessed February 24, 2020, https://www.apple.com/ca/apple -arcade/.

20. "Apple Arcade: 'Loud House: Outta Control' out Now," Macworld, February 14, 2020, https://www.macworld.com/article/3385024/apple-arcade-faq-games-price -compatibility.html.

21. "About Us," Rainway, accessed February 24, 2020, https://rainway.com/about/.

22. Michael Rundle, "Star Wars: The Old Republic Is 'Fastest-Growing MMO Ever' with 1m Users," Huffington Post, December 27, 2011.

10
Collectable Card Games, Role-Play Games, and Miniature Role-Play (Minifig) Games

The gaming genre is vast and encompasses more formats than just video games and board games. This chapter provides an introduction to three additional game genres: tabletop role-play games, collectable card games, and miniature tabletop games. These are all well-established genres that have their own unique advantages and challenges when deciding to incorporate them into a library gaming collection.

Tabletop Role-Play Games

While role-play games (RPGs) can be a type of game mechanic in both digital and analog games, this chapter only discusses analog games that typically have an extensive rulebook or scenario builder and are played among small groups of people on a routine basis. Modern tabletop role-play games (TTRPGs) as we know them today are typically a result of one of the most famous role-play games of all time, Dungeons & Dragons (D&D). Invented by Gary Gygax (a former insurance underwriter) who had a love for tactical wargames using miniatures, D&D was one of the first role-play games when it was released in 1974. Gary stated that D&D was driven by an interested market who asked retailers to carry the game as its popularity spread. By 1982, D&D sales had surpassed the 20-million-dollar mark, and the game continues to be widely popular;[1] the most recent surge may be a result of the game appearing in the popular Netflix series *Stranger Things*. Today, there are several popular RPG series along with one-off titles that appeal to different users.

The best approach for libraries is to have a few core sets and then see what your user group is interested in, as there are literally thousands of titles of TTRPGs. It is impractical to list them all here, so this section will provide some core titles to get your collection started. Besides providing the materials (game books, grid paper, etc.), libraries offer groups a free place to meet and play and by doing this you can use these local experts to help you build a collection to appeal to your patron base. For example, if you run a D&D campaign at the library and the participants are interested in trying something similar, you could look into Pathfinder or something completely different.

Something to keep in mind when running a TTRPG—it may be best to find out what setting and atmosphere players want to play, as opposed to what system you want to play. Do players want to play in a high fantasy to live out adventures similar to *Lord of the Rings* or *Chronicles of Narnia*? Or would they rather take on monsters lurking in the shadows, terrorizing their small rural town? Do they want a good scare or a fun narrative story they build collaboratively? As great as it is to jump into a game like D&D because it's been featured on *Stranger Things* or *The Big Bang Theory*, the best games are those where the objectives, settings, and characters are those you feel a personal connection with.

Some of the more popular TTRPGs include:

- Classic Dungeons & Dragons (it is recommended to get the 5th edition for beginners or 3.5 for seasoned experts)
- Pathfinder (a game based on the 3rd edition of D&D)
- Traveller (a more sci-fi genre game)
- Call of Cthulu (a horror genre RPG)
- The End of the World (based on apocalyptic scenarios)

These core games are popular and represent a fairly diverse audience. The following titles will help you to create a broad collection and provide the necessary information should your patrons come in asking about them.

Game Title: Call of Cthulu
Year published: 1981
Genre: Horror; role-play
Format: Tabletop Role-Play Game
Available Platforms: n/a
Age: 15+
User behavior type: Achiever, Explorer
Description: Call of Cthulhu (CoC) is based on H. P. Lovecraft's work of the same name. The basic series is set in the 1920s similar to the Lovecraft novel, and players can travel to areas that are both on earth and outside, which are called Dreamlands. This is a basic RPG

that is skill based with players building and improving their skills as they play the campaign as long as they stay alive and healthy in the game. The series uses percentile dice to check for success and failure in a player's actions within the game using probability of success. The playable characters are normal humans and as the campaign progresses players start to lose their sanity ("Sanity Points" or SAN) as they experience the true horrors of the world. It is typically common for characters to die in gruesome ways or end up in a mental institution. You can gain a lot of inspiration from Lovecraft's novels, as well as the board game Arkham Horror, which acts very similarly to a CoC game. There are also video games based in this world you can pull from as well.

Gameplay: 3–5 players

Series (Y or N): Yes

Other titles in the series: There are seven editions in the series along with other related versions.

Similar games: Arkham Horror (board game)

Game Title: Dread

Year published: 2005

Genre: Horror; role-play

Format: Tabletop Role-Play Game

Available Platforms: n/a

Age: 10+

User behavior type: Socializer

Description: Dread is one of the easiest TTRPGs to play, as it is essentially RPG Jenga. Instead of dice, the main mechanic of this game is pulling from a Jenga-like tower, and when your pull makes the tower fall, your character dies. This simplicity extends to character creation, as the character sheet is a questionnaire with 13 questions on it asking basic and intrusive questions about your character. These questions give hints about the world and game to be played. Since the game mechanics are so simple, the game setting is nearly infinite in scope, so long as there is a survival element to the story. It can be set in deep space, the old west, zombie apocalypse, modern day with a natural disaster, or Victorian England outrunning ghosts.

Gameplay: 3–5 players

Series (Y or N): No

Other titles in the series: n/a

Similar games: Vampire: The Masquerade, Call of Cthulhu

Game Title: The Dresden Files RPG

Year published: 2010

Genre: Fantasy; role-play

Format: Tabletop Role-Play Game

Available Platforms: n/a

Age: 10+

User behavior type: Achiever, Explorer

Description: Based on the 3rd edition of the Fate system, this game is set in the Dresden File universe from the book series by Jim Butcher. This game's focus is on relationships and your city. The city the game is set in is as important as the characters you play. Magic is a big part of this game, and many character types can use it. Others have special abilities that compensate for their lack of magic so that no one is ever in want of abilities. You can play werewolves, Vampires, Changelings, Wizards, or regular mortals with connections in the city you play in.

Gameplay: 3–7

Series (Y or N): No

Other titles in the series: There is an accelerated version of the game based off the Fate Accelerated game.

Similar games: Fate (Mechanically), Vampire (Thematically)

Game Title: Dungeons & Dragons

Year published: 1974

Genre: Fantasy; role-play

Format: Tabletop Role-Play Game

Available Platforms: n/a

Age: 10+

User behavior type: Achiever, Killer, Explorer

Description: D&D is a fantasy game that allows players to create their own characters based on race and class. They embark on a campaign to solve situations, engage in battle, while gathering knowledge and treasure. As players progress through the campaign, they increase their experience points (XP) and become increasingly powerful; these skills then can be transferred to another campaign as players can keep their characters as long as they stay alive in the game. Playable characters in the game include humans and fantasy creatures who can have magical powers. Players use polyhedral dice to resolve in-game events, using them to gage the success of their chosen actions.

Gameplay: 3–5 players

Series (Y or N): Yes

Other titles in the series: There are six editions (1st, 2nd [Advanced Dungeons & Dragons], 3rd, 3.5, 4th, and 5th) along with other related versions and companion books (e.g., *Monster Manual*).

Similar games: Pathfinder

Game Title: The End of the World

Year published: 2014

Genre: Zombies; science fiction; role-play

Format: Tabletop Role-Play Game

Available Platforms: n/a

Age: 15+

User behavior type: Achiever, Explorer, Socializer

Description: The End of the World has four main books *Zombie Apocalypse*, *Wrath of the Gods*, *Alien Invasion*, and *Revolt of the Machines*. Each book contains five scenarios to play through. Players play as themselves and play through the campaign making decisions similar to what they would if they encountered these situations in real life, within the environment they live, which is quite different from other RPGs that typically transport the players to a fictional world. This game is very accessible and a great entry point for people looking to try out RPGs. The scenarios are quite short in comparison to other RPGs.

Gameplay: 3–5 players

Series (Y or N): Yes

Other titles in the series: Zombie Apocalypse, Wrath of the Gods, Alien Invasion, and Revolt of the Machines

Similar games: None

Game Title: Fate

Year published: 2003

Genre: Any; role-play

Format: Tabletop Role-Play Game

Available Platforms: n/a

Age: 10+

User behavior type: n/a

Description: Unlike most of the games outlined in this section, Fate is one of the few open-source RPGs, meaning anyone can use the rules to publish their own RPG game. Players only roll four fudge dice, two sides with +, two sides with –, and two that are blank. These are then added to your skills to create a number that is matched against a target. The main aspect that makes Fate so different is the concept of a Fate Point. Every time your character makes an action or choice that puts you or your party at a disadvantage, you receive a Fate Point that will give you a boost in your rolls or allow you to change something in your game. This is the heart of Fate, a give and take of advantages and disadvantages.

Gameplay: 2–8

Series (Y or N): Yes

Other titles in the series: There are over five official Fate versions, with Fate Core and Fate Accelerated at their heart.

Similar games: Dresden Files (mechanically)

Game Title: Kids on Bikes

Year published: 2018

Genre: Action-adventure

Format: Tabletop Role-Play Game

Available Platforms: n/a

Age: 8+

User behavior type: Explorer

Description: The newest edition of any game on this list, Kids on Bikes is capitalizing on the current trope that started with the ragtag gang of young friends going on grand adventures. Popularized in the 1980s with movies like *ET*, *The Goonies*, and *Stand by Me*, and more recent shows such as *Stranger Things*, this game has players relive those more innocent years with fantastical twists. With situations such as large government cover-ups, monsters who have befriended your team who are being hunted by misguided citizens, or on the hunt for long lost treasure. The game mechanics are similar to D&D, in that the better you are at something the more sides the dice have.

Gameplay: 2–8

Series (Y or N): Yes

Other titles in the series: Due to its popularity, two adventure books have been put out: *Strange Adventures*, Volume 1 and 2, that are meant to aid players who are exploring the world of Kids on Bikes.

Similar games: Monster of the Week, Tales from the Loop, Bubble Gumshoe

Game Title: Legend of the Five Rings

Year published: 1997

Genre: Asian fantasy; Samurai; Ninja; Magic

Format: Tabletop Role-Play Game

Available Platforms: n/a

Age: 10+

User behavior type: Achiever, Explorer

Description: Set in a fantasy version of Feudal Japan and taking influences from many sources around Asia, Legend of the Five Rings focuses on keeping the justice and order, through maintaining honor. Players who are interested in Asian culture and want to play a magical ninja or samurai character will enjoy this game. It uses similar mechanics as D&D, so those familiar with that system will find the learning curve of this game easier to climb, though this game has a lot more rules than your average D&D game. The Five Rings from the title refer to the different elements that players can tap into: Earth, Wind, Fire, Water, and "Void," which is human potential.

Gameplay: 2+ players

Series (Y or N): Yes

Other titles in the series: There are three other editions of this game, as well as a very intensive card game.

Similar games: Pathfinder

Game Title: Monster of the Week

Year published: 2015

Genre: Urban fantasy; mystery

Format: Tabletop Role-Play Game

Available Platforms: n/a

Age: 8+

User behavior type: Achiever, Explorer

Description: This fairly new RPG has picked up a lot of steam in gaming circles. Based on serial television shows such as *Buffy*: *The Vampire Slayer*, *Supernatural*, *Scooby Doo*, or *Doctor Who*, this game throws a different monster at the players each session. Players face off against a new monster each week, gaining intel about the monster, what the monster is, what it's after, and how to take it down. It has a very simple game mechanic of just two six-sided dice, and either a success, mix success, or failure. Types of characters add to abilities and skills to keep the game interesting and dynamic.

Gameplay: 3–8

Series (Y or N): Yes

Other titles in the series: There's an expansion called Tomb of Mysteries, which adds more playable materials to the game.

Similar games: Kids on Bikes, Blades in the Dark, Bubble Gumshoe

Game Title: Pathfinder

Year published: 2009

Genre: Fantasy; role-play

Format: Tabletop Role-Play Game

Available Platforms: n/a

Age: 10+

User behavior type: Achiever, Killer, Explorer

Description: Pathfinder is based on the 3.5 edition of D&D and uses many of the same mechanics, including polyhedral dice to determine the success of a player's actions within the game. Pathfinder adds additional classes and boosts not found in D&D to make it more exciting. It also changed the balance by altering several spells, the skill system, and some of the combat maneuvers that the creators thought needed modification from D&D 3.5. Some gamers have nicknamed Pathfinder D&D version 3.75.

Gameplay: 3–5 players

Series (Y or N): Yes

Other titles in the series: There are two editions of the game (one released in 2009 and the other in 2018).

Similar games: D&D

Game Title: Star Wars Role-Playing Game

Year published: 2012

Genre: Science fiction

Format: Tabletop Role-Play Game

Available Platforms: n/a

Age: 10+

User behavior type: Achiever, Killer, Explorer

Description: It should come as no surprise that a role-playing game from the Star Wars universe exists, but it's a matter of which one to play. With such a vast history at the game designer's disposal, you can play in any edition that you want. The dice that are used throughout the game systems vary, but most rely on six-sided dice with different designs on each. It's best to find out what era of Star Wars players want to play in (e.g., The Old Republic and Empire Control) and find the setting to match it. Game mechanics are not the simplest to pick up in comparison to the other games listed, but those who are fans of Star Wars will really enjoy the submersion in the world.

Gameplay: 3–6 players

Series (Y or N): Yes, there are several editions taking place throughout the Star Wars History.

Other titles in the series: Star Wars: Edge of the Empire, Age of Rebellion, Force and Destiny, The Force Awakens Beginner Game, Rise of the Separatists

Similar games: Feelings and Lasers, Diaspora

Game Title: Traveller

Year published: 1977

Genre: Science fiction; role-play

Format: Tabletop Role-Play Game

Available Platforms: n/a

Age: 15+

User behavior type: Achiever, Killer

Description: Traveller is a space opera that has players journeying between various star systems to explore, battle, and trade. Playable characters are typically human or "Humaniti" (races include Solomani, Vilani, and Zhodani), but there is the ability to choose an alien or robot character. Players have six primary characteristics that are generated with a dice role and gain their skills through a mini-game where they make choices that ultimately affect their abilities. Traveller uses something called psionics, which is extrasensory perception, typically a psychic-like ability, and depending on the choices players make, their character may have this ability.

Gameplay: 3–5 players

Series (Y or N): Yes

Other titles in the series: There are several other titles in the series, including the most recent Mongoose Traveller: 2nd edition (2016).

Similar games: None

Game Title: Vampire: The Masquerade

Year published: 1991

Genre: Horror; role-play

Format: Tabletop Role-Play Game

Available Platforms: n/a

Age: 18+

User behavior type: Killer, Achiever

Description: Vampire: The Masquerade, often shortened to just Vampire puts players in the driver's seat as a Vampire in a major city.

The game is focused less on hunting people and more about finding humanity in being the monster. The game has a wonderful social mechanic to keep track of all the power dynamics among players and non-playable characters (NPCs). Players are always forced to balance their need to feed, and continue the Masquerade of being human, while maintaining their social power status.

Gameplay: 3–5 players

Series (Y or N): Yes

Other titles in the series: Set in the "World of Darkness," Vampire was the first and most successful of these games. There are five editions of the game, the latest being published in 2018. But there are many others set in the World of Darkness, such as Werewolf, Mage, Wrath, and Changeling.

Similar games: Any World of Darkness game

Collectable Card Games and Miniature Tabletop Role-Play Gaming

These genres of games have similar features, and while libraries may find it difficult to provide access in the library setting, we thought a brief overview of them would be helpful.

Collectable Card Games (CCG) are games that require players to purchase packs of cards in an attempt to collect cards that they desire to add either to their deck for playing or simply just for collecting purposes. This genre of games began in 1993 with the introduction of the game Magic the Gathering and has since grown to incorporate other popular series, such as Yu-Gi-Oh! and Pokémon.[2] It is quite popular to partake in CCG tournaments, and these are typically hosted at game stores along with what are called drafts. While different games have particular rules around their drafts, in general, card drafts are opportunities for players to build their decks and trade cards from packs that are opened. These are very popular events and could be an area for libraries to explore hosting one in the future.

Miniature tabletop gaming is one of the oldest hobby game industries. Teri Litorco notes that "in 1913, the science-fiction writer H. G. Wells published *Little Wars,* a book of rules for playing with military miniatures."[3] Miniature tabletop gaming is similar to CCG in that players need to purchase different miniature figures (referred to as miniatures or minifigs) in order to add them to their playable army. Generally, miniatures are not randomized in the way that CCG cards are, but they do require the player to finish them. Finishing them includes sanding and painting, creating terrain for battles and campaigns, and ensuring you follow the particular rules for the game for creating your armies. Popular examples of miniature tabletop games are Warhammer, Star Wars: X-Wing Miniature Game, and Warmachine.

Due to the nature of these two genres of gaming, it can be challenging for a library to collect in this area. There are many pieces involved, so it can be difficult to maintain a set that can be loaned out to patrons. Often with collectibles, there is the issue of rarity, and the value of some of these items make them more prone to theft, for example, some Magic the Gathering cards can sell for thousands of dollars. Finally, these genres have strict rules about what cards or miniatures are current regulation, and these are constantly updated causing your collection to quickly become out-of-date and no longer desirable to patrons.

There are ways that libraries can engage with fans of CCGs and miniature tabletop gaming. As previously discussed, you could host a miniature paint night and bring in local experts to share their painting techniques. You could also offer space for players to have regular battles or tournaments and provide supplemental material. Another option would be to partner with a local game store and have them donate the leftover cards from a draft night so you can create modest decks to help teach patrons how to play these games to generate their interest in the genre. These two genres of gaming can be very cost-prohibitive so by offering some programming and materials at the library you increase inclusivity.

Here are some CCG and miniature tabletop RPG game collection suggestions:

Game Title: Magic the Gathering

Year published: 1993

Genre: Deck building; card drafting; hand management

Format: Collectable Card Game

Available Platforms: n/a

Age: 13+

User behavior type: Achiever, Killer, Socializer

Description: Magic the Gathering is credited as being the first CCG. Players known as "planeswalkers" cast spells, use artifacts, and summon creatures that are represented on cards within their collectable deck. When creating their deck, players can choose different colors (red, black, white, green, and blue) and create a deck that they think will win. Many players create their decks with a particular strategy in mind: aggro, control, combo, or midrange. These types of decks can also be combined (e.g., aggro-control). Different decks react differently to each other, and some colors work better together than others or certain combinations (e.g., green and white) have cards that require both colors to use. The deck contains 40–60 cards total, and if the players are participating in tournament play, they need cards from the current expansion. Actions in the game require mana and land. The object of the game is to reduce the opponent's life points to zero. Magic cards are highly collectable, and there is a flourishing resale market as some cards are rarer than others.

Gameplay: 2 players (there is a way to play with multiple players, but it is not common)

Series (Y or N): Yes

Other titles in the series: There have been multiple expansions throughout the years.

Similar games: Yu-Gi-Oh!, Speed Duel, KeyForge, Final Fantasy Trading Card Game

Game Title: Pokémon
Year published: 1996
Genre: Deck building; card drafting; hand management
Format: Collectable Card Game
Available Platforms: n/a
Age: 8+
User behavior type: Achiever, Killer, Socializer
Description: Pokémon (the CCG) is based on Nintendo's Pokémon anime and video games. Players (or trainers) collect cards with different creatures on them to use in the deck for battle. Players use their cards to battle their opponent with the goal of weakening them and defeating that particular card. This carries on for the rest of the game with the winner of the battle being the one who has knocked out the most Pokémon from their opponent's deck. A player's deck needs both basic Pokémon and more advanced in order to play the game properly.
Gameplay: 2 players
Series (Y or N): Yes
Other titles in the series: There are eight generations of Pokémon that come from different fictional regions. These generations also correspond to video game releases.
Similar games: Yu-Gi-Oh!

Game Title: Star Wars Miniatures
Year published: 2004–2010
Genre: Science fiction; wargame
Format: Miniature Tabletop Game
Available Platforms: n/a
Age: 12+
User behavior type: Achiever, Killer, Socializer
Description: Although this game was only produced for six years, it is still rather popular, and people are interested in exploring it, especially if they are interested in Star Wars. Gameplay is similar to that of D&D using a d20 system, and it explores different maps and locations within the Star Wars universe. There are 10 different factions that players can choose to play: Rebel, Imperial, Republic, Sith, Separatist, New Republic, Yuuzhan, Vong, Mandalorian, and Fridge. Players pick their faction and build their squads according to Star Wars canon. The objective of the game can vary depending on what factions, scenarios, and maps players choose. The overall objective is to score the most victory points. The game varies from other TTRPGs as it resides in the realm of an existing science-fiction universe and is sometimes constrained by this. Players can use "force powers" like the Jedi and Sith do in the universe, and "commander effects" are held by known commanders in the universe (e.g., Darth Vader and Leia Organa) who have special characteristics from other playable characters.

Gameplay: 2+ players
Series (Y or N): No
Other titles in the series: n/a
Similar games: D&D

Game Title: Warhammer Age of Sigmar
Year published: 2014
Genre: Wargame
Format: Miniature Tabletop Game
Available Platforms: n/a
Age: 12+
User behavior type: Achiever, Killer, Socializer
Description: Warhammer Age of Sigmar replaced the original War-hammer in 2014. Warhammer is heavily influenced by the works of J. R. R. Tolkien and Michael Moorcock.[4] It is set in one of eight mortal realms, and players build their armies to do battle against each other. Each of these realms have different artifacts, spells, and character-istics.) Warhammer is set up to be quite easy to learn, but difficult to master so this keeps players interested in the game. There are story-telling elements along with scenarios, so it has a large appeal along with the ability to customize (paint) your army to your liking; in fact, the art of painting miniatures is a huge part of this particular game.
Gameplay: 2+ players
Series (Y or N): Yes
Other titles in the series: There are several editions to the game. The first was released in 2014 and the second in 2018. There is also War-hammer 40,000 (aka Warhammer 40k), which is set in space.
Similar games: Warhammer 40k

Game Title: Warmachine
Year published: 2003
Genre: Steampunk; wargame
Format: Miniature Tabletop Role-Play
Available Platforms: n/a
Age: 12+
User behavior type: Achiever, Killer, Socializer
Description: Set in the Iron Kingdom, players (warcasters) play against each other (rival factions) in a more aggressive style of tab-letop wargame play. Factions consist of warjacks (steam-powered machines), battle engines (additional war machines), humans, and fantasy races of characters. Warmachine is a bit different from other TTRPGs as its main emphasis is on the rules of the game rather than the storytelling component. Because of this, Warmachine attracts a lot of competitive players and tournaments are quite popular.
Gameplay: 2–5 players
Series (Y or N): Yes

Other titles in the series: There are three expansions to Warmachine: Wrath, Colossals, and Vengeance. Hordes is set in the same universe, but within the untamed wilds and is compatible with Warmachine.

Similar games: Hordes, Warhammer 40k

Game Title: Yu-Gi-Oh!

Year published: 1999

Genre: Deck building; card drafting; hand management

Format: Collectable Card Game

Available Platforms: n/a

Age: 8+

User behavior type: Achiever, Killer, Socializer

Description: Yu-Gi-Oh! (or Yugioh!) is a CCG based on the Japanese manga of the same title and is based on the fictional game Duel Monsters. Players build decks of cards and also create a side deck of 15 cards that they can swap with as the game progresses based on needs. There are three different kinds of cards: spells, monsters, and traps. Monsters have specific attack and defense points. These are used to attack other players, and these cards require specific summoning techniques to summon depending on the card. Trap cards are placed face down and are activated upon certain conditions laid out on the card, whereas spells are used during the turn and vary depending on what is written on the card. The object of the game is to use monster attacks to deplete the opponent's life points. Yu-Gi-Oh! is a popular game for tournament play, and it is also one of the most successful CCGs of all time.

Gameplay: 2–4 players (either 1 vs. 1 or 2 vs. 2)

Series (Y or N): No

Other titles in the series: n/a

Similar games: Pokémon, Magic the Gathering

Notes

1. Brian Tinsman, *The Game Inventor's Guidebook* (New York: Morgan James Publishing, 2008), 9–12.

2. Teri Litorco, *The Civilized Guide to Tabletop Gaming: Rules Every Gamer Must Live By* (Avon, MA: Adams Media, 2016), 14.

3. Ibid., 15.

4. "Warhammer: Age of Sigmar," Wikipedia, accessed February 2020, https://en.wikipedia.org/wiki/Warhammer_Age_of_Sigmar.

11
Virtual Reality and Augmented Reality

While Virtual Reality (VR) gaming has recently exploded in popularity, it does have a rather lengthy history. The term "virtual reality" was first used by Jaron Lanier in the 1980s, the founder of VPL Research where some of the first virtual reality goggles and gloves were created.[1] One of the first mass market VR systems for video games at home was Nintendo's *Virtual Boy*, released in 1995. The *Virtual Boy* was not a commercial success, but it was an important step to at home virtual reality gaming.[2] Sega also designed a VR headset called Sega VR in 1991, but it was ultimately scrapped.[3] In terms of modern, at-home VR systems, Oculus Rift (released in 2013) made it not only more accessible, but produced a level of quality we have come to expect from our VR experiences.[4] Upcoming releases will continue to grow the VR market, including Apple's VR glasses, expected to be released sometime in 2021.[5]

Having access to VR games is something that more patrons may be interested in having, but it does come with some additional challenges and considerations. In order to run most VR games, you will need a console or online account (e.g., Steam) along with a VR headset and additional hardware equipment depending on the particular system you are running. Popular VR headset manufacturers include Oculus, HTC, and PlayStation. Depending on the particular setup and experience you are trying to achieve, you may need to purchase a fairly robust gaming computer or laptop to run some of the games.

Most of the time, a VR experience requires staff supervision and will need to be run in the library rather than being something that can be loaned out. If you're using an Oculus or HTC product, you will need a computer to run an online account, so this is not something that can be easily loaned. You may want to explore loaning out a PlayStation VR system, as it is a little more accessible and has fewer hardware requirements. With PlayStation

VR you will have the games preloaded onto the console that can be loaned or a physical copy of the game.

Whether you loan out the systems or not, you will need to make sure you are regularly updating the software and also disinfecting the VR headset in between uses. If you have never worn a VR headset, you may not be aware of how dirty and sweaty they can get during use. This is especially the case with longer term play. An easy way to keep things clean is to purchase extra washable components within the headset and use disinfectant spray or wipes on the goggles/headset. You will also want to have some form of waiver for people to sign before participating in a VR program that includes information about potential seizures, lightheadedness, motion sickness, and other warnings that are usually outlined in the paperwork that comes with the system. You can find examples of these waivers online from other libraries quite easily or you can create a custom one for your library.

Since the commercial release of the Oculus Rift in Spring 2016, libraries have been experimenting with ways to provide this new technology to their patrons. As we've discussed earlier in this volume, many public libraries have been able to purchase Google Cardboard, which is a far more approachable VR system given its cost and the use of Smartphone technology. The introduction of these inexpensive technologies has allowed public libraries to offer exciting and unique programming to their patrons. Using Google Cardboard and Smartphones, public libraries have begun to offer such programming as build-your-own VR set workshops.

Janine Johnson noted that VR, Augmented Reality (AR), and Mixed Reality (MR) are not going away anytime soon, and libraries would be remiss not to participate.[6] While Janine works in a school-library system and incorporates AR and MR into her collections and programming, there are clear opportunities for other library systems to provide similar services to their communities. Carolyn Foote notes that there are many ways that libraries can apply VR and AR, including wayfinding activities, information literacy, student projects, and preparing students for future encounters with technology.[7] There are many examples of libraries collaborating and using this technology, including Felicia Ann Smith who used VR to teach students about common sense and "fake news" see her article "Virtual Reality in Libraries is Common Sense."[8] While this is a relatively new area, there is a growing community of library professionals who are experimenting with using this technology, including emulating real world or industry applications in the library.

In an academic context, work has been done to try to tie in the use of VR into course curriculum. In Fabio Montella's recent article "Producing Academic Outcomes with Virtual Reality Labs," he outlines the various benefits to students by providing this type of experience. He notes that providing this kind of technology allows students to collaborate and explore new ways of interacting with course material. Montella also advocates for a "starting with fun" approach to entice users to the material before embarking on a more serious curriculum application. Montella not only provides working examples of using VR in visual arts curriculum but also provides some future thoughts on expanding their offerings.[9] Another example of how VR is being used in an academic context is Carleton University in Canada. They are using VR with architecture students to allow them to create interactive, virtual buildings that mirrors what industry professionals are experimenting with VR.[10]

VR Programming and Use in the Library

Earlier in the book, we discussed a successful way of integrating VR technology into programming for seniors; however, there are many different programs that a library can build for a variety of the communities they serve—yet another way to engage patrons and gamers with your collection. It is essential to realize that besides the academic or learning approach discussed earlier, VR can simply be an enjoyable program.

Recognizing the enjoyability of VR as a game is essential if you want to engage patrons in this area of your collection. For instance, some systems have catalogs of free games, allowing libraries with smaller budgets to still utilize VR as a resource. For many gamers, the opportunity to try out VR can be exciting and a new way to experience gaming. It will only benefit you and your collection if you can consider ways to use VR either in your collection or programming.

There are some considerations you will want to take into account before starting any kind of VR-based program.

- First, you are going to have to purchase materials that support your programming desires and also fit within your budget. Some systems can be very expensive and require an extensive hardware commitment, whereas others, such as Google Cardboard, are rather approachable.

- Second, you need to consider how much space is needed. You may need to have a clear space dedicated to this program, and again, depending on the particular VR system your library has, you could either leave the system permanently hooked up or have the option of making it portable.

- Finally, a major consideration is the possibility of patrons developing motion sickness. Some libraries have participants sign waivers or impose age restrictions on VR to minimize the likelihood of negative interactions. Waivers should include a blurb on the possibility of the system causing temporary motion sickness. As the technology improves, this becomes less of a concern, but for now it is definitely something to note when embarking on using these systems.

Virtual Reality Game Collection Suggestions

For this particular section, finding similar games can be challenging to use in gamers' advisory. This is due, in part, to more and more digital games offering either portions of VR or existing games are porting to VR; porting means the games have been released on another platform and are coded to be "ported" to another, but the game as an experience remains the same. If you do encounter patrons who are excited by the concepts around VR, we encourage you to read through some of the video game suggestions (in Chapter 8) to get a better sense as to what type of VR experience your patrons may be interested in having. It can help you target possible games, themes, or plots, as VR offerings are continuing to expand and diversify. Many of these titles are currently one-offs, so there are very few true VR series as the technology is rather new. With the relative newness and growing number of titles in this area, this section presents a representative list of possible titles and genres that you might want to explore.

Game Title: *Arizona Sunshine*
Year published: 2016
Genre: Zombie; first-person shooter
Format: Virtual Reality
Available Platforms: Online, PlayStation VR
Age: M
User behavior type: Killer, Achiever, Explorer
Description: Players awaken in a cave in Arizona to find that the world is inhabited by zombies. Players must navigate through the game, find weapons, and kill the zombies they encounter. This is a one-player game that follows a particular story arch, leading the player through a series of events until the final ending of the game.
Gameplay: Single player
Series (Y or N): No
Other titles in the series: n/a

Game Title: *Beat Saber*
Year published: 2018
Genre: Rhythm game
Format: Virtual Reality
Available Platforms: Online, PlayStation VR
Age: E
User behavior type: Achiever, Socializer
Description: Players hold the two VR controllers that show up as neon lightsabers and they have to use these sabers to hit targets in the game along with the music. The game comes with a set of original songs, but other users have uploaded hundreds of other songs that are available to download to expand the music inventory. The game has different complexity levels making it good for replayability. It is also a good social game to play with friends.
Gameplay: Multiplayer
Series (Y or N): No
Other titles in the series: n/a

Game Title: *Iron Man VR*
Year published: 2020

Genre: Shooter; comic
Format: Virtual Reality
Available Platforms: PlayStation VR
Age: T
User behavior type: Explorer, Achiever
Description: This game is a first-person perspective where players get to embody Iron Man, interact with characters, and enter battle. The game allows players to fly, use missiles, change costumes over the progression of the game, and is a must play for any Marvel fan.
Gameplay: Single player
Series (Y or N): No
Other titles in the series: n/a

Game Title: *Job Simulator*
Year published: 2016
Genre: Simulation; science fiction; action
Format: Virtual Reality
Available Platforms: Online, PlayStation
Age: E
User behavior type: Achiever, Explorer
Description: Players are employees working in a museum in 2050 that is run by robots. Players complete tasks for their robot bosses, and there is a lot of creative freedom on how one can complete the assigned tasks. Players complete tasks doing four "historic" jobs before the robots took over.
Gameplay: Single player
Series (Y or N): No
Other titles in the series: n/a

Game Title: *Keep Talking and Nobody Explodes*
Year published: 2015
Genre: Dexterity; strategy; puzzle game
Format: Virtual Reality and regular digital game
Available Platforms: PlayStation, Android, Online, Xbox One
Age: E
User behavior type: Achiever, Socializer
Description: This is a team-based game that combines the digital and analog worlds. One player is trying to defuse a bomb, but he does not have access to the manual. Other players only have access to the manual, but cannot see the layout of the bomb. The team must work together to make sure that the bomb is defused before it explodes.
Gameplay: Multiplayer
Series (Y or N): No
Other titles in the series: n/a

Game Title: *The Lab*
Year published: 2016

Genre: Action
Format: Virtual Reality
Available Platforms: Online
Age: Varies
User behavior type: Varies
Description: *The Lab* contains eight mini games that players can choose from: slingshot, longbow, xortex, postcards, human medical scan, solar system, robot repair, and secret shop. Slingshot has been compared to the game Angry Birds and has players shooting personality cores at piles of debris. The game longbow allows players to control a bow while they defend a castle from invaders. Xortex is a space-themed game where players move around a spaceship; this game is known for having players be able to only use their upper body to play. Postcards is a game simulation where you are on a mountain that you can explore with your robot dog companion. Human medical scan allows players to peel back layers of a human composed of CT scan images. Solar system is an interactive model of the solar system that players can manipulate. Robot repair is a mini game that follows a set script and has players inside a repair shop for robots used in the game *Portal 2*. Finally, the game secret shop has players inside the item shop for the game *Dota 2*, where they can interact with items from the familiar game.
Gameplay: Single player
Series (Y or N): No
Other titles in the series: n/a

Game Title: *Lone Echo*
Year published: 2017
Genre: Adventure; science fiction
Format: Virtual Reality
Available Platforms: Online
Age: T
User behavior type: Explorer, Achiever
Description: *Lone Echo* is a single-player game that is set in space. Players are transported to a mining operation within the rings of Saturn and play as the character Jack who is an advanced AI with an ultra-powerful synthetic body. As Jack, players complete tasks and try to solve an increasingly threatening mystery while exploring space.
Gameplay: Single and multiplayer (*Echo Arena*)
Series (Y or N): Yes
Other titles in the series: *Echo Arena* is the multiplayer option in *Lone Echo* that became its own stand-alone game.

Game Title: *Moss*
Year published: 2018
Genre: Adventure; family; puzzle
Format: Virtual Reality

Available Platforms: Online, PlayStation
Age: E
User behavior type: Explorer, Achiever
Description: *Moss* is a first-person perspective game. Players meet up with a young mouse named Quill in a fantasy land they discovered in a book. Players can manipulate their character and Quill as they go through the game looking to navigate obstacles and solve puzzles.
Gameplay: Single player
Series (Y or N): No
Other titles in the series: n/a

Game Title: *Rec Room*
Year published: 2016
Genre: Sports; cooperative; maker; adventure
Format: Virtual Reality and digital
Available Platforms: Online, PlayStation
Age: E
User behavior type: Explorer, Achiever, Socializer
Description: *Rec Room* can be played with or without a virtual reality headset. When played in VR mode the game uses full 3D motion capture. Players start in the hub room that looks like the lobby of a recreation center with doors that lead to various games and user-generated rooms. Players can freely explore and choose their destination in the game and also pick up objects in the game. The game has many mini games and also multiplayer game, including first-person shooters, sports games, charades, and cooperative role-play games along with user-generated content. The user-generated content is a fun feature that libraries can use in programming to have their patrons create games they can play with each other giving it a "maker" quality to it.
Gameplay: Single and multiplayer
Series (Y or N): No
Other titles in the series: Formerly known as *Against Gravity*

Game Title: *Superhot*
Year published: 2017
Genre: Action; shooter
Format: Virtual Reality
Available Platforms: Online, Xbox, PlayStation
Age: T
User behavior type: Killer, Achiever
Description: *Superhot* is a first-person shooter game where players navigate through levels trying to kill their computer-generated opponents. The fun mechanic in this game is that time moves only when you do so players essentially play in slow motion allowing them to make Matrix-type moves in the game to avoid getting killed by the computer-generated opponents. Players need to be creative with their tactics as they can use physical combat, shoot weapons, throw

objects, dodge bullets, and even stop bullets in mid-air. This is a really fun game to play with friends as you can challenge each other in how you creatively get through a level.

Gameplay: Single player (but you play in person with friends)

Series (Y or N): No

Other titles in the series: n/a

Game Title: *Tetris Effect*

Year published: 2018

Genre: Puzzle

Format: Virtual Reality

Available Platforms: Online, PlayStation

Age: E

User behavior type: Achiever

Description: *Tetris Effect* is a new spin on the classic game of Tetris. Players need to manipulate blocks in order to clear complete lines before the entire playing field fills up. This is a simple game that many players are already familiar with so it can be an easy way to introduce people to VR for the first time or seasoned gamers will enjoy the challenge of having their favorite game in the VR world.

Gameplay: Single player

Series (Y or N): Yes

Other titles in the series: This is the VR version of the very popular series of Tetris games.

Game Title: *Tilt Brush*

Year published: 2017

Genre: Art game

Format: Virtual Reality

Available Platforms: Online

Age: T

User behavior type: Explorer, Achiever

Description: *Tilt Brush* is a room-scale 3D application that allows participants to create 3D pictures using brush strokes. The pictures they create can then be manipulated and used as stationary images, GIFs, or videos. This particular VR application is not necessarily a game, but it is commonly used in VR programming in libraries for both leisure and more academic applications. It also serves as a great introduction to VR environments and is typically a crowd pleaser for patrons who may not be as interested in immersive gameplay. While this particular game may seem innocuous and could be used for children's programming, there are some suggestive images and content.

Gameplay: Single player

Series (Y or N): No

Other titles in the series: n/a

Notes

1. "History of Virtual Reality," The Franklin Institute, accessed February 2020, https://www.fi.edu/virtual-reality/history-of-virtual-reality.

2. "Virtual Boy," Wikipedia, accessed February 2020, https://en.wikipedia.org /wiki/Virtual_Boy.

3. "Sega VR," Wikipedia, accessed February 2020, https://en.wikipedia.org/wiki /Sega_VR.

4. "Virtual Reality," Wikipedia, accessed February 2020, https://en.wikipedia.org /wiki/Virtual_reality.

5. "Apple Glasses: VR and AR Are Coming," July 21, 2020, https://www.macrumors .com/roundup/apple-glasses/.

6. Janine Johnson, "Jumping into the World of Virtual and Augmented Reality," *Knowledge Quest* 47, no. 4 (2019): 22–27.

7. Carolyn Foote, "Is It Real or Is It VR? Exploring AR and VR Tools," *Computers in Libraries* 38, no. 3 (2018): 33–36.

8. Felicia Ann Smith, "Virtual Reality in Libraries Is Common Sense," *Library Hi Tech News* 6 (2019): 10–13.

9. Fabio Montella, "Producing Academic Outcomes with Virtual Reality Labs," *Computers in Libraries* 39, no. 5 (2019): 4–8.

10. E. Cross, M. Goodridge, and M. Rohweder, "Game Services in Ontario Academic Libraries: Current Issues and Hot Topics," paper presented at the Ontario Library Association Super Conference, Toronto, ON, January 2018.

Conclusion:
"Press Start to Play"

Wait? You mean I can take out any video game for free . . . for two weeks!?
Man, which one should I start with?!
—An MBA student

It is important to realize that the world of games and gaming is constantly changing and growing. Understanding this growth is essential for any librarian working with a gaming collection or advising patrons. This genre of game collections is somewhat new, but it is not showing any signs of slowing down given the rate at which games are being released and the continued growth in sales year after year. If you create a collection that appeals to a wide range of patrons and pair this with knowledgeable staff and interesting programming, you have a much better chance of making this collection one of the star features of your library.

Game announcements can be a daily occurrence, with dozens of new board games being announced every month. In the world of video games, there can be hundreds of highly anticipated titles every year—titles that appeal to all different gamers. This is important with the releases of two new consoles: the PlayStation 5 and the Xbox Scarlett. Some of these games may be exclusive only to these specific consoles, which is something any library considering a gaming collection has to take into account. Do you wait for the new console to be released or do you purchase older consoles, thereby excluding some games and in turn certain gamers? The advice presented throughout the volume on how to stay abreast of trends and releases in the gaming industry can help you work through many of these questions.

This book was never meant to be a comprehensive listing of all the games available as that would be an unattainable feat. Rather, this book had two goals in mind:

1. To help you understand how to work with your game collection and help patrons navigate the widely diverse environment of game genres and titles.

2. To make creating and maintaining gaming collections in a library context more approachable.

Gamers and people who like games can be an incredibly independent community—they know what they like, and they will seek out those games that interest them or which have similar mechanics. However, gamers can also be incredibly curious and will often want to seek out something new and different to try out and explore. Because of these unique motivations and interests, libraries are well situated to adapt and provide informed and engaging services. As a library offering a gaming collection, you need to be aware of those kinds of attitudes and cater to them when working with your patrons. "So, you love the open-world aspect of *Zelda: Breath of the Wild*, well what specifically draws you to those kinds of games. And let's see what board games might appeal to you then . . ."

Who will approach the library information desk and ask for help in finding their next game to play? This is perhaps one of the questions at the heart of this particular volume. And it is not an easy one to answer.

Unfortunately, the obvious answer is—it could be anyone.

Understanding the different types of games, their mechanics, styles, and genres can help you intimately know your gaming collection, especially when applying that to finding the perfect game for your patrons.

Gaming in libraries is an exciting and expanding area, so it is wise for library staff to pick up the controller and join their patrons in the experience. We are not suggesting you become a hardcore gamer—but you can if you want—rather we want you to see how much fun it can be to have a gaming collection. When you have fun with it, we promise your patrons will too!

And now . . . play on!

Appendix: Speed Run: A Quick Reference Guide

This section is meant to be a Quick Reference Guide to help you think about easily answering questions directed toward genre or game features—consider it a starting point to engaging with your users. Before you delve in, a little definition: a speed run is a playthrough (usually recorded) of a whole video game, with the intention of finishing it as fast as possible. Speed runs may actually come in handy as a librarian working to recommend games to patrons, as you can watch a full video game and get a feel for the action and content before even working with a patron.

We would encourage you to take time with your patrons to really understand their player motivations and interests to be able to provide a more accurate list of suggested games they may want to play. Players may want a game because it includes a specific character: "I played *Mario Kart*; do you have more stuff with Mario?" Or they might like a specific game because it includes socialization aspects: "I got to play *Call of Duty* with my friends, are there other games that we can play together?" Players might want to stay in a certain universe and explore all the games included: "I love Lovecraft, and played *Elder Sign*, are there any video games similar to that?"

Using this guide will give you some easily accessible suggestions to offer your patrons, but it is not meant to stand-alone without context and a good gamers' advisory interview (for a full discussion of a gamer' advisory interview, please see Chapter 6). We have included in a fair representation of different genres and formats, but our book is not an exhaustive list of games that are available on the market. So, make sure you use some of the tools and tricks we have talked about to do the extra research.

Consider this Quick Reference Guide as a starting point to engaging with your users, we will provide some possible situations and suggestions. Keep in mind that while some games are listed under a particular category, there are additional considerations that should be noted (e.g., if it's listed as a family game, what ages and abilities do those family members have?). Some genres are harder to pin down (e.g., social games). Almost any board game can be deemed "social," as it requires a minimum of two players to play. Many games have "storytelling" elements, so it is important to know what aspect of storytelling the patron likes: telling others a story, the way the game told a story, the level of communication necessary to succeed in the game, and so on. It is crucial to do a good reference interview before suggesting a game to a patron.

But for all the cautionary tales, consider this as a good way to start your adventure with gamers' advisory. "It's dangerous out there! Take this."[1]

Player's map (a key to reading this quick guide):

VG: Video game

TT: Tabletop game

CCG: Collectable card game

TMG: Tabletop miniature game

TTRPG: Tabletop role-play game

ORPG: Online role-playing game

Action-Adventure

VG: *Assassins Creed*; *God of War*

TT: Mansions of Madness

TTRPG: Kids on Bikes; The End of the World

CCG: Magic the Gathering; Yu-Gi-Oh!

TMG: Star Wars Miniatures

ORPG: *The Elder Scroll Online* or *World of Warcraft*

> **Questions to Consider:** What kind of action do you like in your games? Do you enjoy higher levels of violence or something more cartoonish? Are there certain time periods you like? Do you prefer more fantasy or sci-fi themed action? What is a recent action movie you enjoyed and do you think you might enjoy a game that is similar?

City Building Games

VG: *Cities: Skylines*; *Tropico 6*

TT: Mansions of Madness; Carcassonne

TTRPG: Dungeons & Dragons

CCG: n/a

TMG: n/a

ORPG: *World of Warcraft* has some city building elements

Questions to Consider: What aspect of building a city do you enjoy? Do you like the architecture elements? The puzzle elements of fitting buildings within a city or the idea of making a city for your citizens? Do you prefer realistic cities or fantastical cities?

Cooperative Play

VG: *Mario Party*; *Mario Kart*

TT: Pandemic; Forbidden Island

TTRPG: Dungeons & Dragons

CCG: n/a

TMG: n/a

ORPG: *World of Warcraft*

Questions to Consider: When you play other cooperative games, how do you like to interact with the other players? What kind of novels or stories do you like and do you think you'd like something similar? Do you want to play using a board or something more free form—like a role-playing game?

Educational Games

VG: *Little Big Planet*; *Portal*

TT: Wingspan or Power Grid

TTRPG: Legend of the Five Rings

CCG: n/a

TMG: n/a

ORPG: *World of Warcraft* (this can be a touchy subject as the benefits of *WoW* as an educational game are not immediately apparent. To expand understanding of *WoW* as an educational game, we suggest checking out Sri Ravipati's article, which discusses how online role-playing games can encourage cooperative play and self-accountability for students).[2]

Questions to Consider: Are you looking for a game to teach your children something or to complement something that they recently learned? Are you looking for a game that fits in with a certain curriculum? Do you need a game that is educational but can be scaled up so an entire class can play it together? Do you want a game that can help teach kids (or adults) something specific—like Physics or Geography, etc.?

Family Games

VG: *Mario Kart*; *Lego Star Wars*

TT: Rory's Story Cubes; Scotland Yard

TTRPG: Kids of Bikes; The Monster of the Week

CCG: Most collectable card games could be played with older children

TMG: n/a

ORPG: n/a

> **Questions to Consider:** Would you prefer a party-style family game or something more structured, like a board game? Do you like a family game that is easy to play or something with more rules? What are the ages and abilities of the family members who would be playing together? Do you want to play competitively or work together as a family?

Fighting Games

VG: *Injustice* series; *Mortal Kombat* series

TT: Exploding Kittens; King of Tokyo

TTRPG: Many role-play games have fighting elements in them

CCG: Yu-Gi-Oh!; Magic the Gathering

TMG: Warmachine; Warhammer

ORPG: *Guild Wars 2*

> **Questions to Consider:** Do you enjoy combative play games? Do you want to play against another person or play against non-playable characters in the game? Do you want to battle one on one or large armies or groups? Do you enjoy customizing your characters or armies? Do you like battles based on history or more futuristic scenarios?

Party Games

VG: *Jackbox*; *Mario Party*

TT: Say Anything; Secret Hitler

TTRPG: n/a

CCG: n/a

TMG: n/a

ORPG: n/a

Questions to Consider: How many people do you anticipate will be playing together? What are the ages and experience levels of these participants? Would a game with adult content be fine? Do you want something that is highly interactive or something that is more passive? Do you have some examples of party games you've played in the past that you liked? Are you looking for an analog or a digital experience?

Puzzle Games

Note: Many video games and online role-playing games will include puzzle elements.

VG: *Inside*; *Keep Talking and Nobody Explodes*

TT: Patchwork; Castles of Mad King Ludwig

TTRPG: n/a

CCG: n/a

TMG: n/a

ORPG: *World of Warcraft*; *EVE Online*

Questions to Consider: What kind of challenges or puzzles do you enjoy? Do you want something you solve on your own or with the help of others? Is story and narrative important to you or is a game that is more abstract ok?

Racing Games

VG: *Forza*; *Grand Theft Auto*

TT: n/a

TTRPG: n/a

CCG: Speed Racer

TMG: n/a

ORPG: *Magic Hero's: Lord of Souls*

Questions to Consider: What aspect of racing games do you enjoy the most? Are you looking for a more realistic experience? Do you enjoy racing games that have extra features such as *Mario Kart* with combative and sabotage elements?

Simulation Games

VG: Sports Simulation: *FIFA* series; Social Simulation: *Animal Crossing*; Pure Simulation: *Flight Simulator*

TT: The Resistance; Power Grid

TTRPG: n/a

CCG: n/a

TMG: n/a

ORPG: n/a

> **Questions to Consider:** What types of simulations do you enjoy? Do you want something very much like the real world or something more imaginative? Do you like repetitive tasks or something with more freedom? Do you want a game that progresses in complexity over time?

Social Games

VG: *Animal Crossing*; *The Sims*; *Mario Kart*

TT: The Resistance; Sheriff of Nottingham

TTRPG: Dread; Vampire: the Masquerade

CCG: n/a

TMG: n/a

ORPG: *World of Warcraft*; *Guild Wars*

> **Questions to Consider:** Do you like the idea of a game that you play with your friend s over an extended period of time? Do you enjoy games that are more casual and allow for idle chitchat in between?

Sports Games

VG: *FIFA* series; *NHL* series; *NBA* series

TT: Camel up!

TTRPG: n/a

CCG: n/a

TMG: n/a

ORPG: *Bloodbowl*

> **Questions to Consider:** What kinds of sports do you enjoy playing? Do you enjoy the simulation aspect of a video game or the use of game rules found in board games? If you enjoyed a certain kind of sport game, would you like to try other sports?

Storytelling Games

VG: *Breath of the Wild*; *The Last of Us*

TT: Once Upon a Time; Dixit

TTRPG: Most role-play games have storytelling elements—Dungeon & Dragons, etc.

CCG: n/a

TMG: n/a

ORPG: *Star Wars: Old Republic*; *Guild Wars 2*

> **Questions to Consider:** Do you enjoy making up stories? What kind of stories do you like reading, and would you like a game that allows you to make up something similar? Do enjoy developing a character and leading them through a story?

Strategy Games

VG: *Dragon Age: Inquisition*; *Final Fantasy*

TT: Rising Sun; Dominant Species

TTRPG: Most role-play games involve strategy

CCG: n/a

TMG: Most tabletop miniature games involve strategy

ORPG: *World of Warcraft*; *Final Fantasy XIV*

> **Questions to Consider:** Do you enjoy creating strategies for battles? What kind of strategy games have you played in the past? And what aspect of those games did you enjoy?

War Games

VG: *Call of Duty*; *Assassin's Creed: Odyssey*

TT: Risk; Rising Sun

TTRPG: Dungeons & Dragons; Pathfinder

CCG: n/a

TMG: Warmachine; Warhammer

ORPG: *World of Warcraft*; *Guild Wars*

> **Questions to Consider:** Is there a specific war or historic period you would like to engage with in a war game? Do you prefer more

fantastical war games or more realistic? Do you like the more strategic side of war or battle/action?

Word Games

VG: *Wheel of Fortune* (online based); *Happy Words* (Nintendo Switch)

TT: Word Slam; Funglish

TTRPG: n/a

CCG: n/a

TMG: n/a

ORPG: n/a

> **Questions to Consider:** What kind of word games do you enjoy? Are you looking for something similar to Scrabble or some other type of word game? Are you looking for something to build your vocabulary? Do you want a challenging word game or something that encourages learning?

World Building Games

VG: *Minecraft*; *Lego* series

TT: Tapestry; Terraforming Mars

TTRPG: Most role-play games involve building of imaginary worlds

CCG: n/a

TMG: n/a

ORPG: *Star Wars: Old Republic*; *Elder Scrolls Online*

> **Questions to Consider:** Do you like world building games that exist in a sandbox environment? What kind of worlds do you want to engage with—realistic or fantasy? Do you want to create a digital world or a world within a board game experience?

Notes

1. Nintendo, *The Hyrule Fantasy: Zelda no Densetsu* (Famicom Disk System) (in Japanese), February 21, 1986.

2. Sri Ravipati, "Fantasy Role-Playing Game Motivates Students to Rely on Each Other to Learn," THE Journal, July 7, 2017, https://thejournal.com/articles/2017/07/07/fantasy-role-playing-game-motivates-students-to-rely-on-each-other-to-learn.aspx.

Resources

"About Us." Kickstarter. Accessed September 2, 2020. https://www.kickstarter.com /about?ref=global-footer.

"About Us." Rainway. Accessed February 24, 2020. https://rainway.com/about/.

"About Us." Valve Corporation. Accessed February 23, 2020. https://www.valvesoft ware.com/en/about.

Andreen, Michael Thomas. "Choice in Digital Games: A Taxonomy of Choice Types Applied to Player Agency and Identity." PhD Dissertation, University of Texas at Dallas, 2017.

Andronico, Michael. "The $199 Nintendo Switch Lite Is a Dedicated Handheld with a Smaller Screen, Longer Battery Life." Toms Guide, July 10, 2019. https://news .yahoo.com/199-nintendo-switch-lite-dedicated-122018150.html.

Apple Arcade. Accessed February 24, 2020. https://www.apple.com/apple-arcade/.

"Apple Arcade: 'Loud House: Outta Control' out Now." Macworld, February 14, 2020. https://www.macworld.com/news.

Bakkes, Sander C. J., Pieter H. M. Spronck, and Giel van Lankveld. "Player Behavioural Modelling for Video Games." *Entertainment Computing* 3, no. 3 (August 2012): 71–79.

Bates, Matthew, David Brown, and Wayne Cranton. "Gaming and the Firewall: Exploring Learning through Play via Game Design with Children." *Proceedings of the 3rd European Conference on Games Based Learning*, October 2009, 8–16, University of Applied Sciences, Graz Austria.

Bedford, Emma. "Global Board Games Market Value from 2017 to 2023." Statista, August 9, 2019. https://www.statista.com/statistics/829285/global-board-games -market-value/.

Bergstrom, Frank. "The Top 10 Most Funded Kickstarter Board Games of All Time." Evil as a Hobby. Accessed September 2, 2020. https://www.evilasahobby.com /blog/the-top-10-most-funded-kickstarter-board-games-of-all-time/.

Berserk Games. "Games: Tabletop Simulator." Accessed April 1, 2020. https:// www.tabletopsimulator.com/games?fbclid=IwAR22mGrGKppdsmGrN6hIIv4C wag8vNHRyaVlmV0503m3rwcAYJ4pdknaLA0.

Bolding, Jonathon. "Steam Now Has 30,000 Games." PC Gamer, January 13, 2019. https://www.pcgamer.com/steam-now-has-30000-games/.

"Bring Your Lessons to Life with Expeditions." Google for Education. Accessed September 2, 2020. https://edu.google.com/intl/en_ca/products/vr-ar/expeditions/?modal_active=none.

Buchanan, Kym, and Angela M. Vaden Elzen. "Beyond a Fad: Why Video Games Should Be Part of 21st Century Libraries." *Education Libraries* 35, no. 1–2 (Summer–Winter 2012): 15–33.

"Build & Distribute Your Games on Steam." Steamworks. Accessed February 24, 2020. https://partner.steamgames.com/.

Byers, Fred R. "Care and Handlings of CDs and DVDs: A Guide for Librarians and Archivists." Council on Library and Information Resources, October 2003. https://www.clir.org/wp-content/uploads/sites/6/pub121.pdf.

Castle, Simon. "Board Game Types Explained: A Beginner's Guide to Tabletop Gaming Terms." Dicebreaker, February 12, 2020. https://www.dicebreaker.com/categories/board-game/how-to/board-game-typesexplained?fbclid=IwAR1ot5Exmm42LhDfwEJosxEdpcY97r7VqXy1zcdH2CGfjPzlLX3SEqdV1Vk.

"Classic PC Games." Internet Archive. Accessed September 2, 2020. https://archive.org/details/classicpcgames.

Cloke, Harry. "4 Types of Gamers and Learner Engagement." eLearning Industry, September 26, 2017. https://elearningindustry.com/types-of-gamers-and-learner-engagement-4.

"Country Report: Video Games in the US." Euromonitor International, June 2019.

Cross, Emma, David Mould, and Robert Smith. "The Protean Challenge of Game Collections at Academic Libraries." *Source Information* 21, no. 2 (May 2015): 129–145.

Dewan, Pauline. "Why Your Academic Library Needs a Popular Reading Collection Now More Than Ever." *College and Undergraduate Libraries* 17, no. 1 (March 2010): 44–64.

Doherty, Shawn M., Joseph R. Keebler, Shayn S. Davidson, Evan M. Palmer, and Christina M. Frederick. "Recategorization of Video Game Genres." *Proceedings of the Human Factors and Ergonomics Society Annual Meeting* 62, no. 1 (September 2018): 2099–2103.

Entertainment Software Ratings Board. "Ratings Guide." Entertainment Software Ratings Board, 2019. https://www.esrb.org/ratings-guide/.

Ferguson, Christine L. "Ready Librarian One." *Serials Review* 42, no. 1 (2016): 42–46.

Fogel, Stefanie. "'God of War,' 'Red Dead 2' Lead BAFTA Game Awards Nominations." *Variety*, March 15, 2019. https://variety.com/2019/gaming/news/british-academy-games-awards-2019-nominees-1203163369/.

Foote, Carolyn. "Is It Real or Is It VR? Exploring AR and VR Tools." *Computers in Libraries* 38, no. 3 (2018): 33–36.

Frank, Allegra. "R.I.P., Wii Shop Channel." Polygon, January 30, 2019. https://www.polygon.com/2019/1/30/18203844/nintendo-wii-shop-channel-closed.

The Franklin Institute. "History of Virtual Reality." Accessed September 2, 2020. https://www.fi.edu/virtual-reality/history-of-virtual-reality.

"Gamescom Wiki Guide: Attendance and Stats." April 16, 2020. https://www.ign.com/wikis/gamescom/Attendance_and_Stats.

"Gaming Collection." Wilfrid Laurier University Library. Accessed September 2, 2020. http://library.wlu.ca/research-materials/gaming-collection.

Gick, Natalie. "Making Book: Gaming in the Library: A Case Study." In *Gaming in Academic Libraries: Collections, Marketing, and Information Literacy*, edited by Amy Harris and Scott E. Rice. Chicago: ACRL, 2008.

Goodridge, Michelle. "Conversational Gamers: Developing Language Skills and Connections through Games." In *Supporting Today's Students in the Library: Strategies for Retaining and Graduating International, Transfer, First-Generation, and Re-Entry Students*, edited by Ngoc-Yen Tran and Silke Higgins. Chicago: American Library Association, 2019.

Hansen, D. *Game On!: Video Game History from Pong and Pac Man to Mario, Minecraft and More*. New York: MacMillan, 2016.

Horrigan, John B. "Libraries 2016." Pew Research Centre, September 9, 2016. https://www.pewinternet.org/2016/09/09/libraries-2016/.

Ivan, Tom. "Tokyo Game Show 2019 Attendance Declines, 2020 Event Dated." VGC, September 16, 2019. https://www.videogameschronicle.com/news/tokyo-game-show-2019-attendance-declines-2020-event-dated/.

Johnson, Janine. "Jumping into the World of Virtual and Augmented Reality." *Knowledge Quest* 47, no. 4 (2019): 22–27.

Kirman, Ben. "Play Styles and Personality >> Computer Games Play Styles Applied to Board Gamers." Boardgamegeek. Accessed September 2, 2020. https://boardgamegeek.com/geeklist/18914/play-styles-and-personality-computer-games-play-st.

Laskowski, Mary, and David Ward. "Perspectives on . . . Building Next Generation Video Game Collections in Academic Libraries." *The Journal of Academic Librarianship* 35, no. 3 (2009): 267–273.

Lee, Jin Ha, Rachel Ivy Clarke, Hyerim Cho, and Travis Windleharth. "Understanding Appeals of Video Games for Readers' Advisory and Recommendation." *Reference & User Services Quarterly* 57, no. 2 (Winter 2017): 122–139.

Levine, J. "Broadening Gaming Services in Libraries." *Library Technology Reports* (April 2008): 24–34.

Litorco, Teri. *The Civilized Guide to Tabletop Gaming: Rules Every Gamer Must Live By*. Avon, MA: Adams Media, 2016.

MacKenty, Bill. "All Play and No Work." *School Library Journal* 52, no. 9 (September 2006): 46–48.

Makuch, Eddie. "E3 2019 Attendance Falls Compared to Last Year." Gamespot, September 16, 2019. https://www.gamespot.com/articles/e3-2019-attendance-falls-compared-to-last-year/1100-6467795/.

Mena, Ricardo Javier Rademacher. "Player Types, Player Styles, and Play Complexity: Updating the Entertainment Grid." *International Journal of Game-Based Learning* 2, no. 2 (April–June 2012): 79–85.

Miller, Olivia. "But What about the Librarian? Game Design Students Get a New Player 2." Speaker Deck, January 16, 2015. https://speakerdeck.com/olmiller/but-what-about-the-librarian-game-design-students-get-a-new-player-2.

Montella, Fabio. "Producing Academic Outcomes with Virtual Reality Labs." *Computers in Libraries* 39, no. 5 (2019): 4–8.

"More than Apps, Experiences." Google. Accessed September 2, 2020. https://arvr.google.com/cardboard/apps/.

Neiburger, Eli. *Gamers . . . in the Library?! The Why, What, and How of Videogame Tournaments for All Ages*. Chicago: American Library Association, 2007.

Newman, James. *Videogames*. 2nd edition. New York: Routledge, 2013.

Nicholson, Scott. "Go Back to Start: Gathering Baseline Data about Gaming in Libraries." *Library Review* 58, no. 3 (2009): 203–214.

Nicholson, Scott. "The Impact of Gaming on Libraries." *Library Trends* 61, no. 4 (Spring 2013): 751–754.

Nicholson, Scott. "Playing in the Past: A History of Games, Toys, and Puzzles in North American Libraries." *Library Quarterly* 83, no. 4 (2013): 341–361.

"Nintendo Switch System Launches Worldwide." Free Library, 2017. https://www .thefreelibrary.com/NINTENDO+SWITCH+SYSTEM+LAUNCHES+WORLD WIDE-a0510556297.

Online Audiovisual Catalogers. "Best Practices for Cataloguing Video Games: Using RDA and MARC21." Version 1.1, April 2018. https://www.olacinc.org/sites/default /files/Video%20Game%20Best%20Practices-April-2018%20Revision-a.pdf.

"Online Gaming Market to Grow at 10% CAGR to Hit $79 Billion by 2025—Global Insights on Share, Size, Growth Drivers, Value Chain Analysis, Investments Plans, Key Stakeholders and Business Opportunities: Adroit Market Research." Globenewswire, February 14, 2020. https://www.globenewswire.com/news -release/2020/02/14/1985063/0/en/Online-Gaming-Market-to-grow-at-10-CAGR -to-hit-79-billion-by-2025-Global-Insights-on-Share-Size-Growth-Drivers-Value -Chain-Analysis-Investments-Plans-Key-Stakeholders-and-Business-.html#.

Pasfield-Neofitou, Sarah. "Language Learning and Socialization Opportunities in Game Worlds: Trends in First and Second Language Research." *Language and Linguistics Compass* 8, no. 7 (2014): 271–284. https://doi.org/10.1111/lnc3 .12083.

Quanat, Thorsten, and Sonja Kröger, eds. *Multiplayer: The Social Aspects of Digital Gaming*. New York: Routledge, 2013.

Quantic Foundry. "The Science and Data behind Our Gamer Motivation Model." Accessed March 24, 2021. https://quanticfoundry.com/.

Ravipati, Sri. "Fantasy Role-Playing Game Motivates Students to Rely on Each Other to Learn." THE Journal, July 7, 2017. https://thejournal.com/articles/2017 /07/07/fantasy-role-playing-game-motivates-students-to-rely-on-each-other-to -learn.aspx.

Riedl, Mark Owen, and Alexander Zook. "AI for Game Production." *Proceedings of the IEEE 2013 Conference on Computational Intelligence in Games*, Niagara Falls, Canada. https://www.cc.gatech.edu/~riedl/pubs/cig13.pdf.

Robson, Diane, and Patrick Durkee. "New Directions for Academic Video Game Collections: Strategies for Acquiring, Supporting, and Managing Online Materials." *The Journal of Academic Librarianship* 38, no. 2 (March 2012): 79–84.

Robson, Diane, Jessica Phillips, and Steve Guerrero. "Don't Just Roll the Dice: Simple Solutions for Circulating Tabletop Game Collections Effectively in Your Library." *LRTS* 62, no. 2 (2018): 80–90.

Rundle, Michael. "Star Wars: The Old Republic Is 'Fastest-Growing MMO Ever' with 1m Users." Huffington Post, December 27, 2011. https://www.huffingtonpost .co.uk/2011/12/27/star-wars-the-old-republic-sales-record_n_1171028.html ?guccounter=1&guce_referrer=aHR0cHM6Ly93d3cuZ29vZ2xlLmNvbS8&guce _referrer_sig=AQAAAAzugeWLa3N_qBn_GY7_b8mQFzh64SRSc0e4pYZQ _R465I-h8-KgWrd6idEochF0dovwantH6QCzGWaBdK1YeH7LSlxpYCpSXO2 dvlGnPHcRhaYIxcom_2tUzhrGthkTfhIkI31bvk3WCicgJvqXeFX49gvKV2ps s5IdA-O45AsE.

Schneider, Edward, and Brian Hutchinson. "Referencing the Imaginary: An Analysis of Library Collection of Role-Playing Game Materials." *The Reference Librarian* 56 (2015): 174–188.

"Sega VR." Wikipedia. Accessed September 2, 2020. https://en.wikipedia.org/wiki /Sega_VR.

Senior, Tom. "Team Fortress 2: The Best of the Steam Workshop." PC Gamer, October 19, 2011. https://www.pcgamer.com/team-fortress-2-the-best-of-the-steam -workshop/.

Slobuski, Teresa, Diane Robson, and P. J. Bentley. "Arranging the Pieces: A Survey of Library Practices Related to a Tabletop Game Collection." *Evidence Based Library and Information Practices* 12, no. 1 (2017): 2–17.

Smith, Brena. "Twenty-First Century Game Studies in the Academy: Libraries and an Emerging Discipline." *Reference Services Review* 36, no. 2 (2008): 205–220.

Smith, Felicia Ann. "Virtual Reality in Libraries is Common Sense." *Library Hi Tech News 36,* no. 6 (2019): 10–13.

"Steam & Game Stats." Steam. Accessed September 2, 2020. https://store .steampowered.com/stats/.

"Tanglewood." Accessed March 2020. https://tanglewoodgame.com/index.html.

"This Month in Physics History: October 1958: Physicist Invents First Video Game." *American Physical Society* 17, no. 9 (October 2008). https://www.aps.org /publications/apsnews/200810/physicshistory.cfm.

Thomas, Christopher M., and Jerremie Clyde. "Game as Book: Selecting Video Games for Academic Libraries Based on Discipline Specific Knowledge." *The Journal of Academic Librarianship* 39, no. 6 (2013): 522–527.

Tinsman, Brian. *The Game Inventor's Guidebook.* New York: Morgan James, 2008.

Tucker, Henry. "Gaming Online." *ITNow* 53, no. 5 (September 2011): 12–14.

Verstraeten, Julie. "The Rise of Board Games." Medium, April 21, 2018. https://medium .com/@Juliev/the-rise-of-board-games-a7074525a3ec.

"Virtual Boy." Wikipedia. Accessed September 2, 2020. https://en.wikipedia.org/wiki /Virtual_Boy.

"Virtual Reality." Wikipedia. Accessed September 2, 2020. https://en.wikipedia.org /wiki/Virtual_reality.

"Warhammer: Age of Sigmar." Wikipedia. Accessed September 2, 2020. https://en .wikipedia.org/wiki/Warhammer_Age_of_Sigmar.

Webster, Andrew. "These Are the Developers Creating New Games for Old Consoles: Cartridges Are Back." The Verge, May 9, 2017. https://www.theverge.com/2017 /5/9/15584416/new-games-retro-consoles-nes-snes-sega-genesis-famicom.

Wolf, Mark J. P. *Video Games FAQ: All That's Left to Know about Games and Gaming Culture.* Milwaukee, WI: Backbeat Books, 2017.

Woodward, Jeannette. *Creating the Customer-Driven Library: Building on the Book-store Model.* Chicago: ALA Editions, 2004.

Wright, James. "Xbox One S Release Date, Specs and Price Confirmed for Micro-soft's Slim HDR Ready Console." *Daily Star*, September 26, 2019. https://www .dailystar.co.uk/tech/gaming/xbox-one-release-date-specs-17085516.

Yee, Nick, and Nicolas Ducheneaut. "Gamer Motivation Profiling: Users and Applica-tions." In *Games User Research*, edited by Anders Drachen, Pejman Mirza-Ba-baei, and Lennart E. Nacks. Oxford: Oxford University Press, 2018.

Index

Note: Page numbers followed by *f* or *t* indicate figures and tables, respectively.

About the Authors

Michelle Goodridge, MA, MLIS, is liaison librarian at Wilfrid Laurier University in Ontario. She has authored a book chapter and several journal articles and has presented at conferences on gaming collections and programming in libraries. Goodridge's key areas of interest are game programming in libraries, bridging the gap between public and academic libraries, using games for English as a Second Language learning, representation of law enforcement in video games, and using game simulations in the classroom.

Matthew J. Rohweder, MA, MLIS, is liaison librarian at Wilfrid Laurier University in Ontario. He has been a contributing author to an LGBTQ+ encyclopedia along with author of a book chapter and has presented at dozens of conferences in North America and the United Kingdom on such topics as information literacy, LGBTQ+ issues in libraries, and gaming in libraries. He has been awarded a number of social sciences and humanities research grants through the government of Canada for his work on LGBTQ+ representation in American literature. Rohweder's key areas of interest are games and gaming in libraries, LGBTQ+ representation and outreach in libraries, information literacy and the importance of failure in teaching, and the representation of law enforcement in video games.